LOCAL POLITICS AND INDIAN NATIONALISM MIDNAPUR 1919–1944

Local Politics and Indian Nationalism
MIDNAPUR
1919–1944

BIDYUT CHAKRABARTY

MANOHAR
1997

ISBN 81-7304-158-X

First published 1997

Published by
Ajay Kumar Jain for
Manohar Publishers & Distributors
2/6 Ansari Road, Daryaganj
New Delhi 110002

Printed at
Rajkamal Electric Press
B35/9 G.T. Karnal Road Industrial Area
Delhi 110033

To

my brother

SWAPAN

Contents

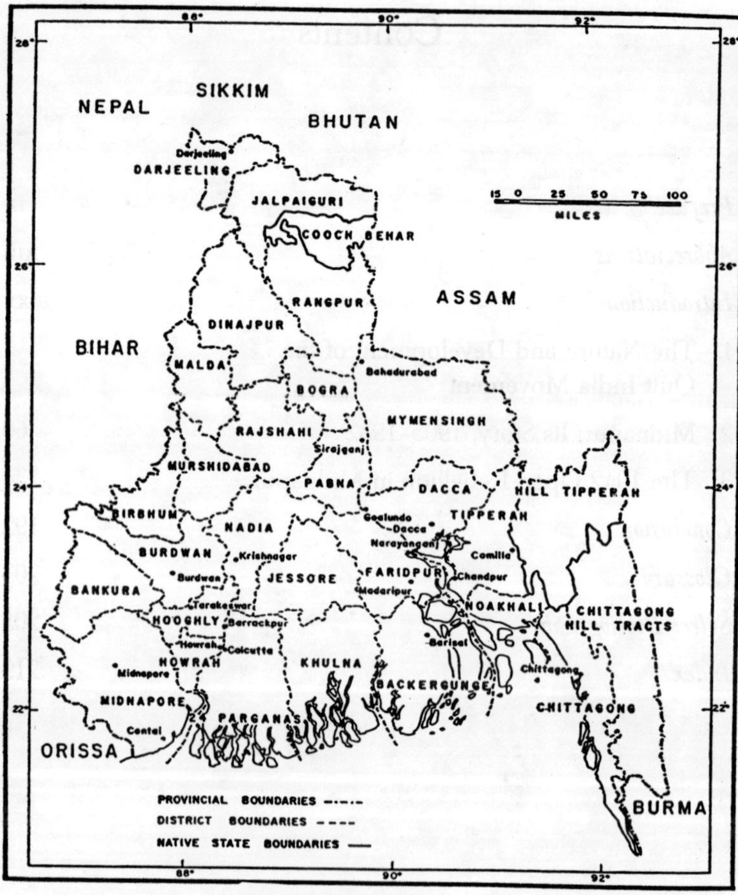

BENGAL, 1912–47

Note: Midnapur (Midnapore) is shown in relation to Bengal

Preface

THE BOOK IS about the 1942 Quit India Movement at the grassroots. Like the earlier Congress campaigns, the open rebellion, as Gandhi, defined, had its varied manifestations in the localities though the Mahatma remained the supreme leader. By focusing on the Quit India Movement in Midnapur, a south-western district of Bengal, the study has underlined the multifaceted dimensions of the nationalist movement in India. Launched by the Congress, the movement however acquired an autonomy of its own as it engulfed the country. What was evident in this Bengal district was vindicated elsewhere in India. A particular case study is thus useful in challenging the unilinear argument regarding the progress of history. Drawing upon the peculiar socio-economic characteristics of the district since they significantly influenced, if not shaped, political articulation the book is merely another attempt to show the limitation of an essentially 'political explanation' of events in the context of imperial rule.

Was India a nation? Probably not, as the events during the Quit India Movement demonstrated. Following the 1940 Lahore resolution, Muslims as a community generally remained aloof with the idea that cooperation with the British during the war would ensure Pakistan. Not only did the Muslims stay away from the open rebellion several Hindu lower castes also decided to oppose the Congress because of its failure to effectively challenge the upper caste hegemony. Given the well-defined political stance of the Muslim League and other political groups, the Quit India Movement, despite its remarkable success in undermining the British power in India, was hardly a national movement. So, the process that culminated in the 1947 bifurcation of the subcontinent of India was politically articulated in the wake of the 1942 anti-British rebellion.

I thought about and wrote various parts of this book over the last couple of years but put it together in its present form during my stay in Cambridge in 1993-4. However, I broached the idea of writing a monograph on Midnapur when I started teaching in Iowa University, USA. Several evening-discussions with Dr Paul Greenough, my colleague in the department of History enabled me to articulate my thought in a more systematic manner. By allowing me access to his work on local politics in India, Dr Swapan Dasgupta of the *Indian Express* has done a useful service to me. It is a particular sadness that Mr Hiteshranjan Sanyal who introduced me to the intricate world of grassroots politics passed away before the completion of this study.

I am particularly grateful to Dr Gordon Johnson, President of the Wolfson College, Cambridge, for his assistance and warm encouragement during the preparation of the manuscript. In fact, when I was uncertain about the feasibility of the project, it was Dr Johnson who inspired me to write a full-length monograph on the subject. I express my gratitude to Professor Mohit Bhattacharyya, Vice Chancellor, Burdwan University, India who with his incisive criticism of my work always brought new dimension to the subject. Despite his busy schedule, Professor Bhikhu Parekh, my colleague at the University of Hull read whatever I gave and offered valuable criticism and suggestions which were of great value in reformulating some of my ideas. My gratitude goes to Professor Tom Nossiter of the London School of Economics who assisted in fine-tuning many of my arguments. I fondly remember Dr Lionel Carter of the Centre of South Asian Studies, Cambridge, who despite being over-burdened with his work, was always helpful.

The book would never have been complete without the assistance of those 'nationalist rebels' who sacrificed their life for a political cause. By allowing free access to the materials in their possession they eased my task considerably. Also, long interviews with them enabled me to put the complex progress of events during the open rebellion in a proper perspective. During my field trips to Midnapur, I had occasions to talk to a large number of people who took part in the nationalist movement. I express my gratitude to them. Of all of them, the followings deserve special mention because without their help I would probably have abandoned the project. Mr Sushil Dhara, Mr Gopinandan Goswami, Mr Ramesh Kar, Mr Billapada Jana, Mr Basanta Kumar Das, Mr Prahlad Kumar Pramanik, Mr Nanigopal Dolui and Ms Kumudini Dakua offered assistance in grasping the growing importance of the Gandhi-led nationalist campaign at the grassroots. I appreciate their contribution without which the project would probably have lost much of its significance.

I am also thankful to Professor Mahendra Kumar and Professor Sushila

Kaushik, my colleagues in Delhi University, for having recommended my application for leave most favourably. Delhi University helped me a great deal in the completion of this project by approving my request for leave because without respite from regular teaching it would have been impossible to write the book within such a short period.

Finally, the book would have taken longer to complete without the cooperation and warm encouragement of my friends and relatives in Delhi and Calcutta who would like to remain anonymous.

Cambridge
December 1995

BIDYUT CHAKRABARTY

Abbreviations

ABP	*Amrita Bazar Patrika*
AICC	All India Congress Committee
AIKS	All India Krishak Sabha
AITUC	All India Trade Union Congress
BCCD	Bengal Council for Civil Disobedience
BLC	Bengal Legislative Council
BPC	Bengal Provincial Congress
BPCC	Bengal Provincial Congress Committee
BNCC	Bengal National Chamber of Commerce
BPML	Bengal Provincial Muslim League
BSRR	Bangladesh Secretariat Record Room, Dhaka
BVSG	Bengal Village Self Government Act
CDC	Civil Disobedience Committee
CPI	Communist Party of India
CSAS	Centre for South Asian Studies, Cambridge
CUP	Cambridge University Press
CWMG	*Collected Works of Mahatma Gandhi*
DCC	District Congress Committee
DM	District Magistrate
EPW	*Economic and Political Weekly*
FR	Fortnightly Report
HMP	Hindu Mahasabha Papers
IAR	*Indian Annual Register*
ICS	Indian Civil Service
IESHR	*Indian Economic and Social History Review*

INA	Indian National Army
INC	Indian National Congress
IOR	India Office Records, London
JAS	*Journal of Asian Studies*
JNP	Jawaharlal Nehru Papers
JNSW	*Jawaharlal Nehru Selected Works*
JPS	*Journal of Peasant Studies*
KPP	Krishak Praja Party
MAS	*Modern Asian Studies*
ML	Muslim League
MLC	Member of Legislative Council
MR	*Modern Review*
MSS	Manuscript
MZC	Midnapur Zamindari Company
NAI	National Archives of India, New Delhi
NMML	Nehru Memorial Museum and Library, New Delhi
OUP	Oxford University Press
PCC	Provincial Congress Committee
RPP	Rajendra Prasad Papers
RSP	Revolutionary Socialist Party
SDO	Subdivisional Officer
TICP	Tamralipta Itihas Committee Papers
TP	*The Transfer of Power Vols. 1-4*
TSS	Typescript
UP	Uttar Pradesh
WBSA	West Bengal State Archives, Calcutta
WC	Working Committee
WPP	Workers' and Peasants' Party

Introduction

FORMED IN 1885, the Indian National Congress launched an anti-British campaign resorting principally to 'moderate techniques', articulating nationalist grievances in such a way as not to disrupt the colonial order. However, the nature of political agitation changed substantially with the arrival of Gandhi on the scene. The constituency of nationalist politics expanded in the aftermath of the 1920-2 Non-Cooperation Movement, and the Congress went far beyond its original elite-institutional confines. Its President, thus, could legitimately claim in 1936 that the Congress had now 'become the largest organization of the common people drawn largely from the village population and counting amongst its members lakhs of peasants and cultivators and a sprinkling of industrial and field workers'.[1] By bringing in hitherto peripheral social groups, the newly emerged leadership radically transformed the nature of the anti-British struggle which became not merely a battle for political freedom but an organized attack on the vested interests in Indian society as well. In other words, though the nationalists strove hard to sustain the multi-class political platform, the Indian freedom struggle provoked different kinds of movements at the grassroots in which attempts were constantly made to do away with the structural impediments to social progress. What was also interesting was that the mass phase of the anti-British struggle, which Gandhi was instrumental in initiating on a large number of occasions, deviated from the basic tenet of his instruction, viz., non-violence. The situation thus created led to manifold possibilities and thereby making history writing more difficult. What is therefore needed is to grasp the complex interplay of factors at various levels of political mobilization entailing not only the actors involved but also the rapidly changing global and domestic socio-economic and cultural milieus.

The national movement gradually expanded in the Gandhian era in both geographical and social terms going beyond Bengal, Maharashtra and Punjab, and enrolling various social groups from all the Indian provinces. Since the principal aim was to wrest political control from the British, the Gandhian leadership of the Congress never allowed ideologies diluting the freedom struggle to thrive. On most occasions, the carefully-nurtured national leadership succeeded in directing even those popular movements that had radical social aims against imperial rule. By striving to maintain the prevalent power relations, the Congress exposed its limitation as a political organization which, despite bringing various contending social groups within its fold, was very careful not to dilute the freedom struggle by discouraging tendencies potentially harmful to the multi-class platform. However, the Congress was radicalized with the participation of the 'marginalized section' of Indian society, namely, peasants and workers, which by demanding the inclusion of their rights in the Congress agenda, both expanded and sustained various new constituencies of nationalist politics. This probably explains why the 1905-8 Swadeshi campaign was substantially different from the later Congress movements between 1919 and 1942 in which anti-British slogans gained a wider currency, principally because of the Congress success in attributing India's socio-economic dislocation to imperialism. The Congress was keen to champion the peasants' and workers' political aims so long as they were complementary to the nationalist goal. The growing participation of 'the subaltern groups' in the freedom struggle suggests the extent to which nationalism appeared significant in accommodating interests clearly contradictory with the carefully-articulated multi-class ideology of the Congress.

The involvement of various social groups in the nationalist movement brings into focus the role of leadership in successfully organizing and directing mass discontent against the alien state. The presence of a foreign ruler was the factor that united the Indian masses regardless of vertical and horizontal differences among themselves. It would however be misleading to ignore the many internal divisions within Indian society. That the Congress leadership succeeded in translating the aspirations of diverse classes and groups into a pre-dominantly anti-imperial movement is significant in this regard. Such an argument allows us to capture the complex dynamics of the nationalist movement which was never unilinear given the steady expansion of its political audience. The anti-imperialist principle articulated however differently by different social groups was the Congress' most important ideological device in giving a unified shape to variegated political movements. It is now evident that through a complex interaction of a relatively elite and a more populist level of politics , there arose a specific pattern in the Indian national movement in which the leadership is as important as mass fervour. Viewing the nationalist movement from this perspective allows us to capture its complex dynamics in the context of a steady expansion of its political audience.

In the context of India's freedom struggle, nationalism sustained mass opposition to British rule. Nations seen as 'imagined communities'[2] appear to be a useful construct in underlining the apparent homogeneity of interest of various sections of society in any struggle against foreign rule. However, Anderson's argument concerning 'modular forms' of nationalist intervention[3] ignores the point that if modular forms are made available nothing is left to be imagined. While exposing the limitation of the conceptualization that hinges on the modular forms of nationalism, Partha Chatterjee argues,

> [t]he most powerful as well as the most creative results of nationalist imagination in Asia and Africa are posited not on an identity but rather on differences with the modular forms of the national society propagated by the modern west.[4]

Such an articulation probably explains why the Gandhi-led national movement contained essentially Indian features. Drawing upon values meaningful to the Indian masses, the freedom struggle developed its own modular form which is characteristically different from that of the West. The distinctiveness of India's freedom struggle lies also in the fact that despite radical tendencies aiming at structural changes, the multi-class Congress platform appeared most effective in streamlining mass oppostion to an alien state which gradually lost its legitimacy and hence authority to rule.

The present work is a study of the nationalist movement as it was conducted at the grassroots between 1905 and 1944. By concentrating on Midnapur, a south-western district of Bengal, the study proposes to bring out the dynamics of India's freedom struggle against a powerful state which wielded the instruments both of coercion and persuasion. Organized by the local political leadership, the anti-British assault channellized mass discontent drawing upon both local and national grievances. Although far away from Calcutta, the nerve centre of provincial political activities, this south-western district of Bengal articulated the nationalist protest more effectively than any other district in eastern India. What deserves attention here is the success the local Congress organizers attained in mobilizing people politically in the face of mass repression. Not only was the district distinctly different in regard to the pattern of mobilization, but had also succeeded in sustaining its independence *vis-a-vis* the provincial and national leadership while challenging the colonial state. In other words, the local leadership supported the wider National

Movement and yet was not amenable to outside pressure. An indepth study of the grassroots movements, initiated and conducted by the district-level political activists challenges the hagiography of nationalism as being centred exclusively around Gandhi. Although the Mahatma set the agenda that the nature of the anti-British struggle varied substantially from one place to another reveals the extent to which local leaders were crucial in significantly altering the course of the freedom struggle at the grassroots. What is suggested here is that a nationalist ideology drawing upon anti-British sentiments remained decisive in organizing the disparate masses though its articulation was contingent on both the leadership and the immediate socio-economic scene. By consistently following the anti-British tradition, manifested in various political activities during the period between 1905 and 1944, Midnapur merely exemplified a specific pattern of mass involvement in politics which appeared likely, given the role of organization in consolidating the nationalist ideology.

By concentrating on the peculiar land relations of the district and its caste structure, there will also be an attempt to find out the extent to which political mobilization is contingent on factors other than ideology and organization. Midnapur is probably one of the few Indian districts where nationalism created and sustained social alliances among the contending classes in the context of an anti-imperial challenge. Rather than underlining the vertical division along caste lines, movements for ensuring a distinct status to those identified as 'Mahishyas' contributed to greater social cohesion that was gradually consolidated by intelligently accommodating the social agendas of substantial ryots, known as *jotedars,* in the Congress-led nationalist movement. With their hegemony in rural areas, jotedars succeeded in harnessing mass grievances into more organized protests challenging the British rule which was singularly held responsible for severely dislocating Indian rural society.

The peculiarity of political mobilization lay in the fact that the attempts to undermine the multi-class Congress platform were never allowed to assume serious proportions. Despite occasional opposition, the radical forces generally cooperated with the Congress because in the battle for freedom they saw steps towards fulfilling some of their political goals. Hence, Midnapur continued to pose a severe threat to the colonial state which was considerably marginalized when the district responded to the Congress call for the 1920-2 Non-Cooperation Movement, the 1930-2 Civil Disobedience campaign and the 1942 August revolution. Even as it caused acute consternation to the British administration, the district was also a source of anxiety to both the provincial and national Congress leadership. Supporting the wider national movement, the local leadership devised its own strategy to contain the alien state disregarding, on a number of occasions, both the Bengal Provincial Congress (BPC) and All India Congress Committee (AICC). During all the three movements, as will be shown below, the provincial leaders were allowed to come to the district after they conceded their role merely as observers. It is not therefore surprising that at the height of the anti-British confrontation in the wake of the 1930-2 Civil Disobedience Movement, the BPC was not willing to sanction funds to the Midnapur District Congress Committee (DCC) until the AICC intervened. Similarly, on the eve of the August revolution, despite being aware of the adverse reactions, the local leadership vehemently opposed the AICC for its attempt to force the DCC to act as a BPC satellite.[5] Annoyed with the local Congress, J.B. Kripalani, the AICC secretary, expressed disappointment since division within the Congress was suicidal in the context of the forthcoming movement.[6]

Given the complexity of political movements at the grassroots, the study of Midnapur and its involvement in nationalist politics will bring out the differences as well as similarities of the local pattern with the pattern of socio-political changes that unfolded at the national and provincial levels. A major focus here is on the Congress-led freedom struggle that articulated a collective voice against imperialism. With its continuous effort, the Congress successfully organized anti-British campaign in the district between 1920-2 Non-Cooperation Movement and the 1942 open rebellion. Although nationalism was translated into a movement opposing the British state it had varied manifestations at different levels of the nationalist politics. So, by accommodating interests of various social groups championing various issues, nationalism projected an umbrella ideology that laid the foundation of the multi-class Congress platform. By itself, ideology may not be decisive; what is important is the role of organization that articulates and directs the popular dissent in the form of movements to attain a set goal. Through sustained activities, the Congress had gradually established a near monopoly in the articulation of local grievances and its role in the anti-British campaign was legitimized in terms of a nationalist ideology.

In the following chapters, our effort will be directed to show how the Midnapur Congress mobilized people at the grassroots for a widespread and unified political movement of protest in adverse circumstances. Chapter 1, focusing on the nature and development of the Quit India Movement at the pan-Indian level will set the scene for anti-British political agitations elsewhere. By concentrating on the socio-economic complexity of Midnapur and the role of the Congress ideology in organizing the nationalist struggle, Chapter 2 will be devoted to the period between 1905 and 1932 when the district was pre-eminent in launching successful political campaigns against the British. As Midnapur figured prominently in the 1942 August rebellion, an attempt will be made in Chapter 3 to analyse the political activities at the grassroots with reference to the factors likely to have significantly influenced the nature of events.

NOTES

1 In his presidential address to the 1936 Faizpur Congress, Jawaharlal Nehru further underlined 'the gradual transformation of the Congress from a small upper class body to one representing the great body of lower middle classes and later the masses of this country. As this drift to the masses continued, the political role of the organization changed and is changing'. See Jawaharlal Nehru's speech in A. M. Zaidi, *The Encyclopaedia of the Indian National Congress*, Vol. 11 (1936-9), S. Chand & Co., Delhi, 1980, p. 196.

2 Benedict Anderson, *Imagined Communities: reflections on the origin and appeal of nationalism*, Verso, London, 1991.

3 For Benedict Anderson, historical experience of nationalism in western Europe, America and Russia had supplied for all subsequent nationalisms a set of modular forms from which nationalist elites in Afro-Asian countires had chosen the ones they liked.

4 Partha Chatterjee, *The Nation and its Fragments: colonial and post colonial histories,* Oxford University Press (hereafter OUP), Delhi, 1994, p. 5.

5 Interview with Sushil Dhara, 15 December 1985.

6 NMML, AICC G 2 (part 2)/1942, J. B. Kripalani to B. C. Roy, 27 July 1942.

CHAPTER 1

The Nature and Development of the Quit India Movement

FOLLOWING THE adoption of the 8 August resolution at Gowalia tank in Bombay, Indian masses rose into revolt which became famous as the Quit India Movement.[1] It was a call for freedom. 'Nothing less than freedom',[2] to quote Gandhi. Unlike the 1920-2 Non Cooperation and the 1930-2 Civil Disobedience Movements which were basically non-violent campaigns against the British rule in India, the Quit India Movement was the ultimatum to the British for final withdrawal, a Gandhi-led un-Gandhian way of struggle since the Mahatma exhorted to take up arms in self defence and resort to armed resistance against a stronger and well-equipped aggressor.[3]

At the beginning, the movement was widespread, affecting almost every corner of the country. With a massive British counter-attack, however, the upsurge which caused alarm to the British administration lost its momentum considerably. Although the pan-Indian counterpart evaporated almost within a couple of weeks after the adoption of the 8 August resolution, the movement continued incessantly in three different locations, viz., Satara (Maharashtra), Talcher (Orissa) and Midnapur (Bengal). By concentrating on the August revolution as it developed following the incarceration of the top Congress leaders, the chapter seeks to set, as it were, the scene. As the work concentrates on political mobilization in Midnapur, a south-western district of Bengal, the chapter, with a chronological sequence, will also situate the experience of a particular locality in the all-India perspective. Challenging the 'spontaneous thesis' an attempt will also be made to reformulate the widely accepted explanations in the light of new theoretical insights and untapped source materials, available in the district archives. Furthermore, interviews with the participants in the Quit India Movement constitute another major source of information which has brought out the complex nature of the last nationalist campaign at the grassroots.

The Quit India: A Different Political Campaign

Galvanizing the masses into action, not only did the Quit India Movement cause alarm to the colonial authority, it also extended the constituency of the nationalist politics by incorporating various new social groups which remained peripheral in earlier political campaigns. Politics here denotes collective action performed with a power perspective in which an attempt is constantly made to gain authority and influence over certain areas of human activity. The role of ideas is important too in this regard for they play a crucial role in political mobilization in adverse circumstances. Politics, thus defined, will be of help in capturing the mass zeal, evident during the August revolution for analytical purposes. Although it is the culmination of the Gandhi-led nationalist campaign which began with the 1920-2 Non-Cooperation Movement, the 8 August Quit India resolution launched a political campaign which is different from the earlier ones in a number of ways. The Quit India Movement was not merely another instance of the Civil Disobedience campaign, it was also 'an open rebellion'. All the past Satyagraha Movements, writes the *Harijan*,[4] were protests against 'the unwanted or unapproved acts' of the Raj, the authority of which was however conceded. Hence, the Congress 'registered protests by breaking the salt laws, forest regulations, the enforcement of section 144 of the Indian Penal Code, curfew orders, executive bans on meetings, etc., and [we] bowed our heads to lathis of the police who represented the collective self of the people—the government, or underwent sentences of imprisonment as model prisoners, etc.'. The situation however changed as soon as 'even the tacit recognition of the government by the people is consciously withdrawn, a government ceases to have any sanction and persons who attempt to exercise governmental authority are usurpers and no obedience is due to them and any punishment meted out having no sanction became the acts of ruffian'. The AICC resolution of 8 August demanding, as Gandhi articulated 'that the British authority should end completely irrespective of the wishes or demands of various parties'[5] is certainly a significant departure from the earlier practices when the authority of the government had 'political sanctions to carry out the laws such as they are'[6] and hence was legitimate. With the onset of the Quit India Movement, the political equation between the government and Congress had undergone a radical change in the context of the Raj being identified as 'a usurper of authority and power'.

In such a situation, the Congress became more militant than ever. Insisting on the immediate British withdrawal, the party therefore exhorted the people, to refuse to recognise government officials and we owe no obedience to them. When a police man appears with a lathi or a revolver, he, having no licence to use such powers, has to be disarmed. We should not bow our heads to receiving the strokes as formerly but pull away their sticks and render them powerless. They have no authority to arrest us. Therefore the present day arrest and detention is on par with kidnapping. All our leaders have [therefore] been kidnapped.[7]

To the Congress, the British therefore had no right whatsoever to rule India and it was a 'sacred duty' of the Congress nationalists to strengthen the anti-imperial campaign by means other than non-violence, if the situation so demanded. In order to contain 'a satanic government' the Congress nationalists were urged to attack the system of communication because 'they use telegraphs and telephones for issuing their illegal fiats, railway to rush troops and armed police, [and] the trunk roads for mechanised forces'.[8] Identifying the government officials as 'mercenaries' aiding and abetting 'a foreign interloper', the Congress appealed to the people for withdrawing 'all social cooperation with them'.[9] As the British government degenerated into a 'fifth columnist government', the resistance to it, as the appeal went, was but 'a sacred duty' of Indians irrespective of religion, class and caste. F. O. Bell, an ICS officer who served Bengal between 1930 and 1947, noted:

Thus the struggle has been animated by violence and terrorism. There should be no surprise to those who preached it as an open rebellion who knew the sorry [sic] history of Mr Gandhi's previous experiments with ahimsa who set the countryside alight with the slogan 'do or die' who pledged on the emotions of callous students who commanded that when the law took its course and Congress committees ceased to function, every individuals must be his own guide in the conflict and who sheltered within the party the revolutionaries and hooligans who are always ready to profit by anarchy.[10]

The discussion pursued so far has brought out that a cursory glance at the movement shows that the Quit India campaign was a popular nationalist upsurge that occurred in the name of Gandhi but went substantially beyond any confines that Gandhi may have envisaged for the movement. Ideologically, the August revolution drew upon non-violence and its concomitant value system, in its actual unfolding however, the movement developed its own dynamics. What it reveals is the tension, prevalent between Gandhi and the participants in the context of the final assault on the imperial power. Although such a tension was there in earlier Gandhi-led movements, in the 1942 campaign it was probably more evident than ever. Hence, it is not counterfactual to argue that Gandhi was the undisputed leader of the movement over which he had little command. Such an assertion draws our attention to the dialectical interconnection between the 'organized' and 'unorganized' worlds of politics highlighting simultaneously their respective separate domains.[11]

The Quit India Resolution and its Aftermath

The 8 August Quit India resolution provoked mass arrest and the alien state, which was stronger than ever due to her military preparedness in the context of the war, left no stone unturned to assert its authority. Not only was there an organized army at its disposal,[12] the all-pervasive imperial state was also getting ready to launch a pre-emptive strike against the Congress. In fact, since 1940, the Government of India warned the provincial government of a possible political campaign challenging the British power in India. The reason was simple: in the context of the war crisis, the state in India was vulnerable and hence it was a golden opportunity for 'the Congress to strike it down when it is the weakest'.[13] Strategically, the situation was ripe for a full-scale political movement, and therefore an immediate state action was warranted to nip the campaign at the bud. Although Linlithgow, the Viceroy, wanted to crush the Congress[14] if it threw down a gauntlet to the government during the war, there was significant opposition from his colleagues who did not think it prudent on the part of the government. Challenging Linlithgow's assessment of the situation as 'flawed and short-sighted', Edward Benthall, an important member of the Viceroy's Council, asked the government not to provoke a political campaign by unleashing repression since the Congress leaders do not want to embark upon civil disobedience for the following reasons:

> (*a*) it might lead to communal trouble; (*b*) the masses are not prepared for such action now and indeed the present economic prosperity of the cultivators and others is not conducive to civil disobedience; (*c*) the businessmen who have influence in the Congress are doing well out of the war; (*d*) there is a general desire for a settlement [with the British] as opposed to civil disobedience which, if launched, would postpone any possibility of a settlement; and (*e*) civil disobedience would lead to violence which would discredit Gandhi in the eyes of the world.[15]

Although the situation was not alarming *per se*, the Executive Council urged the Viceroy to streamline the administration in view of the probable mass-discontent due to the imminent economic crisis in the context of the war. Bentall's advice was most appropriate given the simmering of tension in the provinces due to the fact that 'India's participation in the war was purely a British act imposed on the Indian people without the consent of their representatives.'[16] In such a volatile situation, the Congress leaders, he apprehended, 'may find themselves pushed into civil disobedience against their will and every resolution or pronouncement they make, to some degree makes it more difficult for them to remain inactive'.[17]

Benthall's apprehension was not entirely unfounded because there was constant left pressure for action. Moreover, Gandhi realized that without another anti-British campaign, it would be difficult to manage the 'youth members who were increasingly being attracted to communism'.[18] The 1940 Ramgarh Congress resolved to undertake a civil disobedience 'as soon as the Congress organization is considered fit enough for the purpose' and left entirely with Gandhi the form and timing of the movement.[19] Gandhi agreed on the condition that the first phase of the campaign would be conducted by individuals 'whom he himself would choose as men whom he could trust'.[20] Thus started probably the most limited and largely ineffective satyagraha in the history of India's freedom struggle. For Gandhi however, the movement though restrained, was significant because the anti-war pronouncement of the satyagrahees registered hostility to a war waged without consulting the Indians; and since it was non-violent, the campaign would not provoke a major British crackdown on the nationalists. The 1940-1 satyagraha, despite its tremendous symbolical significance, hardly evoked interests among the people. In its four different phases (between October 1940 and October 1941) the movement reached its peak in April 1941 when 20,000 satyagrahees courted arrests.[21] In relation to the total membership of the Congress, the number was insignificant and hence some Congressmen identified the movement as a failure. In a statement in *The Hindu,* a pro-Congress daily, the leading Congressmen from UP, Tamil Nadu, Bengal and Bihar, urged Gandhi to call off the campaign.[22] The Mahatma was however unmoved and he declared that 'satyagraha must neither be withdrawn nor expanded into a mass movement, as some desired, since mass action would *embarrass the government* (emphasis added), and at this stage without communal unity is an invitation to civil war'.[23]

The individual satyagraha petered away gradually and by the end of 1941, it was virtually over. The Congress on the whole accepted the Gandhian dictum except the Bengal Provincial Congress Committee (BPCC), already crippled due to the division between the Bose group and Ad-hoc committee,[24] expressed dissatisfaction with Gandhi's decision to halt the movement at an opportune moment when it was gaining momentum through gradual but steady mass participation.[25] Bengal was probably an exception but there was a lull in the nationalist campaign which had possibly to do with the relatively stable economic conditions of the people even after the outbreak of the war. Though India joined the war by being part of the British empire it had brought, on the balance, gains rather than losses for a substantial section of the population. The rise in agricultural price was not as yet very sharp and the peasantry had therefore no reason to feel aggrieved.[26] Indian industrial development received a major boost due to the war demand, reducing imports significantly and forced reliance on indigenous products. Employment in Indian industries rose by 31 per cent between 1939 and 1942.[27] Labour unrest was kept in check 'by substantial dearness allowances and supply of essential goods at subsidised rates'.[28] For Indian businessmen and traders in general, 'war meant an opportunity for fantastically quick profits, particularly so long as it remained distant and did not involve the threat of destruction of property through aerial bombardment or evacuation'.[29]

The Indian political situation however changed dramatically with the Japanese conquest of Singapur in February and Rangoon in March 1942. With the rapid Japanese advance in the winter of 1941-2, it was widely believed that 'India's safeguard in the war . . . was lost. After the fall of Singapur, the Bay of Bengal lay open. When Rangoon fell . . . , it seemed as if the tide of Japanese conquest, which had flowed so swiftly and irresistibly over Malaya and then Burma–only yesterday a province of the Indian empire–would soon be sweeping into Bengal and Madras'.[30] Although there was less immediate alarm in Delhi and Bombay due to sheer distance from the Eastern war front, 'it seemed nevertheless quite possible', a note from the Eastern Command apprehended, that 'Japanese army might be able to penetrate as deeply and quickly into India as they had into Malaya and Burma'.[31] The British administration was visibly alarmed. A panic-stricken central intelligence officer at Madras thus recorded,

> The grave news from Malaya and the Far East has entirely eclipsed the reports of Allied successes in Russia and Libya and public confidence in the might of Great Britain and the USA has, I think, deteriorated considerably. . . . There has been much loose talk regarding war developments and many wild rumours have been current. One of the most recent of these is that some Indian Regiments in Malaya have mutinied and gone over to the enemy after shooting their British officers. A considerable number of people, mostly Indian women and children, have left Madras during the fortnight and in many families, arrangements have been made to vacate the city should the present situation deteriorate.[32]

Not only was there preparation for evacuation of the British, the Government of India issued an order to the effect that 'in the event of Bengal being overrun by the Japanese, all officers of District rank and below in all departments were to remain at their posts to administer the district for the good of the people under the control of the enemy'.[33] Furthermore, the government took ample care to suppress the news of the Japanese success in the war.[34] Simultaneously, with the increasing military preparedness in view of an impending Japanese attack, the India Office felt obliged to make some gestures to win over Indian public opinion. The Viceroy was however opposed to the idea of devising a formula to ensure the cooperation of the Indian political parties, Congress in particular. In his view, 'they [the Congress] are entirely ruthless politicians'. . . and hence he did not believe 'that any further move at this stage will likely to improve India's contribution to the war'. He also felt that further transfer of power to Indians would encourage, what he called 'quisling activities' which he substantiated by reference to a note from military authorities in eastern India reporting that 'there is large and dangerous potential fifth column in Bengal, Assam, Bihar and Orissa and that indeed potential of pro-enemy sympathy and activity in eastern India is enormous'.[35]

There was international pressure too. The US President Roosevelt raised the question of Indian political reform during his talk with Churchill in December 1941; in February 1942, Chiang-Kai-Shek during his trip to India publicly expressed sympathy for 'India's aspiration for freedom'. For L.S. Amery, the Secretary of State for India, the decision to send the Cripps Mission 'is to answer the charge that our policy in India is inconsistent with our general profession about fighting for freedom as well as the even more humiliating charge that if we are prepared to make concession to India now, it is simply the result of a decadent imperialism realising that the game is up'.[36] The announcement of the Cripps Mission was essentially a politically expedient device in so far as the Raj was concerned. However, the draft declaration was certainly a positive drive towards resolving the constitutional deadlock by promising post-war dominion status with the right of secession, a constitution making body, elected by provincial legislatures, with individual provinces being given the right not to join it and with states being invited to appoint representatives.[37] Linlithgow, the Viceroy, threatened to resign.[38] because he was unhappy with the draft declaration which was, he thought, unnecessary during the war crisis.[39] Churchill while drawing his attention to its effect on the world opinion, especially the Americans, explained that 'it would be impossible owing to unfortunate rumours and publicity, and the general American outlook, to stand on a purely negative attitude and the Cripps mission is indispensable to prove our honesty of purpose . . . . If it is rejected by the Indian parties . . . our sincerity will be proved to the world.'[40] The Cripps mission was finally withdrawn for not adequately consulting Linlithgow and the Commander-in-Chief, Wavell who expressed concern that Cripps was conceding far too real power to the Congress.[41] That the appointment of the Cripps Mission was essentially a strategy to win the British allies was evident when Churchill congratulated Strafford Cripps on his success in 'proving how great was the British desire to reach a settlement. . . . The effect throughout and in the United States has been wholly beneficial.'[42]

Whatever the reasons, the failure of the Cripps Mission reveals the attitude of the British towards the Congress and future political movement under Gandhi's leadership. During the Non-Cooperation and Civil Disobedience Movements, the British authority was manifestly keen to negotiate with Gandhi at least before the onset of the campaign. In 1942, their attitude had changed dramatically and under no circumstances, the Viceroy and his Executive Council were inclined to open a dialogue with the Congress leadership. The authority became stern than ever with the Congress threat to start 'a mass struggle on non-violent lines on the widest possible scale' unless the demand of 'the immediate withdrawal of the British power from India' was met.[43] Gandhi persuaded himself, as Tottenham, the Home Secretary, Government of India, reminiscensed, 'that the situation gave him an unrivalled opportunity to obtain full independence for India in view of the British difficulty in the war following the Japanese success in the eastern front'.[44] Moreover, there were indications that 'dangerous preparations being pushed by the Congress in the provinces for immediate action, for cutting of telegraph wires, interference with railway services, the organising of strikes, the tampering with the loyalty of Government servants, the picketing of troops and a wide variety of similar unlawful and nefarious activities'.[45] Hence it was agreed upon an immediate crackdown on the Congress leadership because 'any pretence of delay would be for the purpose merely of giving [the Congress] an opportunity to perfect its plans before striking openly'.[46] In its emergency meeting of 8 August 1942, the Executive Council thus decided that (*i*) Gandhi and the members of the working committee should be arrested immediately in Bombay and interned; (*ii*) the agreed orders for the imposition of control on the press should be issued immediately; (*iii*) provincial and All India Congress committees to be declared unlawful; offices and funds seized and all potential organizers arrested and (*iv*) if these measures fail to stultify civil disobedience, the Congress as a whole will be declared unlawful association and emergency power to be promulgated giving fullest powers for dealing with all forms of Congress activity.[47] The action taken, it was officially announced, 'is not punitive but preventive and is directed against those, involved in a movement which if successful, must cripple India's war effort and gravely prejudice the cause of the United Nations. Moreover, this movement in so far as it seeks to undermine legal authority will also handicap India's political advancement'.[48]

Within hours of the passage of the Quit India Resolution on 8 August 1942,[49] the British government arrested all the leaders of the Congress not only at the all India, but provincial and district levels also, and clamped down on the Congress organization to disable it from functioning. Questions were raised in American and British ruling circles about the appropriateness of these measures and L. S. Amery the Secretary of State who was a war cabinet member as well, however was obliged to explain in public as to why such penal measures were necessary. In a BBC broadcast from London, he defended the Government of India's decision for a crack down on the Congress because

> in the face of such a challenge, and of such a menace, there could be only one answer. That was for the Government of India to take firm and above all, swift action to deal with its authors before their preparedness were further advanced or before the campaign could gain momentum . . . by their prompt and resolute action, the Government of India saved India and the Allied cause from a grave disaster.[50]

He also justified the arrest of the Congress leaders since

> . . . the success of the proposed campaign would paralyse not only the ordinary civil administration of India but the whole war effort. It would stop the output of munitions, the construction of aerodromes and above all, shetters against air attack; it would put an end to recruiting; it would immobilise the forces.

The war preparation would have suffered tremendously without incarcerating the leading Congressmen who were reported to have been 'fomenting'

> strikes not only in industry and commerce, but in the administration, law courts, schools and colleges, the interruption of traffic and public utility services, the cutting of telegraph and telephone wires, the picketing of troops and recruiting stations.[51]

Though these kinds of activity were never authorized by the Congress in advance of 8 August, Amery 'inadvertently lent them credibility as Congress policy' by charting it out as clearly as possible.[52] With a wide publicity of the broadcast in the Indian newspapers,[53] the confusion and uncertainty felt by the ordinary Congressmen and Congress sympathizers was suddenly ended: Amery became 'the chief instrument' in broadcasting the supposed Congress programme; what he said was avidly believed by the people.[54] As a result, what Amery said had been the Congress plan 'was accepted as the Congress plan by indignant demonstrators groping for direction. Many wanted to take extreme measures; Amery's charge gave them an excuse for taking them in the name of the Congress . . . what Amery claimed to have prevented, he instead helped to bring about.'[55]

Despite his meticulous plan for press censorship,[56] Amery's speech was widely hailed as that radicalizing text which galvanized the disparate masses into action. Hence, it is not a strange coincidence that the mass unrest hit the nation after the publication of the broadcast in the press on 10 August 1942. What is significant in this context is to underline the importance of a particular type of articulation in organizing a united political movement even in the absence of a central leadership. In his zeal to convince the Allies by providing an inventry of the proposed plan of sabotaging the war effort, Amery unknowingly provided the nationalists with a radicalizing text which probably unleashed the whole process of moving a mass of strangers to united political action under circumstances, favourable to the Congress call. In this respect, this particular speech of the Secretary of State appeared decisive in the absence of the Congress instruction regarding the way, the movement was to be organized; and thus made easy for the Congress leaders to exonerate their responsibility towards 'the disturbances'. The chief irony of 1942 was therefore, as Greenough aptly puts, 'that the awesome power of the press to inspire united action was unleashed by the British government; the radicalising text was the composition of Leopold Amery, not Mahatma Gandhi'.[57]

The Congress Preparedness

The Congress became militant and hence the wave of insurrection activity. Deviating from non-violence, the Congress volunteers resorted to violence indiscriminately on various occasions. The state was equally repressive in view, *inter alia*, of its ready access to an organized army, and yet 'the open rebellion' assumed massive proportions in areas where the state appeared to have been seriously undermined. At the beginning, the movement was widespread, affecting almost every corner of the country; its organization was so well-entrenched that the British left no stone unturned to contain the upsurge which, in a way, caught the administration by surprise. So alarmed and panic-stricken was the administration especially in the context of a probable Japanese attack that the Viceroy demanded a military solution.[58]

Provinces	*Congress Membership*		
	1938-9	*1939-40*	*1940-1*
Ajmer-Marwar	13,151	6,700	6,250
Assam	37,321	56,633	56,300
Bengal	4,83,158	4,40,729	2,44,064
Bihar	5,63,629	2,76,704	1,83,731
Bombay city and suburbs	61,936	60,368	18,631
Maharashtra	1,48,544	1,15,137	87,240
Karnataka	1,72,113	75,426	28,312
Gujarat	92,418	80,101	55,231
Nagpur	44,854	42,418	22,638
Mahakoshal	1,26,554	1,10,119	–
Vidharva	78,396	44,733	14,878
Delhi	19,423	11,956	7,974
Tamil Nadu	3,64,393	2,06,152	–
Andhra	3,35,205	2,05771	–
Kerala	55,031	49,266	–
NWFP	34,397	23,815	15,985
Orissa (Utkal)	1,98,325	1,26,126	45,792
Punjab	1,88,791	1,89,289	1,10,289
Sind	22,303	18,179	12,667
United Provinces	14,72,456	8,33,830	2,58,826
TOTAL	45,11,858	29,73,452	14,81,616

Sources: NAI, Home-Poll(g), 4/7/41; IOR, L/I/1/885: decrease in membership; *The Times*, London, 31 July 1941.

Despite the fear of a severe military clamp down on the participants, the movement acquired the characteristics of a rebellion with a strong organizational backing. What it reveals is that though the Congress was outlawed and its organization was in disarray in the provinces, due to, among other reasons, factional squabbles, the call for an open rebellion organized the disparate masses largely with a single aim of overthrowing the British rule in India. How big was the Congress organization in terms of membership on the eve of the August revolution? It is true that the drive for membership was not as effective as it was in the case of the earlier nation wide campaigns, notably, the Non-Cooperation and Civil Disobedience, though the AICC endeavoured constantly to enlist 'four anna' members. In circulars to the Provincial Congress Committees (PCC), in April 1940, the Congress High Command underlined the necessity of expanding the organizational network at the grassroots 'to conduct propaganda on Congress policies and the programme of satyagraha'.[59] The effort paid off and by May, there was considerable enthusiasm for satyagraha, but the Congress organization was not in a satisfactory condition.[60] What caused consternation to the Congress President, Maulana Azad, was the lukewarm response to the Gandhian call of individual satyagraha. Except United Provinces (UP) PCC, none of the provincial wings of the Congress succeeded in enrolling the allotted number of satyagrahees from the provinces.[61] In fact, there was a sharp decline in membership, as the earlier table shows (p. 11).

The dramatic decrease in membership from 4.5 million in 1938-9 to as low as 1.4 million is probably enough to prove that the Congress became terribly unpopular in course of time. And, the trend was evident: 'the Congress base was shaking, the members drifting away!' Therefore the Quit India declaration, as a commentator argues, was 'a cry of despair' or 'a cry of a party in panic'.[62] The interpretation seems plausible given the decline in membership. What is not explained in the gradual decrease of membership is why such a weak organization became formidable with the declaration of the Quit India demand. Warning that the administration should not feel complacent in view of the membership decline, the Intelligence Bureau made a necessary distinction between 'Congress membership figures' and 'Congress influence'. While attributing the membership decline to (*i*) failure to renew membership, (*ii*) the defection of the leftist from the Congress and (*iii*) success in containing the bogus membership, the official report cautioned that 'it would be unsafe to assume that Congress has become unpopular or noticeably lost its influence over the masses in provinces where it previously held undisputed sway'. Moreover, the anti-Congress activities of the Muslim League, the Hindu Mahasabha and other political parties increased appreciably during the past year and were to some extent responsible for detaching 'waverers' from active association with the Congress.[63] Although the decline of membership was never accepted as a right yardstick to judge the Congress strength, to the British administration, the information was useful to propagate the idea that the Congress popularity as a nationalist anti-British party was on the decline and hence, the Congress had no moral right to speak for India as a whole.[64]

The Quit India Resolution

The apparent decline in membership meant nothing serious in so far as the movement that followed after the adoption of the Quit India resolution on 8 August 1942, was concerned. What became famous as the August movement was the culmination of a process that began with the 1940

Ramgarh session of the AICC Though there was a noticeable lack of enthusiasm of the Congress volunteers in conducting 'the individual satyagraha'[65] the Ramgarh resolution was a significant step towards the adoption of the Quit India resolution. By insisting on an immediate British withdrawal, Gandhi and his associates were reported to have sent signals for the ultimate countdown. The Governor-General thus asked the Secretary of State to issue an order to the effect that 'civil disobedience in time of war will not be permitted and/or a formal warning to them that they will not be permitted to proceed with preparations for civil disobedience'.[66] Justifying a preventive measure because 'there is however no sign of any modification in stiffness of Gandhi's attitude or excessive nature of Congress claims as embodied in Ramgarh resolution with which there is no reason to doubt that he identifies himself',[67] the Governor-General further felt the need to extend the section 93 proclamation[68] to India as a whole. He saw a silver lining in the opposition of 'the moderate right wingers such as Birla & Co.' who expressed dissatisfaction with the Congress militancy which appeared temporary, as will be shown below, given the intimate association between the Congress and the big-business especially in the context of the August movement.

What became Allahabad resolution (1 May 1942) was principally a reiteration of the 1940 list of Congress demands. The intercepted resolution, drafted by Gandhi which was discussed by the AICC at its Allahabad session (27 April 1942) *(i)* demanded 'an immediate British withdrawal' *(ii)* declared that 'no foreign assistance needed for the freedom of this country'; and *(iii)* announced 'if Japan invaded India it shall meet with non-violent resistance'.[69] During the discussion, there occurred an apparent rift among the Working Committee members regarding the attitude towards the Japanese. Jawaharlal Nehru, opposing the fascist aggression, wanted the AICC to condemn the Japanese in categorical terms because 'we do not embarrass the British war effort because that in itself would mean an aid to the invader'.[70] What caused alarm to Nehru was Gandhi's feeling that 'Japan and Germany will win', a feeling expressed clearly in Bapu's statement that 'if India were freed, her first step will probably be to negotiate with Japan . . . and India bears no enmity with Japan'.[71] Distancing himself from what appeared to be Gandhi's position, Nehru emphatically argued that 'if Bapu's approach is accepted we become passive partners of the Axis powers'. This would equally be damaging for India's freedom struggle since 'the Allied countries will have a feeling that we are their enemies'; so the sympathy with the Japanese in whatever form was suicidal too because, elaborated Nehru, 'Japan is an imperialist country [and] conquest of India is in their plan'.[72] Vallavbhai Patel and Maulana Azad saw Nehru's points but found however unnecessary to dissociate from Gandhi's approach because, as Patel articulated, 'he [Gandhi] is instinctively right in the lead he gives in all critical situations'. Moreover, the Allies did not play the expected role in so far as India's freedom struggle was concerned; instead, they declined to accord importance to India's freedom given the war crisis. Although the Cripps Mission was publicised 'as a significant step towards the British withdrawal', in reality, it was an attempt to solicit the Congress cooperation in the British war effort by demanding cessation of political activities and consequently a complete Congress surrender to the British authority in India. So, Patel was not inclined to negotiate with the British at all especially after what he called 'the repeated insults heaped upon us'.[73] Conceding Patel's argument, Rajendra Prasad too expressed his support for 'Bapu's position' as the only practicable means to attain the British withdrawal from India; hence, he urged the Congressmen 'to strengthen Bapu's hands' forgetting the division among them. Azad did not seem perturbed about the possibility of a Japanese aggression because 'nationalism, the only religion for a subject nation' was strong enough to contain any imperialist design however powerful physically.[74]

The proposed resolution sought to cover the points contained in Gandhi's draft, but the approach was different. The discussion showed that the division of opinion revealed in the earlier deliberations still persisted. Nehru was, therefore, asked to prepare a draft of his own, and Rajendra Prasad, the Congress President, prepared another following Bapu's instruction *in toto.* Both the drafts were put to vote and the Working Committee was divided.[75] Given the fact that independence was a greater cause than anything else, the Congress President urged his colleagues to remain united in the context probably of 'the last battle for freedom';[76] his call yielded result since the resolution which was approved unanimously by the AICC on 1 May 1942 underlined Nehru's concern for equivocal condemnation for the Axis design, if there was any, to conquer India. Instead of mentioning the name of a particular country, the 1 May resolution

> repudiates the idea that freedom can come to India through interference or invasion by any foreign nation. . . . In case, an invasion takes place, it must be resisted . . . [through] non-violent non-cooperation . . . [Moreover], the All India Congress Committee is convinced that India will attain her freedom through her own strength and will retain it likewise.[77]

Notwithstanding the differences among the Congressmen, the Allahabad resolution articulated in clear terms the Congress attitude towards the Japanese and possible steps in case of another imperialist aggression. Nehru was happy for having successfully persuaded his colleagues to adopt a resolution condemning Fascism which, he thought, was most apt given the Japanese help in organizing the Indian National Army (INA) under the stewardship of Subhas Chandra Bose as an alternative front in India's freedom struggle.[78] So, it was not surprising that the Wardha resolution adopted on 14 July 1942 linked the defeat of Fascism to India's freedom; it, thus, declared,

> British rule in India must end immediately, not merely because foreign domination even at its best is an evil in itself and a continuing injury to the subject people, but because India in bondage can play no effective part in defending herself and in affecting the fortunes of the war that is desolating humanity. The freedom of India is thus necessary not only in the interest of India but also for the safety of the world and for the ending of Nazism, Fascism, militarism and other forms of imperialism and the aggression of one nation over another.
>
> The Congress would be pleased with the British power if it accepts the very reasonable and just proposal herein made; . . . [otherwise], the Congress will then be reluctantly compelled to utilise the non-violent strength it might have gathered since 1920 when it adopted non-violence as part of its policy for the vindication of the political rights and liberty.[79]

By far the most militant, the Wardha resolution caused alarm to the authority which already began charting out measures to pre-empt the Congress strike. It was clear, as Benthall suggested, that the Congress was aiming at probably 'the most devastating strike', the British had ever experienced 'in its rule'.[80] The Congress leadership was more militant than ever. While interpreting the nature of the forthcoming movement, as enunciated by the Wardha resolution, Nehru was reported to have said,

> The Mahatma's new movement would impose no restrictions as has been the case in the previous movements of 1920 and 1930. Everyone would be free to use his own weapons according to his own choice. Revolutionaries could do as they pleased and also kisans and labour leaders. The Mahatma was not prepared to call-off the movement on account of the acts of such people. . . . If the people took over government buildings, courts, police stations and other places under risk of repression, this too would be our method of assisting in the movement. Mahatma Gandhi was no longer prepared to look upon such acts as 'Himalayan blunders' as he had done in the past.[81]

The proposed Congress confrontation with the British appeared disastrous to the Raj primarily because of the British difficulty in containing the domestic agitation in the context of the war crisis. Hence Linlithgow, the Viceroy sought the Executive Council's permission to undertake steps in advance, so that the movement could be destroyed before it took off.[82] Defending the Viceroy, the Executive Council asked him to publicise 'the views and intentions of Gandhi and the Congress High Command' in order precisely to prove that 'the more recent utterances of the Congress leaders interpreting the intention of the Wardha resolution, were seditious enough to warrant immediate action against them'.[83] India Office gave the Viceroy a free hand in tackling 'the domestic disturbances' and thus L. S. Amery wrote, 'the only answer to my mind in such a situation is to act at once, take up the challenge to our authority and arrest the working committee and many more as you think necessary to show that in India we mean business'.[84] Without such drastic measures as 'immediate arrest and prosecution and very drastic punishment', the movement, Amery apprehended, would assume devastating magnitudes since its object was 'to create a general atmosphere of defiance of government and of ill-feeling in the course of which the Government will be driven to a series of action which will be increasingly misrepresented in order to fan the flame of resistance and to create the kind of situation in which *the American and some of our people will begin to say that there is already a civil war in India and that things cannot be worse if we give Congress what they demanded'* (emphasis added).[85] That the Secretary of State left no stone unturned in combating the Congress assault in all seriousness was made clear through his order 'to take prompt measures with the press to prevent the circulation of resolutions or of information about Congress generally. This may necessitate putting an end to the gentleman's agreement, but that cannot be helped.'[86]

The final countdown began because the Congress leadership, including Gandhi, appealed to the Provincial Congress Committees to remain united in the context of the last battle for freedom. In its circular to the PCCs on the eve of the Quit India call the AICC urged the Congress volunteers to stick to non-violence while conducting the campaign against the continuity of the British power in India.[87] J. B. Kripalani, the Congress Secretary, however expressed anxiety as to whether an organizationally weak Congress was equipped to carry on the struggle to a successful conclusion.[88] A majority of the Congress members was, however, inclined to believe that the masses were ready for the final battle and 'the Congress influence' was at its peak despite the sudden dwindling of Congress membership. The situation was alarming as anti-war sentiments had a firm grip over the masses and the Government of India's Home Department appeared panic-stricken since the government was identified as 'treacherous dishonest and deceitful . . . [and hence] nobody should pay subscription for war, nobody should enlist in the Government forces, nobody should pay rent and canal dues'.[89] Nehru, after his trip to the United Provinces, was convinced that the forthcoming campaign was likely to attain the goal in view of the emotional attachment of the people with the cause of 'independence' and the role of Gandhi in galvanizing the masses into action. In his words.

> the mood of the country had changed, and from a sullen passivity it rose to a pitch of excitement and expectation. Events were not waiting for a Congress decision or resolution; they had been pushed forward by Gandhiji's utterances and now they were moving onwards with their momentum. It was clear that, whether Gandhiji was right or wrong, he had crystallised the prevailing mood of the people. There was a desperateness in it, and emotional urge which gave second place to logic and reason and a calm consideration of the consequences of action.[90]

On 8 August 1942, the AICC met in Bombay and approved what became famous as the Quit India resolution. Harping on the familiar theme of the final British withdrawal from India, the resolution runs thus,

> The perils of today . . . necessitates the independence of India and the ending of British domination. No future promises or grievances can affect the present situation or meet that peril. They cannot produce the needed psychological effect on the mind of the masses. Only the glow of freedom now can release that energy and enthusiasm of millions of people which will immediately transform the nature of the war.
>
> The AICC therefore repeats with all emphasis the demand for the withdrawal of the British power from India. . . . The Committee appeals to the people of India to face the dangers and hardships that will fall to their lot with courage and endurance and to hold them together under the leadership of Gandhi and carry out his instructions as disciplined soldiers of Indian freedom. They must remember that non-violence is the basis of this movement.[91]

The first few paragraphs of the resolution reiterate the spirit of both Allahabad and Wardha resolutions. For the Congress, India's independence was contingent on the British withdrawal and hence the resolution was passed accordingly. What however was different was the Congress instruction to the effect of asking the participants to act independently in the forthcoming struggle in case of the arrests of the leaders. The AICC thus exhorted,

> A time may come when it may not be possible to issue instructions or for instructions to reach our people and when no Congress committees can function. When this happens, every man and woman who is participating in this movement must function for himself or herself within the four corners of the general

instructions issued. Every Indian who desires freedom and strives for it must be his guide urging him on along the hard road where there is no resting place and which leads ultiumately to the independence and deliverance of India.[92]

The message, the resolution conveyed, was categorical in the sense that the AICC urged the people to take part in what was identified as 'the last battle for freedom'. For Gandhi, 'this [was] the last struggle of [his] life' and he did not want to wait any longer because 'delay is injurious and waiting any further would be humiliation for us'.[93] He thus appealed to the people to follow the *mántra*, Do or Die:

> We shall either free India or die in the attempt; we shall not live to see the perpetuation of our slavery. Every true Congressmen or [Congress] women will join the struggle with an inflexible determination not to remain alive to see the country in bondage and slavery.[94]

In a message to the nation just before his arrest, Gandhi spelt the task more precisely. Reiterating his faith in non-violence, he elaborated,

> everyone is free to go the fullest length under ahimsa; complete deadlock by strikes and other non-violent means; satyagrahees must go out to die not to live; they must seek and face death; it is only when individuals go out to die that the nation will survive. *Karenge Ya Marenge* [We will do or die].[95]

Neither the AICC resolution nor Gandhi's last message was allowed to be reported in the press. So, there was less trouble especially immediately after the incarceration of the entire Congress leadership including Gandhi. The government strategy seemed to have worked in snatching the wind away from the Congress sail, as Tottenham misconstrued by preventing the Congress message getting across to the people.[96] Although there were protest marches in Bombay, Gujarat and Bengal following the adoption of the resolution, they did not pose a serious threat to the British administration. In other words, the decision to gag the press paid-off at least initially and a confident Viceroy sought the Secretary of State's permission to deport Gandhi in particular to save India from further crisis.[97] The idea of deporting Gandhi was in his agenda since the adoption of the Wardha resolution on 14 July 1942. When Linlithgow put it before the Executive Council for discussion 'they unanimously and vigorously opposed the deportation which would cause bad reactions in India and would result in Gandhi staging a fast abroad, with a consequent crop of speculation, rumours about his ill-treatment, etc'.[98] Not convinced in view of the strong opposition of the majority of the Executive Council members, L. S. Amery did not press the issue.[99] There were also differences of opinion at the highest level of British administration as to whether Gandhi should be released if he undertook a fast unto death. The Viceroy held the view that Gandhi should not be set free 'even if he fasted to death'. All the Governors except that of Sind opposed the Viceroy vehemently. R. Lumley, the Bombay Governor, for instance, was 'certain that it would be gravest political blunder to allow him to die in detention'. The Governor of the Central Provinces was 'emphatically of the opinion that local reactions would be most unfavourable. . . . We would be left with no friends in India and even some of the Indian members of the Superior Services will turn against us.' And hence, he urged the Viceroy 'that Gandhi should be released and restricted to Sevagram if he embarks on a fast'.[100] Apprehending the disastrous consequences of Gandhi's death during the imprisonment, Churchill's war cabinet appeared inclined to shift Gandhi to his Ashram in case of fast provided 'he could still be isolated from the outside world at Sevagram'.[101] As there was no categorical support for his view at the highest level of the Raj, Linlithgow had no alternative but to accept that 'we must be prepared in the event of a fast to set Gandhi at liberty (leaving it to himself to decide where he wants to go or whether he prefers to remain in Aga Khan's house at Poona) once fast begins to endanger his life and I feel, in the circumstances, this is the best alternative, one could think'.[102]

With the arrest of the Congress leaders, the movement, Linlithgow felt, would fizzle-out soon. In his letter to Amery, he thus conveyed 'we may congratulate ourselves upon our having struck at Congress before their preparations are completed'. He further added, 'we have . . . far more important reason to be thankful: that we have brought on this business at a time when the war position is not such as to offer any immediate threat to India whether from the West or from the East'. He was emphatic that without such pre-emptive arrests, the situation could have been worse because 'Gandhi's plan was to wait for bad war news before raising the standard of revolt'.[103]

To stop the publication of news regarding arrests and the development of the movement, the Government of India imposed press censorship. Defending the decision, Reginald Maxwell, the Home Member, argued that two objective considerations governed the government stipulation in this regard: first, disorder of this character 'are infectious and news of what has occurred in one place may lead to its repetition in a number of other places which might otherwise have remained quiet'; and, secondly, 'much that has occurred would, if it were known to the enemy, be of great value to his plans for an invasion of this country'.[104] In view of the war crisis, the plan for censorship was probably apt, but it would be a mistake, as R. Tottenham warned, 'to attempt any such general pre-censorship order on the press in India as a whole. It would annoy the Press intensel–even the pro-British Press–and would probably result in our losing quite an appreciable amount of useful spontaneous criticism of the Congress plan.'[105] Challenging the government policy, fourteen of the Calcutta newspaper, excluding the loyalist *The Statesman* and *The Star of India,* ceased publication indefinitely. Although the Viceroy seemed happy because the press, to him, was 'a great nuisance',[106] some of the Executive Council members were inclined to withdraw the restriction in phases precisely to dispel the popular fear that it would contribute to the emergence of a state, 'not different from a fascist one'.[107] There was, in fact, a serious argument, as M.O. Carter, the Secretary to the Governor of Bengal, put forward in favour of a gradual withdrawal of restriction. 'The stopping of publication for one week was', as Carter elaborated, 'intended to give full force to the campaign of leafleting, i.e. to force the public to read the leaflets'. There were reasons to be alarmed because 'arrangements for the printing and distribution of leaflets were . . . made with the connivance of the nationalist press'. By drawing attention to the disastrous consequences of such a campaign aiming at 'spreading alarm and panic by means of false rumours and exaggerated statements', Carter also underlined the importance of streamlining the overall intelligence network in the country.[108] The suggestion did not appear feasible because it was felt that 'any concession to the press at this time are a sure sign of Government weakening in its original determination'.[109]

Not only was the press generally sympathetic to the Congress cause, the Indian big-business too was ready to support the Congress-led nationalist movement. In fact, with the beginning of individual satyagraha following the 1940 Ramgarh resolution, Indian business magnates were reported to have appreciated the Congress demand for 'swadeshi', i.e. home-produced goods and Indian mill owners naturally actively supported a movement so 'beneficial to their business interests'.[110] For any movement to succeed, what was required most was financial backing and thus 'the Congress has relied and still relies on', the Viceroy had no doubt, 'the large Indian financial and commercial interests for support, both political and financial'. The Congress needed that support to maintain its position and its influence 'and is only too glad to receive it notwithstanding its professed democratic if not socialistic creed'. Big industry, on the other hand, 'is only too willing to furnish that support in ample measure so as to have the advantage of the Congress organization and machine of its side and as *a valuable insurance for the future*' (emphasis added). Hence, the Viceroy concluded, 'it suits both sides equally well to work up an insistent agitation for the liquidation of British business and commercial interests in India'.[111] What thus governed the intimate association between the big-business and Congress was conditioned largely, if not exclusively, by the possibility of mutual advantage: on the part of the Congress, money was 'a necessary expedient to provide the sinews of war'; and on the part of the big business support to nationalist politics was 'a grand scale speculation with fabulous profits to follow the attainment of power by the Congress'.[112] The Congress had thus no difficulty to raise money from the Congress sympathizers among the trading community as and when the need arose. Just on the eve of the Quit India declaration, the Congress was reported to have collected Rs.30 lakhs (three million) from renowned millowners like Birla, Tata, Dalmia, Singhania and others including millowners of Ahmedabad.[113] Similarly, in Bombay, the millowners particularly from the Marwari and Gujarati community, contributed significantly to the funds that were collected by Vallavbhai Patel before the movement started.[114] Not only did the Intelligence Bureau fail to ascertain as to where this was deposited, there was also no trace of these transactions as 'the merchants are adepts at writing off big amounts which they do not want to show in their books'.[115] In fact, the big business support to the open rebellion despite its adverse effect on production *per se* was attributed to the possible Japanese victory. The UP central intelligence officer thus wrote 'that the degree of financial backing for Congress has been in direct proportion to the morale of the Hindus and their belief in the invasion of India by the Japanese and the breakdown of the British government'.[116]

There were two ways in which the big business tried to help the open rebellion: on the one hand, they were reported to have encouraged strikes despite the loss involved, to (*a*) champion the non-violent struggle and (*b*) embarrass the British administration which was held responsible for such a breakdown. In fact, 'a whip was issued by the Ahmedabad millowners who', as an Intelligence Bureau report suggests, 'have decided that the owners of mills should encourage strikes in their own mills and should pay two months wages to the labourers'.[117] On the other hand, there were evidences to show that the industrialists provided the Congress with funds. The Indian Chamber of Commerce (ICC), controlled by Birla brothers, found the movement inevitable given the British intransigence in undertaking a fruitful dialogue with the Congress. In a resolution, adopted on 10 August 1942, at its meeting in Calcutta, the ICC expressed affinity with the movement and its leader, Gandhi, and agreed to sanction money to the Marwari Relief Committee[118] which was, as the Intelligence Bureau report demonstrates, nothing but a garb to extend monetary help to the movement and its organization.[119] Apart from its contribution, the ICC asked its constituents to financially help the movement as and when it was needed. Thus Karan Chand Thaper of the Thaper Brothers Ltd, an important Calcutta-based Punjabi business house, 'gave Rs. 10,000 to Jai Prakash Narain' who was assured of more financial help from the same source.[120] S. J. Desai, the Secretary of the ICC, was authorized to draw money any time for the Congress activity in view of its urgency.[121] Likewise, the Bengal National Chamber of Commerce (BNCC), though declined considerably with the consolidation of the Marwari business interests through the ICC, deplored that 'the Government of India should not have precipitated a crisis by not giving an opportunity to Mahatma Gandhi to come in contact' with the Viceroy and explore the possibilities 'of a satisfactory solution of the political deadlock'.[122] Holding the British government responsible for having caused 'a serious dislocation in trade and commerce in many industrial centres of India',[123] the BNCC urged the administration to initiate a dialogue with the Congress leadership as the only way to defuse this grave crisis. Generally sympathetic to the Congress, the BNCC too was identified as another source for fund for the movement. In his daily report, the Deputy Commissioner of Police, Calcutta, advised the government to freeze the BNCC capital for alleged financial support to the rebellion.[124]

The above summary shows the extent to which the big business acted as a motive force behind the movement by providing funds as and when necessary. Thus it is not surprising that there operated a very ingenious working arrangement between the Congress High Command and a number of Hindu business interests in Calcutta and Bombay. Governed by the logic of national democracy, the Congress leadership was generally found to support the Indian industrialists even at the cost of damaging its prospect among the workers. In order to secure India's economic future, the Congress was inclined to gamble in favour of the industrialists; while the big business invested in Congress presumably to ascertain its future in the days to come when the Congress was likely to rule the state. There was an immediate benefit too for Gandhi was alleged to have been instrumental 'at least on more than four or five big occasions for the personal benefit of certain Hindu millionaires in Calcutta and Bombay'.[125] So, the apparent intimacy between the Congress and big business was largely conditioned by the prospect of mutual benefit to both the actors who strove to defend their respective interests out of such an association.

Opposition to the Quit India Resolution

Although the 1947 transfer of power is the culmination of various movements, launched by the Indian National Congress, the 1942 August revolution is perhaps the greatest mass mobilization, based on nationalism. Notwithstanding the fact that Gandhi reigned supreme during the movement, the Quit India resolution provoked opposition to the decision from among his colleagues within the Congress and other major political parties. In a way, the adoption of this resolution is a watershed in India's nationalist movement for a variety of reasons: first, the Quit India call was an ultimatum to the British which itself is significant given that in neither the Non-Cooperation nor Civil Disobedience campaign, the Congress insisted on a complete British withdrawal from India; moreover, the campaign began when the apprehension of a Japanese invasion gripped the Raj following especially the downfall of Malaya and Singapore; its implications were disastrous on the British Indian army, stationed in the Rangoon front and elsewhere, and more particularly on the public opinion in India, underlining the probable Congress victory against the British which lost completely its credibility. The second consequence of the August resolution is more important because it brought out, in clear terms, the schism within the political parties involved in the nationalist struggle; not only does the event highlight the ideological differences between the Congress and other contending parties, it also draws our attention to the division within the Congress over fundamental issues relating to the Hindu-Muslim question.

The 8 August resolution was adopted when the Congress was already divided following the acceptance of the 14 July Wardha resolution. Four prominent Congress activists, headed by C. Rajagopalachari, criticized the resolution on the ground that British withdrawal without a Hindu-Muslim settlement would lead to anarchy. They, thus, argued, 'it is essential that before a demand for withdrawal can be reasonably made, the major political organisations of this country namely, the Indian National Congress and the Muslim League, should evolve a joint plan with regard to the provisional government which can take over power and preserve the continuity of the state'.[126] Moreover, it was not even remotely probable that, as they insisted, 'the movement would be able to install a national government capable of resisting Japanese aggression'. Instead, it would only produce 'more intense and large-scale repression and suffering which would facilitate Japan's invasion and occupation'. Given the British access to a well-entrenched administrative apparatus, the authority, the signatories were confident, 'would not allow the movement to proceed under central direction and the enemy might take advantage of the lack of proper control to convert into a fifth column activity'.[127] Gandhi did not seem persuaded because, to him, the fear of Japanese invasion appeared to have clouded their vision and hence their inability to comprehend the potential of the forthcoming movement.[128] Whatever the validity of the logic, the decision to remain indifferent to the Congress campaign caused a fissure among the Congressmen at a time when the saga of independence drew to a close.

Similarly, B. R. Ambedkar, representing the minority interests, felt that the Quit India resolution was an attempt 'to do away with the intervention of the British government in the discussion of the Minority Question and thereby securing for the Congress a free hand to settle it on its own lights'.[129] Upset with the Congress attitude towards the minority question at a crucial point of India's history, Ambedkar characterised the Quit India campaign as 'a mad venture' which was 'in effect, if not in intention, an attempt to win independence by bypassing the Muslims and other minorities'.[130] Declaring in rather strong terms that Gandhi's civil disobedience was 'both irresponsible and insane' and since this movement 'may be the best way to serve the best interests of the Congress party . . . and not the country', he therefore exhorted that 'duty requires that those who do not believe in his movement must take steps to prevent it from taking place'.[131]

Ambedkar's rather uncompromising stance appeared to have been influenced, if not determined, by the negligence of the Congress of the minority issue in all its political resolutions since 1940. For him, on the solution of the minority problem, including that of the *Harijans,* depended India's future. Hence, political independence, freedom from the British control, appeared insignificant in view of 'the atrocious social practices dividing human beings following an artificial logic'.[132] So, for a constitution to work in India, the foremost pre-condition, as Ambedkar articulated, was to accommodate the minorities on an equal basis in any discussion for India's political future.

Ambedkar's opposition was largely due to the Congress indifference to the minority cause. The Hindu Mahasabha however denounced the satyagraha campaign as 'sterile, unmanly and injurious to the Hindu cause', and expressed its willingness to cooperate with the war effort.[133] The Working Committee thus passed a resolution declaring,

> . . . that in view of the opportunity that the present war offers for the general militarization of the Hindus and for the organization of the system of India on sound and up-to-date modern lines so that India be converted into a self-contained

defence unit, the Hindu Mahasabha is prepared wholeheartedly to work out the schemes of the expansion of Viceroy's Executive Council, but on honourable terms of equity and justice.[134]

The terms included (*i*) the rejection of the proposal for partition [of India] by the government and (*ii*) allotment of six seats to the Hindu Mahasabha in the Executive Council which was legitimate given the Hindu demographic strength. So, in a way, by agreeing to support the war effort, the Hindu Mahasabha leadership strove to sharpen the attack on the Muslims which was articulated clearly in its 1940 annual session, held between 28 and 30 December at Madurai in the south. V. D. Savarkar, the president, thus gave a call to begin a movement unless the demands were conceded.[135] The 1941 annual session, slotted to be held at Bhagalpur, Bihar, led to a confrontation between the government and the Mahasabha. Since Bhagalpur was a riot-prone area, the Bihar government advised that the arrangement might be altered because the date would coincide with that of the Baqr'Id festival and Bhagalpur was notoriously 'liable to outbreaks of communal strife'.[136] The Mahasabha refused to make this concession and the session was thus banned. In an emergency meeting, the Mahasabha working committee decided to ignore the ban and accordingly about 1,200 volunteers, mostly from Bombay and Bengal, began their march to Bhagalpur to attend the 1941 December annual session. All of them were arrested and released in early 1942.

Though the Hindu Mahasabha failed to attain what it tried, it nonetheless projected its strength by mobilizing a large group of people in its opposition to the alleged government favouritism to the Muslims. On the whole, however, the Mahasabha upheld its decision to cooperate with the British during the war despite the so-called governmental policy of Muslim-appeasement. Accordingly, it was decided to challenge the open rebellion, launched by the Congress which would undoubtedly cripple the British war effort. In an appeal to the people, B. S. Moonjee, the president defended the need to abstain from the movement damaging 'the possibility of the rise of an agreed-constitutional system by undertaking such an undemocratic campaign'.[137] Savarkar too found the position ideologically defensible because the Quit India Movement would neither protect the Hindu interests nor that of the country, but would allow the Japanese and other anti-Indian forces to fulfil their evil design.[138] His statement was a mere reiteration of the argument offered by Shyama Prasad Mookherjee in opposition to the Congress campaign at the Mahasabha Working Committee deliberations. Mookherjee had no doubt that the movement should be stopped immediately by any means because 'from the way in which the movement was developing it appeared that it aimed at crippling the production of war materials, military supplies, etc. If that happened, the Axis would be directly helped.'[139]

Mookherjee's unequivocal support to the government's repressive measures in containing the movement however caused a division among his colleagues. There was voting on the action taken by the Government of India to suppress the Congress movement which had already resulted in loss of lives. Out of 26 working committee members, 20 voted against the step pursued; three, including Mookherjee himself, supported, and three remained neutral.[140] A group, led by N. C. Chatterjee, insisted on a resolution expressing sympathy with the Congress movement as a first step, to be followed by an active participation in it.[141] For the majority of the Hindu Mahasabha members, the Congress movement had captured the Hindu sentiments and it would therefore be suicidal to oppose. Seeking the permission of the High Command to join the movement in Bengal, Chatterjee thus argued,

> . . . the present situation [in Bengal] is that the entire Hindu population is in sympathy with Gandhiji and his movement and if anybody wants to oppose it, he will be absolutely finished and hounded out of public life. The unfortunate statement issued by V. D. Savarkar made our position rather difficult in Bengal. It is rather amusing to find that Mr. Jinnah wants the Mussalmans not to join the Congress movement and Mr. Savarkar wants the Hindus not to join the same. Even then, *the Congress movement has made a great stir and it shows that it has got thousands of adherents*[142] (emphasis added).

As it was a rare opportunity to strike roots among the Hindus, Chatterjee further asked Shyama Prasad to lead the movement in Bengal and elsewhere. Despite the risk of causing a permanent fissure among the rank and file Hindu Mahasabha members, the leadership did not seem inclined to join the movement as it resulted in severe dislocations in the war efforts. In order not to antagonize those supporting the open rebellion, it was thus resolved that 'Hindu Mahasabha shall support the demand for the termination of the present system which keeps India in bondage. . . . In spite of the policy of responsive cooperation followed by the Hindu Mahasabha, the elementary fact is to be appreciated that unless the freedom of India is recognised and effected, the Defence of India can not be supported by the mobilisation of the national will.'[143]

The Hindu Mahasabha decision to withdraw participation was conditioned largely by consideration that opposition to the war efforts was tantamount to supporting the Axis powers, particularly the Japanese; the Communist Party of India (CPI) defended its arguments condemning the open rebellion by drawing upon the ideological implications of joining the fascist camp. In other words, for the CPI, the challenge to the state power through a mass mobilization was unwarranted at a time when the fascist aggression was imminent. So long as Soviet Russia was not involved in the war, it was *an imperialist war* and the CPI professed a policy of neutrality which was probably indefensible in view of the Congress attempt to launch a mass struggle for freedom. Although there were CPI activists who complemented the Congress endeavour by organizing movements at the grassroots along the Gandhian line, the leadership however determined its plan of action more in accordance with the international situation than with domestic compulsion. Hence, the imperialist war was transformed into *a people's war* following the German attack on the USSR. And the Soviet victory was the guarantee of people's liberation all over the world. In the context of the August movement, the CPI did not seem puzzled and decided its line of action according to its commitment to defend the Soviet land even at the cost of being alienated from the people in India. Expressing its loyalty to the anti-fascist war in which the British aligned herself with the Soviet Union, the CPI declared,

> The war is India's great opportunity to fight for national liberation, no more in isolation, no more single-handed but as part of the battle for world liberation. It is the war of the Soviet peoples whom we pledged to support against an imperialist attack. It is the war of the heroic Chinese people whose five years of lone struggle we have admired with veneration. It is war of the British people with whom we have preached friendliness and cooperation despite the British imperial domination over us. It is the war of the enslaved people of Europe for whom our hearts bleed. It is an All-Peoples' war against Fascism and for freedom.[144]

The war therefore became a people's war and its victory was a certain guarantee to the emancipation of the enslaved nations. In other words, by way of contributing to the anti-fascist war, Indian masses would, in fact, advance the cause of national freedom. As India's independence was contingent on the Allied victory, 'we can no more fight', the CPI insisted, 'for our freedom by opposing this war. We will be cutting our own throats by doing so. *We will [therefore] not be hitting at British imperialism at all*'[145] (emphasis added). Such an assurance made the British task easy especially in the context of the open rebellion; no longer, the CPI was a threat and the administrative apparatus was now geared to tackle the Congress activists with a renewed vigour. It was therefore not an exaggeration when O.M. Martin, the Bengal Home secretary, stated that 'the only good result of the Japanese entry into the war was that the communists ceased to give trouble'.[146] In consonance with the government policy of utilizing the CPI for the war, the ban on the party was lifted in July 1942. The CPI ensured its freedom in exchange of a guarantee that, as the government communique lifting the ban mentions, 'they have decided, if permitted, to throw their energies into the task of cooperating with existing war effort [which meant that] they will devote all their energies to teaching people what war means and organising them for self defence and resistance to the enemy'.[147]

The pro-war strategy caused a schism among the CPI activists. 'Those of the younger generation', as an official report claims, were not inclined to 'committing them to support the government'.[148] In a note to Amery, the Viceroy urged to reconsider the decision allowing the CPI to function legally as a party because 'CPI remains a doubtful factor. Its official policy is still pro-war but behaviour of many of its members prove what has always been clear, namely, that the CPI is composed far more of anti-British revolutionaries.'[149] Corroborating the Viceroy's apprehension, the Bihar Governor categorically stated that 'I have my suspicion that the communists are playing a double game. On the surface, they are anti-fascist and pro-war; below the surface, they are anti-imperial and their demand for arms may have as much relation to one as the other of these lines of thought.'[150] Similarly, John Herbert, the Bengal Governor, cautioned about the consequences of lifting the ban because 'it is quite clear from the speeches that have been made at the anti-Japanese meetings that some of the members have no intention of stopping anti-government subversive propaganda. Members of the CPI are carrying on anti-British propaganda under the cloak of anti-fascist speeches.'[151]

The above official notes show that the CPI activists continued to pose a threat to the British by championing the nationalist goal even at the cost of deviating from the well-publicized pro-war strategy. Alarmed by its decision to organize students of Bengal for the Quit India campaign, the government found it imperative to demobilize the students by closing the hostels.[152] What caused panic was the successful organization of strikes in and around Calcutta following the announcement of the open rebellion. In attempting to gain what was lost due the pro-war call, the CPI activists were reported to have consistently organized the workers for the freedom struggle. 'It is [therefore] extremely dangerous', the Calcutta Police Commissioner noted, 'to encourage CPI activists in Calcutta. Their chief demand is now for the release of Congress leaders–they hope to force this by a general strike (or threat of one). If they accomplish this, the CPI influence in the Congress organization and with general public will be paramount.'[153] Not only among the jute workers, the CPI-influenced trade union organized strikes in the tea gardens to champion the Quit India call; though the strike lasted for three days, the Jalpaiguri district authority asked for more policemen given the well-entrenched anti-government feelings which might flare-up any time as a gigantic movement.[154] Such a situation, contrary to the pro-war strategy, draws our attention to a different kind of process operating at the grassroots. For the workers, independence meant cessation of exploitation and thus their amelioration. Well-tuned to the needs of the day, the organizers too picked-up those issues which strengthened the workers consolidation against the tea garden owners who were largely Britishers. So, it was perfectly logical for the workers to join the August revolution following the Congress call as it meant their emancipation; for the leaders, the call to rally by the Congress was defensible for it challenged the immediate exploiters who figured prominently in the workers' perception than the distant fascist powers. Underlying this remains a significant reason as to why the people's war largely fizzled out at the level of unorganized politics[155] once the Quit India call created a mass fervour.

The CPI opposition to the August revolution followed the grand strategy of helping those including the British for combating the fascist forces. The Muslim League abstained from the Congress-led Quit India campaign for reasons connected with the call for Pakistan.[156] Hence, the League deplored the decision to launch an open rebellion 'in pursuance of the objective of establishing Congress-Hindu domination in India'. Condemning the movement, it was resolved at a hurriedly called meeting,

> . . . this movement is directed not only to coerce the British Government into handing over power to a Hindu oligarchy . . . but also to force Mussalmans to submit and surrender to Congress terms and dictation.
>
> [The Muslim League is] firmly convinced that the present Congress movement is not directed for securing the independence of all the constituent elements in the life of the country but for the establishment of Hindu Raj and to deal *a death blow to the Muslim goal of Pakistan* (emphasis added). . . . if the Congress demand is accepted it would bring the 100 million of Muslims under the yoke of a Hindu Raj which must inevitably result either in anarchy and chaos or complete strangulation and annihilation of Muslim India and all that Islam stands for.
>
> . . . in these circumstances, the working committee of the All India Muslim League . . . call upon the Muslims to abstain from any participation in the movement initiated by the Congress and to continue to pursue their normal peaceful life.[157]

The carefully worded resolution has three important dimensions reflecting the extent to which the Muslim leadership realized the importance of helping the British during the war crisis probably as the most significant guarantee for a Muslim homeland. First, by attributing the Quit India Movement to the Congress motive of establishing Hindu domination/Hindu Raj, the League successfully projected itself as a dependable ally of the Raj; secondly, by floating the idea that the success of the Congress movement meant an abject submission and surrender of the Muslims to the Hindus, the League employed an effective strategy drawing on the age-old Hindu-Muslim fissure to dissociate the Muslims from the campaign; the strategy paid-off for a variety of complex reasons[158] at a time when the distinctiveness of the community was championed consistently at the cost of the nation and the freedom struggle. Finally, the resolution also underlines the Congress failure to take the Muslims into confidence in such a gigantic effort like the Quit India Movement which thus remained weak from the outset. By their withdrawal and opposition to the movement, the Muslims consolidated their claims as a separate community which was crucial in the context of the British endeavour to resolve the constitutional deadlock through negotiation.

As a resolution, its impact on the nationalist movement was far-reaching. Jinnah's characterization of the Congress as merely a Hindu organization drew heavily upon the 1940 Lahore resolution in which the Pakistan demand was articulated. So, it was logical for Jinnah to oppose the Quit India campaign which, by championing the goal of India's independence, struck at the foundation of the two nation theory and its manifestation in the call for Pakistan. Reiterating that 'Gandhi's sole aim is the revival of Hindu India and establishment of Hindu raj',[159] he identified the Quit India Movement as 'a declaration of internecine civil war'[160] which had nothing to do with Muslims and hence, 'let the Hindus fight it out'.[161]

Jinnah's insistence on the Muslim aloofness from the movement did not gain an easy acceptance in the Bengal Provincial Muslim League (BPML). During the discussion, there were two groups opposing each other : one led by Abdur Rahman Siddiqui urged the League 'to join the Congress to get rid of the British which had always destroyed the Muslim powers and solidarity';[162] the other, under Nazimuddin's stewardship, defended the opposition to the movement because 'they will have to fight with the Hindus sooner or later for Pakistan and this is the best time in their own interests'.[163] Nazimuddin succeeded in winning the majority support and thus it was decided not to merely remain aloof, but to oppose directly in view of the severe dislocation and act of sabotage, encouraged by the Congress. The resolution which was adopted, thus *inter alia,* insists,

> . . . the League must manage all resources to defeat and break Gandhian move or be prepared for its own doom . . . it must declare an open war on the Congress move of sabotage, violence, loot and anarchy in the name of order, peace and freedom of the country from Congress fascism . . . unless the League

boldly takes the field of Mass Action with a programme to actively oppose, counteract and frustrate the Congress move the machinery of Government will be very soon paralysed and the British distressed as they are . . . will be forced to yield to Congress.[164]

As the avowed object of the movement was to subvert the government established by law, the BPML was emphatic that 'if the British and Muslims combine they (with the help of other cooperating parties) can smash both Gandhi and Congress and the axis on behalf of who they are fighting a war of planned sabotage in India'.[165] John Herbert, the Bengal Governor, felt assured and asked the Viceroy to utilise such a sentiment to the British advantage at a convenient time.[166]

The articulated Muslim opposition to the August movement provided the British with a strong argument challenging the Congress claim of representing India as a whole. What is now clear, as the above discussion shows, that the Quit India call instead of unifying, brought the well-entrenched division among the Indians on various counts, to the forefront. Drawing on such a scene, it was not difficult for Churchill to defend that 'the Congress does not represent all and [hence] is not India's mouthpiece [because] outside this party and fundamentally opposed to it are ninety million Moslems in British India who have their rights of self expression, forty-five million depressed classes or the untouchables as they are called, because they are supposed to defile their Hindu co-religionists by their presence or by their shadow and ninety million subjects of the principalities. In all, 235 million out of 390 million in all India. This takes no account of large elements among Hindus, Sikhs and Christians in British India who deplore the present policy of the Congress party.'[167] So, the Congress was accused of nurturing 'the false we' in view of the fact that 'there are large minorities in India that are bitterly opposed to its plan of cutting loose from the British empire'.[168] Though Gandhi insisted on a different occasion that 'the Congress remains the sole representative national organisation in India with a mass following',[169] the British streamlined the administration in such a way as to gain maximum by publicizing the opposition to the Quit India Movement: not only was the information flashed selectively in the media, the revitalized Information Department was also asked to collect news in association with the Intelligence Bureau to prove their authenticity.[170]

The Movement and its Development

The Quit India Movement was the melting point of the struggle between the Raj and the Congress which surfaced with the institutionalization of nationalist politics through the formation of the Indian National Congress in 1885. With the adoption of the 8 August resolution, the entire top leadership was incarcerated which unleashed an unprecedented country wide mass anti-British campaign. It is plausible to argue that the role of the Congress in mobilizing people politically was significant. Equally important was the entire atmosphere which was already a tinder box, ready to be ignited owing to the war crisis and its concomitant socio-economic and political consequences.

In general, three interrelated phases of the movement can be discerned. First, with the adoption of the 8 August 'Do or Die' resolution and incarceration of Gandhi and his lieutenants in Bombay, the all India upsurge which was massive and violent, sparked-off. Within just a week between 9 and 15 August, the movement which appeared to be a civil rebellion comparable to the magnitude of any mass revolution, was smashed fast, reassuring the Raj's hegemony in India and simultaneously warning the British ruling elite of the possible strength of any future Congress-led movement which was so well-coordinated. Bombay and Calcutta were the storm centres undertaking principally the Gandhian method of opposition. There were casualties in Delhi, and Patna witnessed a violent Congress attack on the British police in front of the Secretariat on 11 August.[171] Along with urban upsurges in which students took a prominent role, there occurred labour strikes in Lucknow, Kanpur, Bombay, Nagpur and Ahmedabad[172] which might not have been sympathe-tic strikes *per se* but posed serious threats to the continuity of the empire. The Tata Steel workers, for instance, resolved not to resume work 'until a national government is formed'.[173] Strike at Ahmedabad textile mills, which lasted for three and a half months,[174] made the administration look vulnerable at a time when the British authority was being severely challenged. Hence, the Secretary of State urged the Viceroy to immediately resolve the strike[175] before it became a serious threat by initiating workers' unrest elsewhere. As there were multiple centres of anti-British assault, it would have been impossible for the British to control the movement without an organized army on the spot which was readily available under the pressure of war.

The movement entered its second phase from about the middle of August. In the face of brutal oppression, the Quit India upsurge as an all India phenomenon evaporated rather abruptly; however, there emerged regional centres which sustained the momentum with a greater vigour. Northern and western Bihar, eastern UP, western Bengal and a number of areas in Maharashtra, Karnataka and Orissa witnessed mass attack on the symbols of British authority. Though the local Congress leadership prepared the groundwork, a wholehearted mass participation sustained the 'Do or Die' spirit to a large extent. The second phase also saw the formation of provisional national governments to conduct the struggle. Not only did these governments, though short-lived, consolidate the anti-British sentiments, they also projected the competence of a subject nation to organise its own affairs by evolving a parallel administration. For a variety of complex reasons, though the number of national governments decreased over time, the idea itself provided sustenance to those nationalists continuing the anti-British campaign successfully despite severe torture.

In the third phase, the Quit India Movement was confined to Talcher in Orissa, Satara in Maharashtra and Midnapur in Bengal where the provisional national governments ran successfully for almost two years defying the British. Whatever the impact of the continuity of these parallel governments on the Raj as such, these attempts caused alarm to the respective provincial governments.

The Open Rebellion in Talcher and Satara

The Quit India Movement evoked a favourable response from the state of Talcher which continued to remain a storm centre in the nationalist movement. With the formation of the Prajamandal (parallel government) in the wake of the August revolution, the Congress leadership strove to establish a *chasi-mula* (i.e. peasant-worker) raj in response to the 'Do or Die' call. By mobilizing the people for a movement which meant a direct confrontation with the British, the Congress built its support base drawing heavily upon the local grievances. For Talcher inhabitants, the local ruler exploited them in connivance with the British authority; hence, an attack on him is equally an effective campaign against the British. As the movement gained momentum, there were incidents of the destruction of telephone and telegraph lines in order to prevent the movement of the troops; the railway track, connecting Talcher with the rest of the country, was severely damaged for miles. With the consolidation of the chasi-mula combination as a parallel system of governance in Talcher, the Orissa government expressed concern and troops were requisitioned immediately; flag marches were conducted too in the Congress stronghold areas.[176] Arrests, lathicharges, canning and firings were resorted to indiscriminately to dispel the popular feeling that the British were no longer ruling the country and the Congress-swaraj was established. To disperse the crowd who seized the palace, the military undertook machine gun firing from the air. In the face of an organized military attack, the movement lost its momentum considerably and it was finally withdrawn by the end of 1943.

The Prajamandal, though short-lived, projected an alternative governance drawing essentially on different considerations from those of the British. Championing what can be called 'a popular peasant utopia', the proposed chasi-mula raj, 'aimed to provide food, shelter and clothing to all, reduce rents, helped the employed with jobs and land, and improved the system of education, health and water supply'. Given the presence of mines and factories in the state, 'it also planned to increase wages and take over these from foreign companies'.[177]

In Satara, a high point of radicalism was reached in the setting up of what came to be known as the 'Prati Sarkar' or parallel government. Two phases may be distinguished in the unfolding of the Quit India Movement in Satara. The activity of the first phase followed the usual tactics of satyagraha with its boycotts, strikes and morchas,[178] accompanied by underground activity–chiefly attacks on Government property, namely banks, government buildings, bridges, trains and post offices.[179] The first phase of sabotage and underground resistance lasted till the beginning of 1943 with local groups functioning separately and with Y. B. Chavan as overall leader or 'dictator' (in Congress terminology). Police repression was heavy and the end of 1942 saw 2000 people from Satara in jail.

In the next six months, the underground activists at Karad and Walva taluka made two major decisions: to continue the movement in spite of the repression and to carry it forward with the setting-up of 'people's power' in the villages. This included the creation of a new ethic of struggle: the ideal freedom fighter was no longer to be the *moral satyagrahi* but one who succeeded in remaining free from British jail while continuing the work of resistance. In this second phase, the peasantry who had played only a supportive role in the first phase, became directly involved through the campaign against the dacoity. Organized by the Congress activists, the peasants engaged in a struggle to curb banditry which was undermining the underground organization of civil disobedience. It was in the struggle with the dacoits that the Prati Sarkar established itself. Dacoit power ended in the region by the end of 1943, and the path was cleared for the Prati Sarkar to focus its activity on peasant problems. It is at this point that the Quit India Movement flows into a peasant issue-oriented agitation. The Prati Sarkar was thus committed to conducting a struggle on three fronts, (*a*) the Quit India front against the British government, (*b*) against dacoity, (*c*) the solution of peasant problems–particularly indebtedness and land disputes.

The structure of the Prati Sarkar as it evolved by 1943 was essentially a loose one comprising three village-based institutions: (*a*) Nyayadan Mandals, (*b*) Gram Samitis, (*c*) Toofan Senas. The Nyayadan Mandals constituted the judicial arm of the Prati Sarkar. They were 'people's courts' which dealt with cases of fraud, land disputes between peasants, sales of land and cases of moneylenders charging exorbitant rates of interest. They also tried and punished traitors and informers. The court's decisions were taken by a popular consensus. The main function of the Gram Samitis or the village communities was constructive activities, finance and welfare. Popularly elected, the Samitis were expected to raise funds and set-up cooperative societies, education societies, village libraries and health centres and also to conduct anti-liquor and anti-untouchability propaganda. Finally, the Toofan Sena were youth militia drawn from village wrestling clubs or *Talims*. Toofan Sena village units were generally responsible for the protection of the peasant from the moneylenders' harassment, and though they meted out punishment to offenders they did not make decisions independently of the Nyayadan Mandals.[180]

Another successful experiment in this regard was conducted in Midnapur (Bengal) where the parallel national government survived till September 1944 despite natural devastation and British torture. The Midnapur nationalists never succumbed to the British repression and their government was dismantled only in response to a call from Gandhi. In Chapter 3, a detailed discussion of the Quit India Movement in Midnapur will be undertaken to gauge its intensity there.

The August Revolution: A Radical Movement

The August movement was probably most radical both in its attitude towards the British and in terms of methods employed. Gandhi's 'Do or Die' slogan was an ultimatum to the British leaving no space for negotiation at all. Such an attitude was not there in either the Non-Cooperation or Civil Disobedience Movements when the Congress leadership was always keen to settle the disputes through some kind of compromise. Gandhi too agreed to accept this even at the cost of undermining the cause he fought for; its consequences were far-reaching: on the one hand, masses who took part in the anti-British campaign felt betrayed–which was likely to adversely affect the future Congress mobilization. Just as Gandhi opposed radical social movements which tended to disrupt social equilibrium, he was identified as a conservative political activist who declined to disturb the alien rule. On the other, the failure of the past Congress movements, led by Gandhi or his success in containing them at his will, strengthened the Raj in two ways: (*a*) in its drive to challenge effectively the Congress campaign, the British had in Gandhi a friend who, due to his commitment to non-violence, steered the political agitation in such a way as not to cause severe disruption in the British rule and (*b*) once the major organized political force was thus neutralized, the British administration could concentrate on controlling other radical socio-political movements challenging its continuity. So, despite the apparent threat to the Raj, both the Non-Cooperation and the Civil Disobedience Movements let lose a political process, conducive to the prevalent rule which shaped, to a large extent the anti-imperial movement before the onset of the open rebellion.

Whatever the implications of the past Congress-launched political movements, their significance cannot be denied especially in gradually radicalizing the Congress which loomed large in the August revolution. The Congress had anticipated that the nature of the movement would be different and hence, it was not surprising that the instructions to the Congress workers were tuned to capture the heightened mass radicalism, evinced since the adoption of the 1940 Ramgarh resolution. In his address to the UP Congressmen, Nehru, the UP PCC President, urged, 'Congressmen should be made to realise that the proposed movement is likely to be of a far intenser and more widespread character than any of the previous civil disobedience movements'. Aware of factional feuds impairing the Congress mobilization, he also exhorted that 'all local disputes must forthwith be ended. Complaints over petty matters should not be sent to the PCC. *Even those against whom disciplinary action has been taken are free to join the movement*' (emphasis added).[181] While moving the 8 July resolution, Nehru thus confidently announced that 'the Congress is plunging into a stormy ocean and it would emerge either with a free India or go down. Unlike in the past, it is not going to be a movement for a few days, to be suspended and talked over. *It is going to be a fight to the finish.*' (emphasis added).[182] Gandhi also became far more radical than ever. As early as 9 July 1942, in a draft of the resolution which was to be discussed in the Wardha AICC meeting (14 July), he underlined that

> the struggle thus would have to resolve itself into a mass movement on the widest scale possible involving voluntary strikes, voluntary non-cooperation on the part of all those who are in government employment or in the departments connected with government in any shape or form and it may involve also non-payment of land revenue and taxes.[183]

That the August revolution was qualitatively different from the earlier campaigns was evident from the Congress circulars, reported to have been distributed by the Central Congress Directorate.[184] during the movement. In order to enlist the support of various social groups confronting the British, the underground Congress Directorate took up issues which demonstrate the extent to which the Congress was radicalized in the wake of the August campaign. For instance, in the AICC instruction to the peasants, they were asked 'to obstruct the revenue and police officers to collect the tax, [and] in fact, to enter the village unless in the form of a military invasion. The invaders can be harassed in the meantime by cutting their communications and supplies'.[185] On another occasion, it was insisted on mobilizing the people on the immediate local grievances to launch a direct attack on the British and their supporters. While charting the programme of action, it was thus stipulated,

> Let the peasants select the initial targets of assault in each village or groups of villages. Let the rising and simmering discontent against the immediate grievances be churned up into an angry ferment.
>
> . . . the more extreme and militant spokesmen of the peasants should be helped to take the lead and prepare the men for direct action: by organised and orderly seizure of stocks of essential goods; by refraining payment of rent and debts; by refusing to part with crops; by ignoring court processes for distraint and refusing to attend or bid at sales; by taking possession of the machinery of local administration, such as Union Boards, Chowkis, Thanas and running it themselves; by setting-up new machinery where necessary. If the developments can fairly be synchronised in a number of areas from the centre–and to a great extent, this will be helped by the natural infectiousness of the process–the forces of the state will be helpless to check this progress, the disturbances will be too widespread and scattered.
>
> . . . [for the industrial workers], unrest must be brought to a head on immediate economic issues . . . [d]earness allowances can never keep pace with prices which will soar higher and higher with a progressive inflation of the currency. Price control will show-up as the senseless deception it is. Strikes should be easy to organise in this context. Propaganda should be meanwhile passed home on the capitalist front, appealing to this class on emotional patriotic grounds to view strike programme with favour. The bourgeoisie must be exhorted to keep-up political discontent at high pressure; declasse members of the petit bourgeois sections must be recruited to lead militant demonstration of students and labourers.[186]

There were innumerable AICC bulletins[187] including the famous six commanders of Gandhi Baba–Gandhi's message to the nation before he was taken to prison–which was interpreted as Gandhi's instruction to resort to direct action in what was called 'the final battle for freedom'. Hence, the participants were urged (*a*) not to acknowledge 'any power other than public' and (*b*) 'to completely paralyse communications and transport, dislocate trams and bus services, uproot telegraphic and telephonic posts, dig up roads, cut railways, tear out motor and bus tyres and dislocate the Government machinery in every possible way'.[188]

For the participants, the message was articulated in the form of destroying the institutions of governance, means of communicat-ions and attacking those who sustained its continuity. Local police stations were thus an obvious target. The situation was worse in the district of Ballia, UP where 'all police stations except three were lost to the rebels',[189] and the people were led to believe that 'a Congress Raj had already been established'.[190] Thus in Ballia, there was a rumour that Lucknow had fallen, and the impression soon got around that the Government had collapsed.[191] The movement assumed massive proportions as the fragility of the colonial state gained ground. And the crowd behaviour took a dramatic turn which caught the administration by surprise. Proclaiming the downfall of the British, the rebel leaders made an announcement that the 'Congress Raj had taken over Ballia and all cases and complaints [should be taken] to them'.[192]

There was another aspect of the open rebellion which requires emphasis, viz., the significance of the Congress flag. Unfurling a flag in the government buildings meant an inauguration and subsequently formalization of the Congress rule. Thus R. H. Niblett, the Azamgarh, (UP) District Magistrate reported that the rebels 'had not come to fight their Indian brethren, they only wished to plant the Congress flag on the thana'.[193] Similarly, students who captured a train fixed a flag in its engine which, as it were, registered the arrival of the Congress.[194] Thus, it was stated in the official report that the students turned the train 'into a Congress train with a flag and allowed movement under their direction and carried destruction to the control instruments of every Railway stations'.[195] The police appeared helpless and the British administration was also largely undermined. On the part of the rebels, this was an occasion to effectively challenge the alien state; the policemen, once captured 'were made to wear Gandhi caps and carry Congress flags at the head of the crowds'.[196] The extent of the damage and destruction of the government property[197] clearly shows the degree to which the British state was eclipsed at least temporarily in the eastern UP. What is however significant is that despite well-entrenched radicalisation manifested in the programmes of action, the newly emerged leaders draws, to a large extent, on the top Congress leaders, including Gandhi. So, it never appeared to be a problematic to the rebels who labelled bombs and other explosives as 'Gandhi blasting stick, Jawahar granade, Subhas blasting jelly and so on'.[198] Such an endeavour reveals the importance of the incarcerated Congress leaders in mobilizing the masses who resorted to means which neither Gandhi nor other leading Congress leaders would have approved. This also demonstrates the strategic sense of the rebel leaders who articulated the anti-British feeling in the form of a different kind of movement deriving inspiration from the nationalist leaders and thus linked the campaign at the grassroots with its all India counterpart. It was not therefore surprising for the Home Department, Government of India to note that though Gandhi reigned supreme, there was not 'any master hand behind the disturbances [which were] largely the cumulative effect of anti-British agitation which has been deliberately intensified by the Congress leaders since the failure of the Cripps mission'.[199] Had the Congress leaders committed to non-violence been around, the movement would perhaps not have assumed such alarming proportions. Attributing the violent nature of the rebellion to the second rank Congress leaders, not particularly concerned with the nature of means, adopted to attain the goal, the Benaras District Collector thus bitterly noted, 'the well-known and mainly moderate Congressmen were escorted to gaol leaving those whom we found later to be the real plotters of the rebellion, still happily plotting away'.[200] So, it was a battle of a different kind in which the participants undertook several measures to establish a counter authority–which may not have survived long enough though it had its symbolical value regarding the possible emergence of a free India.

The situation was thus unprecedented and the newly emerged Congress leadership strove to exploit the immediate local grievances connected with the war to organize an effective political campaign against the British which looked vulnerable especially after the fall of Malaya and Singapur. Having prepared so carefully to stop the movement before it started, the government was appalled at the common pattern of disruption that developed almost simultaneously in widely separated parts of the country. Hinting at the growing radicalization of the Congress, Linlithgow thus bitterly expressed that 'we have found ourselves faced with an extremely awkward situation, wholly revolutionary in character, well-organised by people working underground and deterred by non considerations of non-violence or the like'.[201]

The Nature of the Movement

The nationalist upsurge which sparked off following the Quit India resolution on 8 August 1942 is different from both the 1919-22 Non-Cooperation and the 1930-2 Civil Disobedience Movements[202] in a number of ways: first, the Quit India Movement assumed massive proportions in the absence of the top-ranking Congress leadership, thereby bringing a new type of leadership which sustained the movement even beyond what the imprisoned leaders could perceive when they launched it. Secondly, as in the case of leadership, the August resolution brought a new constituent of supporters to the national movement who, though they partici- pated in the earlier anti-British campaign, asserted themselves more vigorously in what was perhaps the final battle for independence. That new groups were politically mobilised is indicative of the widening of frontiers of the freedom struggle. Not only was the campaign effective from the point of view of participation it also introduced new dimension to the nationalist movement itself by incorporating new actors at various levels. Thirdly, although the movement absorbed anti-landlord sentiments which had been manifest in scattered peasant attacks on the landlords, it never assumed the form of a mass peasant uprising drawing on the age-old rift between the landlord and peasantry. This is possibly due to the intensity of anti-British feeling which prevailed over other contradictions. Here lies the success of the Congress in containing and directing popular turbulence towards the attainment of freedom. The Quit India revolt thus perhaps provided 'a safety valve' among the peasants against the British.[203] Fourthly, what really marks off the Quit India Movement is its continuity in Midnapur in Bengal, Talcher in Orissa and Satara in Maharashtra, when it completely withered away elsewhere. Apart from indicating the autonomous nature of the movement in specific regions, it demonstrates the ability of the local Congress organizers to sustain popular zeal in the face of inhuman torture unleashed by the British to control the movement. The continuity of the movement in three different and completely unrelated geographical locations refer to a process of mass mobilization–though started earlier and drew upon the 1922 Gaya Congress resolution[204] to incorporate peasants and workers in order to widen the Congress base–which not only integrated the disparate anti-British struggle with its national counterpart, but also brought local Congress leaders with organic links with the grassroots political activists, onto the political scene.

Although the Quit India Movement was the final battle for India's freedom, there has been debates as regards its nature. According to Francis Hutchins, what emerged in 1942 following the adoption of the 8 August resolution by Congress in Bombay was 'a spontaneous revolution',[205] because even with the imprisonment of top Congress leaders, the movement assumed massive proportions far beyond their expectation. Inspired by the Congress call, people participated spontaneously in the campaign against the British. To argue his point,

Hutchins draws our attention to the mobilization pattern during the movement which was done fairly quickly despite the absence of the established Congress leadership. This, in fact, is substantiated by the assertion that the mobilization pattern varied widely from one locality to another just because in the absence of specific Congress directives to the revolutionaries at the grassroots level, participants carried on the anti-British campaign primarily in accordance with the exigency of the situation.

The spontaneity thesis seems plausible in another respect: unlike during the 1919-22 Non-Cooperation and the 1930-2 Civil Disobedience Movements, the Congressmen in the localities resorted to violence and justified their actions as being in tune with Gandhian thought. In the light of Gandhi's decision to halt the Non-Cooperation Movement following the Chauri-Chaura incident, whether Gandhi would have approved of violence is a matter of conjecture; it, nonetheless, refers to the autonomous nature of the uprising which started with non-violence but drifted away completely in a number of instances as the movement progressed. Here lies the role of local Congress leaders who guided the movement in accordance with their ideological preferences. As a result, in both Midnapur and Satara,[206] where the influence of revolutionary terrorism was substantial, participants often clung to violence; and in Talcher, the movement never became violent, primarily because non-violence prevailed over other ideological leanings.

In terms of its actual manifestation, the movement had the characteristics of a spontaneous outburst, though the Congress was getting ready to launch the final battle for freedom since the 1940 Ramgarh Congress. So, there was a preparatory phase which culminated in the 1942 revolution. In other words, though the movement erupted following the incarceration of the Congress leaders, it was the product of consistent Congress efforts which resulted in the mass upsurge. R. Maxwell, the Home Member, who never believed in 'the spontaneity thesis', thus argued, 'the ordinary characteristics of spontaneous disturbances have almost entirely been absent. The first object of riotous mob is generally loot. There have, of course, been cases of looting but on the whole this form of activity has been far less common than might have been expected'. Moreover, by referring to the simultaneous attack on railways and other communications in widely separated parts of India, he further substantiated the claim that 'these disturbances were not spontaneous outbursts arising out of the arrest of the Congress leaders'.[207] The disturbances themselves had appearances, to start with, of being spontaneous and unregulated but remarkable resemblance of objectives of attack in different parts of India (mainly communications of various kinds) draws our attention to the presumption of pre-organization. It is possible, as an assessment of the Home Department shows, that 'activities selected were outcome more of ideas that had been spread about regarding the plans of Congress than of deliberate instigation by the Congress leaders on the spot'.[208] The Viceroy did not seem convinced and while defending the spontaneous thesis, he attributed the movement essentially to 'the highly strung and excitable character of some of these young men [who took part] and the amusement which it is so easy to get from smashing things or setting something on fire'.[209]

Given the evidence, it is difficult to conceptualize the movement in terms exclusively of 'a spontaneous outburst'. What is plausible to argue here is that the movement was the product of a process, unleashed with the 1940 Ramgarh resolution and the Congress efforts over time yielded results. So, it was the culmination of an organized attempt on the part of Congress; there were other factors too which contributed to such an unprecedented campaign: the apparent difficulty of the British after the fall of Rangoon, for instance, strengthened the idea that Raj was coming to an end; the emergence of a new set of leaders who appreciated openly 'violence' as opposed to 'non-violence' to attain independence.

Along with Hutchins' spontaneous thesis, there is a counter-thesis characterizing the Quit India uprising as mere 'disturbances intending to give notice to quit to British rule in India'.[210] According the N.C. Chaudhuri who puts forward this view, the Quit India Movement was 'a freak and an impulsive outbursts of anger at what the Indian people took as an exhibition of outrageous impudence on the British administration in India in arresting the Congress leaders'.[211] He went on: 'the movement was more or less a face saving gesture . . . [because] the Congress leaders had to counteract the impression which was growing after the rejection of the Cripps' offer that they were powerless to do anything against British intransigence'.[212] He admitted that the movement was relatively more serious in the eastern UP region because it was a backward area in which 'the blind xenophobia' was stronger than elsewhere. Attributing a movement which was widespread at least temporarily to economic backwardness is bound to provoke controversy when it is more or less established that politics has an autonomy of its own, and reducing politics to economic determinism invites serious methodological problems. Besides, the fact that apart from eastern UP[213] the movement assumed gigantic proportions[214] in areas which did not suffer economically, shows the limitation of 'the economic backwardness thesis', and substantiates the autonomy of politics.

The sudden collapse of a movement which had the potential of surpassing the intensity of both the 1919-22 Non-Cooperation and the 1930-2 Civil Disobedience Movements led Judith Brown, a Cambridge School exponent, to characterize Quit India as 'a flotilla of rafts colliding with a battleship'.[215] Though the movement evaporated soon, the interpretation seems to have been derived from a particular bias. According to the available documents, not only had the rulers an access to an army; they had also a well-prepared plan for immediate imprisonment of the Congress leadership and pre-emptive strike against the Congress.[216] So, the British had both the motivation and the necessary manpower to destroy the movement fast in a way they could not have thought in 1919-22 and 1930-2.

Similarly the characterization of the Quit India campaign as nothing but 'a fifth-columnist conspiracy' is equally misleading. In order to win the world anti-fascist opinion, the British ruling elite attributed the violent nature of the movement to secret pro-Axis sympathies.[217] The explanation which was readily acceptable by the highest level of British administration, including Churchill who found in the Quit India Movement a Japanese design to cripple the Indian economy and paralyse the state.[218] The idea probably gained ground in view of Intelligence reports that the Congress plan 'is to organise collective civil disobedience in zones immediately threatened by the Japanese'.[219] Moreover, the British allegation may have been derived from Gandhi's original draft for the 1942 Allahabad session of the AICC (held in July) which included: 'if India were freed, her first step would probably be to negotiate with Japan . . . India bears no enmity with Japan'. Later during the session, Jawaharlal Nehru's argument clarifying that 'it is Gandhiji's feeling that Japan and Germany will win [which] unconsciously governs his decision' confirmed the British apprehension.[220] Yet, the Congress' apparent pro-Axis tilt which influenced its political stance temporarily was transitional because the leadership came out heavily against the fascist powers on a number of occasions. Apart from his open letter to Hitler in which he was held responsible for the devastating war,[221] Gandhi was so emphatic in his assessment of the Japanese that he appealed to his countrymen to oppose Subhas Chandra Bose who was reported to have aligned with the Japanese. In a press interview, he thus made clear: 'well Subhas has risked much for us; but if he means to set up a Government in India under the Japanese, he will be resisted by us'.[222] So, the interpretation attributing the movement to a Japanese-inspired conspiracy does not seem to capture the complexity of a largely popular outburst like the August campaign. And the charge was consequently withdrawn; Wavell, the Viceroy thus wrote to Gandhi mentioning that 'I do not accuse you or the Congress party of any wish to aid the Japanese. But you are much too intelligent a man . . . not to have realised that the effect of your resolution must be to hamper the prosecution of the war; and it is clear to me that you had lost confidence in our ability to defend India, and were prepared to take advantage of our supposed military strains to gain political advantage.'[223]

The entire top Congress leadership was put behind the bars and the oft-quoted 8 August resolution was equally vague about the details of ensuing upsurge. And yet there was a massive counterattack in retaliation to the British policy of repression. The fact that more than 50 battalion of troops were deployed in the early suppression of the movement,[224] confirms the extent to which it threatened the overall security of the Raj. Linlithgow thus labelled the August upsurge as 'by far the most serious rebellion since that of 1857, the gravity and extent of which we have so far concealed from the world for reasons of military security'.[225] However the comparison is not quite apt. The Indian sepoys who mutinied in 1857 had some arms and ammunition and training; simple village folk of Ballia, Azamgarh and other small towns and villages in Bihar and UP who had risen in revolt at the bidding of boys fresh from schools and colleges, wielded nothing more lethal than sticks and stones: their violence was sporadic, unplanned and suicidal. The British response was predictably ruthless. According to official figures which could well be underestimates, by the end of 1942 over 66,000 persons had been convicted or detained; and the army had fired on 538 occasion.[226]

The movement was radical for the Congress volunteers resorted to open violence in a number of cases. It is debatable whether Gandhi would have allowed such a movement to continue in view of his strong antipathy towards violence. There is evidence to show that the movement became violent gradually and British provocation had played a significant role. In fact, this also introduces another dimension to the structure of politics during the open rebellion. The movement's deviation from a true Gandhian path shows the autonomy of the unorganized level where political articulation and mobilization were being carried on through different idioms which were meaningful only in the context of a completely different ideological perception. Here lies the viability of the argument highlighting the autonomy of unorganized politics following a unique pattern and demonstrating new dimensions of the structure of grassroots politics. The argument seems convincing in the light of the 8 August resolution and the transformation of the movement after the incarceration of the top Congress leadership. Given the 1921-2 Chauri-Chaura instance, Gandhi might have withdrawn the August revolution, once the movement became violent. In fact, the Congress urged its volunteers to 'be ready, organise at once, be alert, but by no means act . . . till Mahatmaji decides'.[227] The six stage programme mentioned in the Andhra Pradesh Congress Committee circular included only the traditional Gandhian means like salt preparation, boycott of courts, schools, colleges and government services, picketing of foreign cloth and liquor and no tax and no rent as 'the last resort'. There was just a Congress plan for disrupting communications: stopping of trains 'by pulling chains only'. Drawing on this, the Congress volunteers might have been inspired to launch a massive and violent attack on communications. Although the attack was not pre-planned the sudden eruption seems to suggest that had the masses not been ready psychologically to fight 'the last battle', under no circumstances would the movement have assumed such alarming proportions. Given the military preparedness of the British, the Quit India campaign did not pose as serious a threat as it was apprehended. What had caused consternation was the fear that 'the movement will the destroy "the will" to resist or even the very idea of resistance'. Once this was accomplished, the UP government's note underlined, 'it will be easy for the Japanese to find people to commit acts of sabotage [and to] become spies etc.' Congress was thus identified with 'the counter-part of Lavel's party in France and equally, if not more, dangerous'.[228]

The government statistics provide an indication of the extent of mass participation and an intense British repression to smash the movement fast. By the end of 1943 when the movement at the all India level waned, 91,836 had been arrested with the highest figure coming from Bombay Presidency (24,416), UP (16,796) and Bihar (16,202); 208 police outposts, 332 railway stations and 945 post offices had been destroyed or severely damaged and there had been 664 bomb explosions; 1060 were killed by police or army firing, while 63 policemen had died fighting the upsurge and 216 had defected.[229] That the British felt threatened is evident from Linlithgow's order of 'machine gunning from air' against crowds disrupting communications around Patna and, in fact, aeroplanes were employed to fire from the air to disperse the Congress rebels in Bhagalpur and Monghyr in Bihar, Nadia and Tamluk in Bengal and Talcher in Orissa.[230]

Concluding Observations

So, it was a confrontation of a different type, for the Congress clung to violence, if necessary to counter the British attack. It was a mismatch battle though, because the unarmed Congress volunteers fought the British forces equipped with most modern weapons. This, *inter alia*, is indicative of the spontaneity of the participants who rose in revolt despite adverse consequences of undertaking an anti-British onslaught.

Although the morale of the rebels was high, neither the British police nor the army, composed predominantly of Indians, expressed sympathy for the civil rebellion. Except for the Bihar police, which declined to cooperate with the authority when the movement was at its zenith[231] the police was generally loyal to the Raj. As regards the army, apart from those who defected to the Japanese to form the INA abroad[232] not a single instance is there showing that the 1942 upsurge cut the ground even under the Raj's main instrument of coercion. This certainly enabled the British authority to bring the all India movement under control within a short period. The rise of dissidents among the Bihar police was, however an indication of shifting loyalty from the imperial ruler to the indigenous Congress-led authority: it was felt even at the highest level, R. Maxwell, the Home Member noted thus, 'our officials–and especially the Hindus among them–must naturally, in considering their future prospects, look towards the rising rather than setting sun. The one thing quite certain to them is that we shall not be here to employ or protect them in future . . . and we cannot [therefore] expect our servants to do more for the present government than their duty actually requires'.[233] Change was also evident among the Indian Civil Service officers, a majority of whom were Indian by 1940: 614 as opposed to 587.[234]

Although the loyalty of the Indian ICS men to the Raj was never in doubt, they seemed to have felt threatened with the prospect of Congress coming to power which was in the air since the arrival of the Cripps Mission. Naturally, they began to wonder what would happen to them after the winding-up of the empire. Lord Wavell, who was presiding over a fast dismantling imperial authority appreciated the Indian officers' apprehension. He told his cabinet colleagues that Indian ICS men could not be expected to carry out 'a firm policy unless they were assured of the continuity of the Raj for at least a decade afterwards'.[235]

Not only was there a prospect of the breakdown of the imperial edifice, 'the informal part of collaborative network of support'[236] was also beginning to show signs of collapse. The alarming proportions which the 1942 rebellion assumed, even with the pre-emptive British strike, are indicative of the extent to which British reliance on those Indians who chose for a variety of reasons to give it informal support, advice and information and to guarantee it the backing of their own followers[237] proved abortive.

So, in the final years of the Raj, the entire British network of Indian allies both in formal and informal sectors was fast weakening. The war crisis and their adverse consequences, the prospect of British withdrawal, the communal schism affecting adversely the law and order situation, and finally the dubious loyalty of the Indian ICS officers to the Raj itself, were the factors contributing to the decline of the empire. Viewed thus, the 1942 Quit India was an important signpost of the Raj's disintegration, for it made the ruling elite aware of the possible strength of any future Congress movement which struck at the empire's foundation, particularly if it occurred after the war when the imperial authority had neither the legitimacy nor was well-equipped psychologically or materially to ensure its continuity.

NOTES

1 The term 'Quit India' is itself an American journalist's invention, suitable for compact headlines; Gandhi's initial phrase was 'an orderly British withdrawal' though he too in time used the expression. P. N. Chopra (ed.), *Quit India Movement: British Secret Report*, Thompson Press, Faridabad, 1976, p. 10.

2 *Collected Works of Mahatma Gandhi* (*CWMG* hereafter), Vol. LXXVI, Ministry of Information and Broadcasting, Government of India, 1979, p. 392.

3 *Harijan*, 15 March and 29 March 1942.

4 *Ibid.*, 16 August 1942.

5 *Ibid.*, 21 June 1942.

6 *Ibid.*, 16 August 1942.

7 *Ibid.*, 16 August 1942.

8 *Ibid.*, 16 August 1942.

9 *Ibid.*, 16 August 1942.

10 Centre of South Asian Studies, CSAS hereafter Cambridge, F. O. Bell Papers (TSS), p. 18.

11 For details, see Bidyut Chakrabarty, *Subhas Chandra Bose and Middle Class Radicalism, 1928-40,* I. B. Tauris, London, 1990, Chapter 1.

12 India Office Records (IOR hereafter), L/WS/1/1337, note on internal defence, 15 January 1943: 'the army had provided the equivalent of fifty-seven and a half battalions of infantry for a period of six to eight weeks to prop up the British rule following the declaration of the open rebellion'.

13 IOR, R/3/1/293, note by D. A. Brayden, Deputy Inspector General, Intelligence Bureau, Bengal, 15 June 1942.

14 IOR, R/3/1/293, R. Tottenham's note of 14 July 1942 underlines Linlithgow's plan of action in case there was a Civil Disobedience campaign during the war.

15 CSAS, Benthall Papers, Box No. XIX, Benthall Diary, political situation in 1940.

16 *Amrita Bazar Patrika* (*ABP* hereafter), 3 May 1941.

17 CSAS, Benthall to Reginald Maxwell, Home Member, 3 June 1941. This letter shows the extent to which the Congress was subject to various pulls and pressures from within itself. Hence, Benthall warned that it would be strategically suicidal to undermine the importance of various groups opposing Gandhi and non-violence. He further added, 'it is difficult to balance up the strength of the left and right wings for although the right wing is still apprehensive of the left wing, it claims to be growing in strength; on the other hand, the left wing equally claims that its strength is increasing; Gandhi also claims that his position is stronger than ever'.

18 Nehru Memorial Museum and Library (NMML hereafter), Purshottam Thakurdas Papers, File No. 177, Gandhi to G. D. Birla, 1 January 1940.

19 NMML, All India Congress Committee Papers (AICC hereafter) AICC G 32/1940: Papers relating to the Ramgarh Congress.

20 NMML, AICC, G 32/1940, A note by J. B. Kripalani, 2 March 1940.

21 National Archives of India (NAI hereafter), Home-poll 4/7/41, Home Department's note, 11 November 1941.

22 *The Hindu*, 15 April 1941.

23 *Leader*, 21 April 1941.

24 Bidyut Chakrabarty, *Subhas Bose and Middle Class Radicalism*, Chapter IV.

25 NMML, AICC G 31 (Part 1/1941-2): B. C. Roy to Jawaharlal Nehru, 1 March 1942.

26 IOR, R/3/2/31, Fortnightly Report (FR hereafter), from the Chief Secretary, Government of Bengal for the second half of July 1941.

27 Wadia and Merchant, *Our Economic Problems*, 6th edn., Bombay, 1959, p. 335.

28 NMML, Purshottam Thakurdas Papers, File No. 177. It was decided in one of the meetings (17 April 1941) of the Indian Chamber of Commerce to enhance the dearness allowances of the workers due to increase in the annual turnover.

29 Sumit Sarkar, *Modern India,* Macmillan, Delhi, 1990, p. 384.

30 R. Coupland, *Indian Politics, 1936-42: Report of the Constitutional Problem in India,* Part II, OUP, Madras, 1944, p. 263.

31 IOR, L/WS/1/317: monthly intelligence summary, war situation, July 1941.

32 IOR, L/I/1/777, Central Intelligence Officer, Madras to the Home Department, Government of India, 4 January 1942.

33 CSAS, Memoirs (TSS) of S. G. Taylor, Inspector General of Police, Bengal, 1941-3, pp. 5-6.

34 IOR, R/3/1/293, R. Tottenham's note of 14 July 1942 on 'press censorship'; L/I/1/777, Press censorship in India; CSAS, Reginald Maxwell Papers, Reginald Maxwell to the Provincial Governors, 15 April 1942.

35 *The Transfer of Power,* London, 1971 (*TP* hereafter), Vol. 1, No. 23.

36 IOR, MSS. Eur. F 125/11, Linlithgow Papers, Amery to Linlithgow, 17 June 1942.

37 For detail of the Cripps Mission, see R. J. Moore, *Churchill, Cripps and India, 1939-45*, Clarendon Press, Oxford, 1979.

38 IOR, MSS. Eur. F. 180/9c, Memoirs of W. H. J. Christie, ICS, p. 11. In his memoirs, W. H. J. Christie notes, 'this impetuous but untimely gesture of conciliation (the appointment of the Cripps mission) by Winston Churchill, probably the result of pressure by Roosevelt, was produced without consultation with the Viceroy and showed astonishingly little appreciation of the situation in India'. It caused great embarrassment to Linlithgow and nearly resulted in his resignation.

39 IOR, L/PO/6/102A, Linlithgow to Churchill, 3 March 1942.

40 *TP*, Vol. I, London, 1970, Churchill to Linlithgow, 10 March 1942, pp. 394-5.

41 *TP*, Vol. I, A war cabinet telegram to Cripps, April 1942, p. 670.

42 *TP*, Vol. 1, Churchill to Cripps, 28 April 1942, pp. 707-8.

43 *ABP*, 7 August 1942; *The Statesman*, Calcutta, 7 August 1942.

44 CSAS, Tootenham memoirs (TSS), p. 7.

45 CSAS, Benthall Papers, Box No. XIX, Secretary, Executive Council to Benthall, member, Executive Council, 6 August 1942.

46 CSAS, Benthall Papers, Box No. XIX, Minutes of the meeting of the Executive Council, 8 August 1942.

47 IOR, L/PO/6/102A, Secretary of State's note ratifying the Government of India's decision, 8 August 1942.

48 CSAS, Benthall Papers, Box No. XIX, Secretary to the Government of India to all Provincial Governors and Administrators, 11 August 1942.

49 A detailed discussion of how the resolution was broached and phrased and passed is given later.

50 IOR, L/PO/6/102A, L. S. Amery's broadcast in the BBC, 9 August 1942.

51 *Ibid.*

52 Paul Greenough, 'Political Mobilisation and the Underground Literature of the Quit India Movement, 1942-44', *Modern Asian Studies* (*MAS* hereafter), Cambridge, 17 March 1983, p. 359.

53 *The Hindu,* 10 August 1942; *The Statesman,* 10 August 1942; *ABP,* 10 August 1942; *The Times* (London), 10 August 1942.

54 A.C. Bhuyan, *The Quit India Movement, the Second World War and Indian Nationalism,* Manas, New Delhi, 1975, p. 90.

55 F.G. Hutchins, *Spontaneous Revolution: The Quit India Movement,* Manohar, New Delhi, 1971, p. 272.

56 The Secretary of State states, 'the press has been forbidden to do anything which could give publicity to the Congress or to those who may attempt to carry on the movement without them'. IOR, L/PO/6/102A, Secretary of State's broadcast, 9 August 1942.

57 Paul Greenough, 'political mobilization', *op. cit.*, p. 360.

58 IOR, L/WS/1/1247, Telegram (Tgm hereafter), Linlithgow to the Secretary of State, 14 August 1942.

59 NMML, AICC G 25/1940: the circular to the Provincial Congress Committees, No. 6, 10 April 1940.

60 NMML, AICC G 28 (Part 3)/1940. The AICC appointed inspectors to look into the organizational matter at the provincial level. Their report reveals the lack of co-ordination between the Provincial Congress Committees (PCC) and District Congress Committees (DCC) and hence the inspectors expressed uncertainity about the forthcoming satyagraha.

61 NMML, AICC G 28 (Part 2)/1940: Azad's note, 17 June 1940.

62 Indivar Kamtekar, *The End of the Colonial State,* unpublished Ph.D. dissertation, University of Cambridge, 1988, p. 25.

63 NAI, Home-Poll (G), 4/7/1941. Intelligence Bureau's note, 20 May 1941.

64 NAI, Home-Poll (G), 4/7/1941. A note by R. Tottenham, 23 May 1941. Tottenham was aware that 'the decline in membership does not necessarily mean decline in Congress influence'. He argued that 'one can say that the resignation of Congress ministries and the consequent damage to the prestige of the Congress in the public eye and the loss of prospect of benefiting from membership have been the main causes of the decline'. He felt, that 'proper use should be made of information without disclosing the sources of information or bringing the government into the picture'.

65 Only 31,345 satyagrahees (merely 1.2 per cent of a total membership of 29,73,452) were recruited and the lack of Congress zeal was noticed. See, NMML, AICC G 28 (Part 2)/1940: Papers relating to the Congress Working Committee meeting at Wardha, 17 January 1940. See the table below:

SATYAGRAHEES, ENROLLED IN DIFFERENT PROVINCES TILL MAY 1940

Provinces	*Number of Satyagrahees*	
Andhra	1370	
Bihar	1991	(in 12 out of 16 districts)
Bombay	156	
Delhi	10	
Gujrat	1771	
Karnataka	524	
Kerala	260	
Mahakoshal	75	
Maharastra	545	
Nagpur	174	
Tamil Nadu	2765	
United Provinces	15,200	
Utkal (Orissa)	250	
Vidarbha	254	
TOTAL	31,345	

Note: Only a mere 1.2 per cent out of a total membership of 29,73,452 were enlisted as 'individual satyagrahees'.

Source: NMML, AICC, G28/Part 1/1940.

66 IOR, L/PO/6/102C, Governor-General to the Secretary of State, 5 April 1940.

67 *Ibid.*

68 Emergency powers of the Governor-General.

69 CSAS, Benthall Papers, Box No. XIX, The draft resolution, sent by Gandhi from Wardha and was brought by Miraben.

70 R. Tottenham, *Congress Responsibility*, records of the Allahabad meeting of the Congress Working Committee, p. 44.

71 *ABP*, 23 April 1942; *The Statesman*, 23 April 1942; *The Hindu*, 23 April 1942; also, IOR, L/I/1/777 contains newspaper clips to show the Congress inclination.

72 R. Tottenham, *Congress Responsibility*, records of the Congress Working Committee meeting, pp. 42-3.

73 *Ibid.*, Patel's defence of Gandhi's view, p. 45.

74 *Ibid.*, p. 46.

75 NMML, AICC G 32/1942: Working Committee draft resolution. Those who voted for Gandhi's draft as modified by Rajendra Prasad were Patel, Rajendra Prasad, J. B. Kripalani, Shankar Rao Deo, Sarojini Naidu, Prafulla Chandra Ghosh. Those who voted for Nehru's draft were Nehru himself, G. B. Pant, Bhulabhai Desai and Asaf Ali. Among the invitees, Jairamdas Daulatram, Narendra Deo, Achyut Patwardhan, Bardoli and Biswanath Das voted for Rajendra Prasad's draft while Satyamurti and Mrs R. S. Pandit supported Nehru's draft.

76 *Ibid.*, Rajendra Prasad's speech on 1 May 1942.

77 *Ibid.*, and *The Hindu*, 3 May 1942; *ABP*, 3 May 1942.

78 NMML, Jawaharlal Nehru Papers, File No. 133-4, Nehru to Asaf Ali, 7 June 1942.

79 NMML, AICC G 32/1942: Working Committee's resolution, 14 July 1942. The resolution was widely publicized in the newspapers on the following day. *The Hindu*, 15 July 1942; *The Statesman*, 15 July 1942.

80 CSAS, Benthall Papers, Box No. XIX, Benthall to the Viceroy, 27 July 1942.

81 IOR, R/3/1/350, T. Wickenden's report on the Congress disturbances, p. 21. Nehru's statement of 20 July was quoted in the report.

82 IOR, L/I/1/777: The minutes of the meeting of the Executive Council, held on 29 July 1942.

83 CSAS, Benthall Papers, Box No. XIX, Secretary to the Executive Council to Benthall, 31 July 1942.

84 IOR, MSS. Eur. F 125/11, L. S. Amery to Linlithgow, 15 July 1942.

85 *Ibid.*

86 NAI, Home-Poll (g) 3/16/42: Amery to Linlithgow, 17 July 1942.

87 NMML, AICC P 1/1942: AICC circular to the PCCs, 31 July 1942.

88 NMML, AICC G 2 (Part IV)/1942, Kripalani to Prasad, the Congress President, 29 July 1942.

89 NAI, Home-Poll 3/16/42, Tgm, Home Department, Government of

India to the Secretary of State, 14 July 1942.

90 Jawaharlal Nehru, *The Discovery of India*, OUP, Delhi (centenary edition), 1989, p. 475.

91 *TP*, Vol. II, London, 1971, The Quit India Resolution, p. 622.

92 *Ibid.*, p. 624.

93 Gandhi's press interview of 6 August 1942, quoted in R. Tottenham, *Congress Responsibility*, p. 62.

94 *CWMG*, Vol. LXXVI, April 1942 – December 1942, Gandhi's speech at the AICC meeting, 8 August 1942, p. 392.

95 Gandhi's message to the country, 5 a.m., 9 August 1942, see *ibid.*, p. 403.

96 CSAS, Tottenham Memoirs (TSS), p. 7.

97 IOR, L/PO/6/102A, Tgm, Viceroy to the Secretary of State, 6 a.m., 9 August 1942.

98 IOR, L/PO/6/102, Tgm, Viceroy to the Secretary of State, 7 August 1942.

99 *Ibid.*, Tgm, Secretary of State to the Viceroy, 9 August 1942.

100 IOR, L/PO/6/102A Tgm, Viceroy to the Secretary of State, 9 August 1942–reporting the view of the Governors on the question of Gandhi's fast.

101 *Ibid.*, Tgm, Secretary of State to the Viceroy, 10 August 1942. The Secretary of State reported to the Viceroy the decision of the War Cabinet in a meeting, held on 9 August 1942.

102 *Ibid.*, Tgm, Viceroy to the Secretary of State, 10 August 1942.

103 IOR, MSS. Eur. F. 125/11, Linlithgow to Amery, 17 August 1942.

104 CSAS, Maxwell Papers, Legislative Assembly debates, Tuesday, 15 September 1942, Vol. III (2), Government of India Press, New Delhi, 1942, p. 145.

105 IOR, R/3/1/293, A note by R. Tottenham, Additional Secretary, Home Department, Government of India, 14 July 1942.

106 IOR, MSS. Eur, F, 125/11, Linlithgow to Amery, 17 August 1942.

107 IOR, L/PO/6/102C: the minutes of the Executive Council's meeting, held on 19 August 1942.

108 IOR, R/3/2/37, M. O. Carter, Secretary to the Governor of Bengal to the Viceroy, 29 August 1942.

109 IOR, R/3/2/37, R. Maxwell to the Bengal Governor, 3 September 1942.

110 IOR, L/I/1/885, J. F. Gennings, former Commissioner of Labour to B. Engert, Private Secretary to Parliamentary Secretary, Ministry of Aircraft Production, London, 17 October 1941.

111 IOR, R/3/2/46, Linlithgow to John Herbert, Bengal Governor, 2 March 1943.

112 NAI, Home-Poll 125 (64) GG/1942, B.J. Glancy, the Punjab Governor to Linlithgow, 6 March 1943.

113 IOR, R/3/2/33, Central Intelligence Officer's report, 14 August 1942.

114 Central Intelligence Officer's report of 11 November 1942, quoted in P. N. Chopra (compiled), *The Quit India Movement: The Role of Big-Business*, Vol. II, Interprint, New Delhi, 1991, p. 61.

115 *Ibid.*

116 Note by the Central Intelligence Officer, UP on the role of the business community in mobilizing funds; see P.N. Chopra (compiled), *The Quit India Movement*, pp. 93-4.

117 Report by the Central Intelligence Officer, Calcutta, 14 August 1942; see *ibid.*, p. 19.

118 NMML, Purushottam Thakurdas Papers, File No. 178; the copy of the resolution of the Indian Chamber of Commerce, adopted on 10 August 1942.

119 IOR, R/3/2/33, Deputy Commissioner of Police, Calcutta to M. O. Carter, Secretary to the Bengal Governor, 16 August 1942.

120 West Bengal State Archives (WBSA hereafter), Home-Poll No. 58, 17/42, Central Intelligence Officer's report, 9 November 1942.

121 NMML, Purushottam Thakurdas Papers, File No. 178; a note by Jugal Kishore Birla of the Birla Brothers & Co.

122 IOR, R/3/2/33, a copy of the Bengal Chamber of Commerce resolution, adopted on 12 August 1942.

123 *Ibid.*

124 IOR, R/3/2/33, Deputy Commissioner of Police, Calcutta to M. O. Carter, 16 August 1942.

125 Gandhi was reported to have exercised his influence in securing war contracts for particular business houses. See NAI, Home-Poll 125/64/GG/42; a note by H. J. Hallet, the Governor of UP, 9 March 1943.

126 IOR, L/I/1/755, Rajagopalachari to Gandhi, 18 July 1942; this letter was signed by three other Congressmen, K. Santhanam, S. Ramanathan and T. S. S. Rajan.

127 *Ibid.*

128 *Ibid.*, Gandhi to Rajagopalachari, 20 July 1942.

129 B. R. Ambedkar, *Pakistan or Partition of India*, Thacker and Co, Bombay, 1945, p. 407.

130 *Ibid.*

131 IOR, L/PJ/7/1816, Ambedkar's press statement on 18 August 1942; *The Hindu*, 28 August 1942.

132 *The Statesman*, Calcutta, 2 September 1942.

133 NMML, Hindu Mahasabha Papers; C 26—V. D. Savarkar's correspondence; Savarkar's note, prepared for the press, 9 September 1940.

134 NMML, Hindu Mahasabha Papers, C 30—Working Committee resolution, 23 September 1940.

135 N. Mitra (ed.), *Indian Annual Register*, Vol. II, 1940, pp. 270-6.

136 NMML, Hindu Mahasabha Papers, C 30; the Bihar Governor to Savarkar, 7 November 1941.

137 IOR, R/3/2/33; B. S. Moonjee's appeal to people, 14 August 1942.

138 *Ibid.*, Savarkar's statement of 15 August 1942, meant to be given the press.

139 *Ibid.*, Shyama Prasad Mookherjee's speech in the Mahasabha working committee meeting, 10 August 1942.

140 *Ibid.*

141 *Ibid.*, Intelligence Report on the meeting; D. A. Brayden, Central Intelligence Officer, Bengal to M. O. Carter, Secretary to the Bengal Governor, 11 August 1942.

142 *Ibid.*, the intercepted letter of N. C. Chatterjee, the Working President, Bengal Hindu Mahasabha to B. S. Moonjee, President, All India Hindu Mahasabha, 14 August 1942.

143 NMML, Hindu Mahasabha Papers, C 32/42; Working Committee resolution, 18 August 1942.

144 IOR, L/I/1/1116; P. C. Joshi, *The Indian Communist Party: Its Policy and Work in the War of Liberation,* (pamphlet), Communist Party of Great Britain, London, 1942, p. 12.

145 *Ibid.*

146 CSAS, Martin Papers, Memoirs (MSS), p. 234.

147 IOR, L/I1/1116; the Government communiqué of 23 July 1942.

148 IOR, R/3/2/37; daily report of the Commissioner of Police, Calcutta, 10 August 1942.

149 *TP*, Vol. II, Viceroy to Amery, 5 September 1942, p. 906.

150 *TP*, Vol. II, Bihar Governor to Linlithgow, the Viceroy, p. 46.

151 WBSA, Home-Poll 235/42; Herbert to Linlithgow, 25 August 1942.

152 *Ibid.*, Daily Report, Commissioner of Police, Calcutta, 25 August 1942.

153 IOR, R/3/2/37, Report of the Commissioner of Police, Calcutta, 11 October 1942. Strikes in and around Calcutta were alarming.

154 WBSA, Home-Poll 235/42; District Magistrate, Jalpaiguri, to the Chief Secretary, Bengal, 26 October 1942.

155 IOR, R/3/2/37: In his note of 9 September, 1942, D. A. Brayden, Central Intelligence Officer, Bengal, complains, 'the CPI or its associates by encouraging strikes in Calcutta and in the districts, are damaging the war efforts'. He thus insisted on a ban on the CPI and other communist groups; otherwise, they, he apprehended, would turn their anti-British campaign into a civil war.

156 With the adoption of the 1940 Lahore resolution, the Muslim League articulated the demand for Pakistan more sharply than before; the demand for a separate Muslim state was defended by Jinnah's 'two nation' theory.

157 The Muslim League Working Committee resolution of 20 August 1942, *TP*, Vol. II, p. 771.

158 See for details Suranjan Das, *Communal Riots in Bengal,* OUP, Delhi, 1992; Joya Chatterjee, *Class, Culture and Communal Conflict: The Second Partition of Bengal, 1932-47*, unpublished Ph.D. dissertation, University of Cambridge, 1990.

159 *The Dawn*, 9 November 1942; Jinnah's press statement of 8 November 1942.

160 Jinnah's press statement on 13 September 1942; see *TP*, Vol. II, p. 956.

161 *The Dawn*, 9 November 1942.

162 IOR, R/3/2/33; a report of a special branch secret agent the Bengal Provincial Muslim League Working Committee, held on 14 August 1942.

163 *Ibid.* Both *Dhaka Prakash* (Dhaka) and *Azad* (Calcutta) defending Nazimuddin, argued strongly against the Quit India Movement. Condemning the movement weakening the Raj, *Dhaka Prakash* insisted on cooperating with the British to strengthen its attack on the Congress trying to establish Hindu hegemony; moreover, to *Dhaka Prakash,* since the war was fought to protect human beings against the fascist design, it was incumbent on 'the sensible mortals to support the British'. See *Dhaka Prakash*, 16 August; 23 August 1942. Similarly, *Azad,* in its editorials, exhorted the Muslims to oppose the movement aimed at establishing 'a Hindu raj' and consequently to undermine the movement for Pakistan. See *Azad,* 11, 12, 16 and 21 August 1942.

164 IOR, R/3/2/33, Raghib Ahsan, BPML, to Jinnah, 14 August 1942.

165 Bangladesh Secretariat Record Room, (BSRR hereafter), Dhaka, Police B proceedings, bundle no. 32, BPML meeting on 19 August 1942. Fazlul Haq also expressed his willingness to help to the British in the war. In his words, 'there are the Muslims of India–hundred million strong–who are most anxious to help the British in the war'. See IOR, R/3/2/33, Fazlul Haq to G. Laithwaite, Private Secretary to the Viceroy, 13 May 1942.

166 IOR, MSS. Eur. F 125/11, Herbert to Linlithgow, 6 November 1942.

167 IOR, MSS. Eur. F. 125/145: Prime Minister's statement in the House of Commons, 10 September 1942.

168 IOR, L/I/1/1116, Alfred Watson, 'Is it the Parting of Ways,' *The India Affairs,* London, 25 September 1942.

169 Gandhi, 'To My Critics', *Harijan*, 26 July 1942.

170 IOR, L/I/1/1116, R. Maxwell's note of 18 August 1942.

171 IOR, R/3/2/37, Tgm, Home Department, Government of India to the Secretary of State, 14 August 1942. It was reported that the government authority was undermined for two days after the famous seize of 11 August.

172 *TP*, Vol. II, pp. 669, 682-3.

173 *TP*, Vol. II, Linlithgow to Amery, 21 August 1942, p. 777.

174 CSAS, V. L. Mehta, Oral Transcript, p. 11. Mehta was arrested for his involvement in the Ahmedabad textile mills strikes.

175 IOR, L/PO/6/102A, Amery, the Secretary of State, to Linlithgow, the Viceroy, 28 August 1942.

176 NAI, Home-Poll 3/16/42, Governor, Orissa, to the Viceroy, 21 August 1942.

177 Biswamoy Pati, 'The climax of Popular Protest: The Quit India Movement in Orissa', *Indian Economic Social and Historical Review*, 29, 1, 1992, p. 26. For details, see, Biswamoy Pati, *Resisting Domination: Peasants, Tribals and the National Movement in Orissa, 1920-50,* Manohar, New Delhi, 1993; and Biswamoy Pati, 'Storm over Malkangiri: A Note of

Laxman Naiko's Revolt in 1942' in G. Pandey (ed.), *The Indian Nation in 1942*, K. P. Bagchi, Calcutta, 1988, pp. 185-206.

178 There were four major marches at taluka centres in Satara (between 24 August and 10 September 1942) at Karad (4000), Targaon (8000), Wadiy (700) and Islampur (6000). In Shirala taluka, 32 patils resigned from their posts. The Reserved forest in Shirala was declared open to the public.

179 Congress Youth Squads conducted these attacks. In Kundal, a bank was robbed and in Shirala, grain from government stores was distributed to the public (1941-2 had been a year of famine and in 1942, there was a price inflation).

180 See, for details, Gail Omvedt, 'The Satara Prati Sarkar' in G. Pandey (ed.), *The Indian Nation in 1942;* Livi Rodrigues, *Rural Protest and Politics: A Study of peasant movement in Maharastra*, unpublished Ph.D. dissertation, University of London, 1984, pp. 400-19.

181 NMML, AICC P 22/1942, Jawaharlal Nehru's address to the UP PCC, 24 July 1942.

182 NMML, AICC G 22/1942; Nehru's speech at the AICC meeting while moving the 'Quit India' resolution, Bombay, 8 August 1942.

183 CWMG, Vol. LXXVI (1 April 1942–17 December 1942), p. 284.

184 The Central Congress Directorate comprised Sadiq Ali, Sucheta Kripalani, Aruna Asaf Ali, B. K. Keshkar and Rammanohar Lohia. See, F. G. Hutchins, *Spontaneous Revolution*, pp. 310-11.

185 The AICC instruction for no tax, 'no rent and no grain campaign' in R. Tottenham, *Congress Responsibility*, Appendix VI, p. 64.

186 Another instruction, no date? in R. Tottenham, *Congress Responsibility* Appendix VII, pp. 67-8.

187 Appendix XV in R. Tottenham's *Congress Responsibility* contains a list of the Congress pamphlets during the movement, pp. 81-6.

188 Appendix XIII in R. Tottenham, *Congress Responsibility*, pp. 80-1.

189 IOR, R/3/1/359, *The Congress Rebellion in United provinces*, Government of UP, Lucknow, 1943, p. 5.

190 *Ibid.*, p. 3

191 *Ibid.*, p. 5.

192 *Ibid.*, p. 6.

193 R. H. Niblett, *The Congress Rebellion in Azamgarh*, Allahabad, 1957, p. 13.

194 IOR, MSS. Eur., F 161/4/File n. 5, Indian Police collection, A note by G. Waddel, no date?

195 *Ibid.*, p. 1.

196 *Some Facts of the Disturbances* (printed report), Government of India, New Delhi, 1943, p. 3.

197 IOR, R/3/1/359, *The Congress Rebellion in United Provinces.* This report mentions, about 250 Government buildings were destroyed or severely

damaged, apart from 104 railway stations. Sixteen trains were derailed and there were 15 incidents of serious damage to railway tracks. Over 400 cases of destruction or serious damage to telegraph and telephone communications were reported; . . . the damage to property is estimated at between 7 and 8 lakhs, p. 11.

198 R. Tottenham, *Some Facts of the Disturbances*, p. 8.

199 *TP*, Vol. II, Tgm, Home Department, Government of India to the Secretary of State, 5 September 1942, p. 904.

200 NAI, Home-Poll 18/9/42 (1), Viceroy to the Secretary of State, 16 August 1942, quoting the report of the Benaras District Collector.

201 IOR, R/3/2/37, Linlithgow to Amery, 17 August 1942.

202 There is a plethora of literature on these movements. See, for instance, on the Non-Cooperation Movement, P. C. Bamford, *Histories of the Non-Cooperation and Khilafat Movements,* Government of India, New Delhi, 1925; N. Mitra (ed.), *Indian Annual Register 1922;* Judith Brown, *Gandhi's Rise to Power, Indian Politics, 1915-22,* CUP, Cambridge, 1972. For the Civil Disobedience Movement, see, Judith Brown, *Gandhi and Civil Disobedience: The Mahatma in Indian Politics,* CUP, and Judith Brown, *Gandhi: Prisoner of Hope,* Yale University Press, New Haven, 1991.

203 Stephen Henningham therefore argues, 'The collapse of the British rule seemingly provided suitable conditions for the development of agrarian protest. But prevailing economic conditions made rich peasants and many middle peasants disinterested in agitation against their landlords. Without their leadership and despite harsh economic circumstances the poor peasants failed to initiate agrarian protest'. Stephen Henningham, *Peasant Movements in Colonial India: North Bihar, 1917-42*, Australian National University, Canberra, 1982. The argument, though plausible, may not have captured the complexity of the situation by insisting on the leadership of rich and middle peasants when a myriad of factors contributed to the way the poor peasants behaved.

204 In his presidential address, C. R. Das declared at the 1922 Gaya Congress, 'Let us organise Labour and Peasantry from the point of view of their own special interest and also from the point of view of higher ideal which demands satisfaction of thier special interest and devotion of such interest to the cause of swaraj'. A. M. Zaidi *et.al., The Encyclopaedia of the Indian National Congress,* Vol. VIII (1921-4), p. 136.

205 F. G. Hutchins, *Spontaneous Revolution: The Quit India Movement*, Manohar, Delhi, 1971.

206 Gail Omvedt, 'The Satara Prati Sarkar' in G. Pandey (ed.), *The Indian Nation in 1942*, pp. 223-61.

207 CSAS, Maxwell Papers, Legislative Debates, Maxwell's statement on 12 February 1943, pp. 143-4.

208 IOR, R/3/2/37, Tgm, Home Department to the Secretary of State, 17 August 1942.

209 IOR, MSS. Eur. F125/11, Linlithgow to Amery, 17 August 1942.
210 N. C. Chaudhuri, *Thy Hand Great Anarch India: 1921-52*, Chatto and Windus, London, 1988.
211 *Ibid.*, p. 704.
212 *Ibid.*
213 Chandan Mitra, 'Popular Uprising in 1942: The Case of Ballia', in G. Pandey (ed.), *The Indian Nation in 1942,* pp. 165-84.
214 For details, see the contributions in G. Pandey (ed.), *The Indian Nation in 1942.*
215 Judith Brown, *Modern India: The Origin of an Asian Democracy*, OUP, Delhi, 1985, pp. 311-12.
216 IOR, R/3/2/25, Bengal Governor's note of 7 November 1940.
217 R. Tottenham, *Congress Responsibilities for the Disturbances,* p. 11.
218 IOR, R/3/1/293, proceedings of a war cabinet meeting held on 25 July 1942.
219 R. Tottenham, *Congress Responsibility*, p. 8.
220 R/3/1/293, D/O letter from the UP government to the Home Department, Government of India, 19 May 1942.
221 IOR, L/I/1/886, Gandhi's open letter to Hitler quoted in a Tgm, Governor General to the Secretary of State, 26 December 1942.
222 *The Statesman,* Calcutta, 16 May 1942.
223 Wavell to Gandhi, 28 March 1944, in *CWMG*, LXXVII (17 December 1942–31 July 1944) , Government of India, 1979, Appendix XX, p. 464.
224 IOR, MSS. Eur F 125/11, Tgm, Linlithgow to Churchill, *TP*, Vol. II, p. 953.
225 IOR, MSS. Eur. F 125/11, Tgm, Linlithgow to Churchill, *TP,* Vol. II, p. 853.
226 *ABP,* 18 January 1943; *The Hindu,* 21 January 1943.
227 NMML, AICC 31/42, Andhra Pradesh Congress Committee Circular, 29 July 1942.
228 IOR, R/3/1/293, Extract from a DO letter from the UP government, 19 May 1942.
229 NAI, Home-Poll 3/52/43, Bihar Governor to the Viceroy, 7 March 1943.
230 CSAS, R. Maxwell Papers, Memoirs (TSS), pp. 146-8.
231 *Ibid.*, p. 141.
232 Milan Hauner, *India in Axis Strategy: Germany, Japan and Indian Nationalism in the Second World War*, Klett Cotta, Stuttgart, Germany, 1981, Bidyut Chakrabarty, 'Subhas Chandra Bose, Indian National Army and the Axis Strategy, 1941-43'. *MAS* (forthcoming).
233 R. Maxwell to G. Laithwaite, private secretary to the Viceroy, 24 October 1942, *TP*, Vol. III, p. 157.
234 CSAS, J. M. G. Bell Papers, an ICS who served Bengal between 1940 and 1950; see his Memoirs (TSS).

235 *TP*, Vol. IV, p. 334.

236 Ashis Nandy, *The Intimate Enemy: Loss and Recovery of Self Under Colonialism*, OUP, Delhi, 1988, pp. xiv, 10-11.

237 Judith Brown, *Modern India,* p. 317, Stephen Henningham's study of Bihar situation corroborates the argument: '. . . the failure of the zamindars actively to support the British in 1942 which was based on an accurate assessment that their best interests lay with the Congress'. See Stephen Henningham, *Peasant Movements in Colonial India: North Bihar, 1917-42*, p. 195.

CHAPTER 2

Midnapur: Its Story, 1905–1932

MIDNAPUR a south-western district of Bengal figured prominently in the 1942 open rebellion. Inspired by Gandhi's 'Do or Die' call, the Congress nationalists spearheaded attacks on the British and their representatives deviating, on occasions, from 'non-violence'. The August Movement was a continuity at least in terms of organizing anti-colonial movements based partly on local grievances and partly in conformity with the all-India campaign. Although Midnapur was the only district in Bengal where the anti-British sentiments were articulated in movements since 1905 it is nonetheless difficult to capture them in a single theoretical framework because there was a break with the past in the movements, at least in terms of social background, that unfolded with the 1920-2 Non-Cooperation Movement. In fact, one notices a pattern in the post-1920 Congress-launched campaigns in which the local leadership consciously strove to articulate the interests of the 'well-to-do' cultivators, especially the *jotedars* and tenure-holding *ryots*, and established its hegemony on its basis. This probably accounted for the success of the Congress in both the Non-Cooperation and Civil Disobedience Movements when Midnapur, almost alone in Bengal, was able to challenge the colonial state most successfully. What it demonstrates is significant from the point of nationalist politics: first, Midnapur is probably the only locality where there was an effective merger of both the 'organized' and 'unorganized' worlds of politics. Championing the local issues, the Midnapur district Congress committee developed a movement which, though related directly to the local grievances, succeeded in infusing anti-colonial sentiments in such a campaign by attributing the difficulties in the localities to the colonial state. In other words, by intelligently mingling the local issues with the prevalence of an alien state, the organizers introduced new dimensions to the nationalist politics by incorporating new social groups which remained peripheral in the erstwhile Congress mobilization.

Moreover, the British administration failed to make an inroad in rural Midnapur because of its inability to secure its traditional political base, based on zamindars.[1] Rural power lay in the hands of petty landlords and intermediaries who, over time, consolidated their position in the economic environment of growing commercialization of agriculture. This was reinforced by another significant event, viz., the emergence of the Mahishyas as a well-knit caste group which sustained its hegemony by, *inter alia*, injecting the district with its own version of peasant pride. The aim of the chapter is to articulate the complex processes that contributed to the distinctiveness of the district, especially in the context of political mobilization between 1905 and 1930-2; although its focus is on the Congress-led political movements, an attempt will also be made to unfathom their peculiarities in terms of both the constituents and issues. Such an endeavour will invariably demonstrate the extent to which movements in the localities constituted an integral part of the pan-Indian campaign, though they had their own dynamics showing probably the validity of the studies of the localities.

PART I

Midnapur: Its Social and Economic Distinctiveness

Situated in the south-western part of Bengal, Midnapur was essentially rural. According to the 1911 Census, 96 per cent of the total population of 2.82 million lived in rural areas. Agriculture supports 77.2 per cent of the population, industries 9.8 per cent, the profession 2.9 per cent and commerce 0.5 per cent.[2] The population was more distinctively agricultural than in any other part of west Bengal or central Bengal.[3] Like any other agrarian society, in Midnapur too, it was the control of land that was the crucial determinant in locating political power. The horizontal differentiation never appeared a significant issue in political mobilization presumably because of vertical loyalties of caste; the caste-homogeneity provided the district Congress leadership with an advantage in political mobilization against the alien rule.

In Midnapur, there were ten large zamindari estates, but the bulk of the settlement was made with more than 3,000 petty zamindaries.[4] With the multiplicity of zamindars, there was not a decisive centre of power. Furthermore, as Rajat and Ratna Ray have shown, real control of rural society did not rest in the hands of the zamindars; political power was more localized, and zamindars while having control over revenue had only limited control over land.[5] It will however be a mistake to assume that rural society in Bengal was divided into two well-defined categories: with a parasitic zamindar at the top and a body of landless labourers at the bottom. Between these categories was an intermediate stratum of non-zamindar tenure-holders with varying degrees of income and influence. Unlike certain east Bengal districts such as Bakarganj where there often existed 20 different intermediaries,[6] the land tenure system in Midnapur, as Swapan Dasgupta has shown, 'was relatively simple: there was rarely more than one or at most two intermediaries between the zamindar and the actual cultivator. In fact, 66 per cent of the land was held in 1911 by *ryots* who had security of tenure, who took some personal part in cultivation and who paid rent directly to the zamindar or government in case of *khas mahals* or government estates.'[7] The tenure-holder or *jotedar*, as he was identified in the lexicon of revenue administration 'did let out sections of their holdings to underryots or *bhagchasis* (sharecropper) who were tenant-at-will and consequently had no rights under the law. They thus combined the dual roles of producer and exploiter'.[8] So, price rises did not benefit the peasantry as a whole but the tenure-holders, and especially *jotedars* who had the maximum disposable surplus whether acquired from their cultivation or acquired as rent from under *ryots* or *bhagchasis*.

The *jotedar* or substantial peasant consolidated his hold on rural society through his control over credit and marketing operations. As the Bengal Provincial Banking Commission shows, there were just 27 professional moneylenders per 100,000 of Midnapur population though the degree of rural indebtedness was extremely high.[9] In the absence of professional money-lenders, the rural credit was supplied by the *jotedars* and occasionally the zamindars.[10] The credit advanced took two different forms: first, in order to meet the dire necessity of existence, a huge chunk of rural population was compelled to negotiate paddy loans on clearly disadvantageous terms. The Banking Enquiry Commission notes that peasants received unsecured paddy loans at interests ranging from 25 per cent to 50 per cent.[11] In such a transaction, the *jotedar* who provided loans gained overwhelmingly. Not only did he extract a year's interest on what was in reality a six months loan,[12] but given the economic climate of rising prices, 'he [also] benefited by having at his disposal an even greater saleable surplus'.[13] Secondly, there were loans in the form of liquid cash. A contemporary estimate shows that only 10 per cent of cash loans were used for purely agricultural purposes; while the bulk of it was utilized in special social ceremonies, like marriage and *shradh,*[14] and the interest-rates were as high as 75 per cent on occasions.[15] Most of these cash loans were unsecured which automatically pushed the interest rates and left the interpretation of the terms of credit solely with the money-lenders.[16] Although the relationship is geared to extraction of surplus from the peasants, the fact that credit was supplied whenever needed contributed to a symbiotic network between the *jotedar* and indebted cultivators.[17]

In addition to credit, the *jotedars* maintained a hold over the marketing of the agricultural produce in Midnapur. Traditionally, Midnapur was a rice-surplus region. The smaller cultivators had to part with their surplus to meet their liabilities; to repay the loan and attend to other needs, he had to sell the produce immediately after the harvesting when the prices were, for obvious reasons, at their lowest. Given their stark needs, the indebted cultivators did not have adequate resources to hold out some months when the prices would rise again. This left the *jotedar* with an unassailable position who could easily wait for the price rise to sell his surplus.[18] Moreover, due to lack of means for, or expenses involved in, transporting surplus to Calcutta, the *jotedar* or the local merchant (*paikar* in the local parlance) appeared to be the only buyer in the localities. The prevalence of such a structure in rural economy explains largely the nature of transactions which bind the small cultivators/or landless labourers with *jotedars* who rescued them from severe economic hardships either by offering credit in need or in exchange of surplus produce.

The above discussion shows the importance of *jotedar* in Midnapur who were, though exploiters, hailed for their help, economic and otherwise, in the day-to-day existence of the bulk of the rural population. In other words, the peculiar agrarian economy of Midnapur, characterized by the nature of the rural credit and the conditions of marketing, led to the rise of *jotedar* as a distinct community which had maximum manoeuvrability at the grassroots; since Midnapur was a permanently settled area for revenue purposes, zamindars and not *jotedars* were accountable to the state; this left *jotedar* who had a safe tenure holding with a free hand in so far as the management of rural society was concerned. So, it was therefore not surprising that in Midnapur, *jotedar* played a crucial role in political mobilization probably because of its hold over the people due to his role as a saviour during the crisis; such an idea was reinforced more so in the context of absentee landlordism: interested merely in revenue collection, the zamindars remained a distant object to the rural masses who therefore found in the *jotedar* a natural ally in their day-to-day existence and emergency.

The Role of Mahishya Caste

A peculiarity of Midnapur was the numerical preponderance of the Mahishya–a caste group–which played a prominent part in the nationalist movement. Unlike the Namasudras of east Bengal who failed to project themselves as a homogeneous group vis-a-vis the British,[19] the Mahishyas succeeded immensely in organizing effective political movements at the grassroots against the alien state. That the Congress was well-entrenched in the district was attributed largely to the Mahishya caste solidarity. Thus it is not surprising that while explaining the cohesion and discipline of the Congress organization, the government sources mention,

> The cultivators who form the backbone of the Congress movement mostly belong to one single community, namely, the Mahishya. It is a well-knit community. . . . Any order which goes out to the villages from the town leaders is obeyed without question. If, for example, the order be given that no food-stuff is to be exported from a village, everybody follows that rule, some through conviction and others through fear of social boycott.[20]

Predominantly an agricultural caste, Mahishyas in Midnapur were a locally dominant caste which included petty landlords and *jotedars* as well as poor. In 1896, the Mahishyas were identified as the local aristocrats: since, in Midnapur, the number of high caste Brahman and Kayastha was very small, the Kaibartas (Mahishyas), as the President of the college of Nadia pundits declared , 'may be said to form the upper layer of the population. A great many of them are zamindars and holders of substantial tenures.'[21] As such, their social position was not commensurate with their economic position. Moreover, in the absence of other strong caste groups, the numerically preponderant and economically secure Mahishyas thrived in an atmosphere, free from caste antagonism and confrontation. In other words, the rise of the Mahishyas as a well-knit caste group was largely attributed to the fact that there 'was no solid community above or below them nursing resentment'.[22]

Before 1921, the Mahishyas were not recognized as a separate caste, but were categorized with the Jalia Kaibartas as the Kaibarta caste. The identification of the Mahishyas as distinct from other castes came as a result of an organized movement since 1901. By the turn of the nineteenth century, the better-off Kaibartas of Midnapur, led by some zamindars and a few Calcutta-based lawyers and traders, began calling themselves Mahishyas and started a *Jati Nirdharani Sabha* in 1897 and central Mahishya Samiti during the 1901 census.[23] Not only were they organized to support their claim, they justified their higher status with reference to 'the ancient texts in which they were represented as the offspring of

Kshatriya father and Vaishya mother'.[24] Furthermore, at least among the Mahishyas there was some material basis to the claim for Kshatriya status. Not only were they the leading group in the district of Midnapur their wealth had also ensured for them an access to English education which was a passport to higher status. According to the 1931 census, 2.71 per cent of Mahishyas were literate in English.[25] In the neighbouring 24 Parganas, they constituted the bulk of *lathdar* landholders of Sundarbans. In Nadia, they formed the lower middle class and some had become rich by working as *sarkars* to the European indigo planters; in Calcutta, there was a large Mahishya contingent functioning as traders, manufacturers and lawyers.[26] So, the drive to gain a higher status was strengthened partly by wealth and partly by social position acquired through English education and serving the British state in respectable position. By deciding to categorize the Indian population in terms of caste and thus preference, the 1901 census merely provided the occasion to the Mahishyas to articulate the claims–that would have happened given their consistent efforts to attain a separate caste status since the formation of Jati Nirdharani Sabha in 1897.

In the 1921 census, their demand for Mahishya status as distinct from Jalia Kaibarta was conceded. Their claim for a separate identity was justified on two factors: (*a*) they were a distinct group as opposed to Jalia Kaibarta in terms of 'a somewhat better social position than the latter'; and (*b*) they constituted a majority among the castes in Bengal. As the 1921 census shows, the Mahishyas (2,210,684) are the largest Hindu caste in Bengal, beating the Namasudras by nearly 200,000 and the Rajbanshis by nearly 500,000.[27] In Midnapur, with their demographic preponderance, their position was strong as the table which follows shows (p. 66).

Once the higher status was accorded to the Mahishyas, attempts were made to maintain their distinct and separate identity by preventing other low castes from attaining the status of Mahishyas. Looking upon the census as 'an opportunity for pressing and perhaps obtaining some recognition of social claims which were denied by castes higher than their own', the 1921 census noted, 'each individual community was claimant to obtain a step upward on the ladder of society, *but it was equally insistent that those who stand below it should not be permitted to do something'* (emphasis added).[28] This was particularly noticeable in the attitude of the Mahishyas who devoted their energies to ensure 'that such castes as the *Jalia Kaibarta Patnis* and others who claimed to use the same term or a variant of it should not be permitted to do so'.[29] Referring to their function as *dom*, i.e. to burn the dead, the Mahishya

Name of the Subdivision	Total Population	Total Mahishyas
Sadar	860,622	145,836 (16.9%)*
Jhargram	389,130	7436 (1.9%)
Ghatal	273,308	96,701 (35.4%)
Tamluk	643,157	353,544 (54.9%)
Contai	632,836	229,848 (44.2%)
TOTAL	2,799,093**	883,367 (31.6%)

* Figures in the parentheses indicate the percentage of the Mahishyas in relation to the total population.

** This figure does not correspond with the census figure probably because of the confusion of the enumerators regarding the Mahishya category during the 1921 census when the separate caste status was accorded to the Mahishyas.

Source: The table, prepared from the information available from the Midnapur District Gazetteer, District Statistics, 1921-2 to 1930, Calcutta, 1933, pp. 2-3.

mouthpiece, *the Mahishya Samaj,* disputed the patni claim as nonsense because they were in fact lower in ritual status than even the Muslims. When certain Brahman pundits offered to defend the patni status as equivalent to that of the Mahishyas by reference to the ritual texts, *the Mahishya Samaj* wrote bitterly,

> The brahman pundits might be able to uplift the Patnis on paper, but they cannot reward them with maids, bearers and barbers. If the Patnis manage to get themselves recognised as Mahishyas, then arrangements should be made to call a *Munchi* (cobbler) a Brahman . . . the mercenary pundits by giving sanction to the unjustified claims of the Patnis are paving the way for a social revolution.[30]

On the one hand, the Mahishyas were keen not to identify with lower castes; there had been consistent efforts, on the other, to inject a sense of pride among the Mahishyas as tillers of the soil. Since manual labour was looked down upon by the higher castes, cultivation was never considered respectable enough in the social hierarchy. Hence, the *Mahishya Samaj* published numerous articles and poems to instil a sense of pride in being a *chasa* (peasant) who and 'not the babus nurtured the society and its members'.[31] Since *chasas* were demographically preponderant in a country like India which was essentially an agricultural country, the Viceroy was urged to give them a share in the governance of the country. The *Mahishya Samaj* exhorted, 'every land-owning proprietor without limitation or restriction, every tenure holder, every occupancy ryot, actual cultivator of the soil, each of whom has a stake in land, may possess a right to vote in the election of members of council'.[32]

The crystallization of 'peasant pride' was to have a serious impact on the future political mobilization in Midnapur. The formation of a homogeneous peasant community, regardless of horizontal differentiation, reveals the extent to which caste and class merged to create a separate identity among the Mahishyas which was hitherto unknown. What lay in this process was the origin of a socially coherent and politically agile group which became formidable particularly in the context of 1920-2 and 1942 Congress movements. So well-entrenched was the pride in being a *chasa* that during the 1921 election to the Legislative Council, a candidate for the Tamluk-Contai seat lost his creditability when he referred, in a derogatory way, to Midnapur being a land of *chasas*.[33] Such a well-defined identity of an already well-knit social group especially after Mahishyas were accorded a separate caste status in 1921, appeared crucial in political mobilization in Midnapur. So, in Midnapur, the attempt of the Mahishyas for a distinct social status unfolded a process which led to the articulation of caste-peasant identity among them. This was probably responsible for the development of 'the idyllic notion of an all-embracing peasant community' which served to conceal and undermine the horizontal differentiation in rural society. In effect, caste along with the harsh reality of a colonial agrarian economy contributed to reinforce, if not strengthen, the position of the *jotedars* and some zamindars as 'leaders of society in Midnapur'.[34]

PART II

The Nationalist Campaign in Midnapur, 1905-32

The period between 1905 and 1932 is significant in Bengal's political history for at least three important reasons: first, following the 1907 Surat split between the moderates and extremists, Bengal emerged as an important barometer of the degree to which Congress lacked ideological homogeneity. A fairly well-articulated ideological tradition opposed to the Congress High Command grew up initially around C. R. Das, a prominent Bengali politician, and this tradition continued even after his death in 1925. Secondly, Bengal saw during this period the advent of mass politics in the wake of a successful merger of the Non-Cooperation and Khilafat causes which, despite conceding the Muslims as a separate community, brought about new dimensions to the freedom struggle by expanding its boundary beyond the bhadralok-dominated elite politics. Finally, as politics was no longer confined to Calcutta, localities became crucial in the Congress-launched nationalist campaign; the involvement of the localities unfolded two significant consequences: (*a*) what developed in the localities in response to the pan-Indian campaign reveal the extent to which different layers of politics merge at one level and (*b*) although political movements in the localities drew essentially upon anti-imperial sentiments, local issues gained prominence; such an intermingling of national and local issues underline the importance of local political activists in selectively choosing issues which would allow them maximum mileage. A careful study of the political movements in the localities will thus be useful to gauge both the importance of particular issues in political mobilization and significance of a particular type of leadership which was readily acceptable due, *inter alia*, to a broad uniform social background of the leaders and the led.

Midnapur and the 1905 Bengal Partition

Curzon's partition of Bengal provoked what is famous as the Swadeshi agitation which upset the 'settled fact' of partition and during which various new techniques of political mobilization were successfully attempted.[35] Viewing partition as a Machiavellian device to strike at the roots of the Bengali nation and its nationalism, the bhadraloks of east Bengal organized themselves against the vivisection of the province. Although the Swadeshi Movement aimed at crippling the British, both economically and politically, it was confined primarily to Calcutta and east Bengal where partition threatened 'entrenched vested interests of the bhadralok minority'.[36] The movement, though a success from the point of view of its object of annulling the Bengal partition, was not as popular as the organizers expected because its Hindu character alienated the Muslims. The anti-partition agitation was, as Gordon Johnson points out, 'a Bengal High caste Hindu affair'.[37] Nonetheless, it permeated large areas of Bengal and introduced hitherto unknown devices of political mobilization to India's freedom struggle by directly confronting the British state.

Midnapur was relatively quiet during the anti-partition agitation probably because it was not affected by Curzon's plan. There were two different ways in which Midnapur bhadraloks expressed emotional solidarity with those fighting to rescind the partition. First, various meetings and conferences were organized to champion the swadeshi goal. Immediately after the announcement of the partition plan on 19 July 1905, a conference, attended by at least 1,000 students, was held at the Belly Hall in Midnapur town. It was decided that so long as the partition remained, 'nobody would participate in any public function . . . and would accept any foreign goods'.[38] To organize picketing in the district, a voluntary organization was founded at the behest of Satyendranath Bose who was politically baptized by Barin Ghose,[39] brother of Aurobindo Ghose, an important leader of the Swadeshi campaign. With the implementation of the partition on 16 August 1905, Midnapur like other Bengal districts saw processions, picketing and conferences. On 25 September 1905, a public meeting was organized in Midnapur town which attracted a crowd of 10,000 people;[40] another followed on 1 November which argued strongly for the implementation of the boycott slogan of the Swadeshi Movement. This caused a dissension among the organizers: the extremist section of the local Congress leadership, particularly Trailakyanath Paul, was in favour of adopting the economic swadeshi primarily because 'not only would it affect the colonial state adversely, it would also help build India as a self-sufficient economy by encouraging indigenous industries to grow and thrive'. The moderate leader, K. B. Dutta, found Paul's suggestion as futile and persuaded most of those who took part in the campaign to accept his point of view.[41] So, between 1905 and 1907, Swadeshi Movement in Midnapur was confined to the holding of ritualistic protest meetings.

What unfolded in the debate between the moderate and extremist sections over the acceptance of boycott was articulated clearly in the annual meeting of the local Congress in December 1907. Outnumbered by the Trailakyanath Paul-led extremist section, K. B. Dutta left the meeting after having been accused of using the police to prevent the extremists from attending the meeting.[42] 'With the moderates' withdrawal, picketing and boycott became far more intense and widespread in Midnapur in 1908. The contemporary government report shows that outlets were opened in Tamluk and Mahisadal for selling swadeshi goods. A notice was circulated by the participants declaring that those who offered swadeshi articles for sale would be honoured and not taxed and those who bought and sold foreign goods would be punished and made to pay a tax of Re. 1.[43] Despite the extremist initiative and effort, boycott and picketing never became a threat to the state power as they were, for instance, in east Bengal presumably because of the well-entrenched hostility of the local shopkeepers, manifested in frequent physical confrontation with the local Congressmen.[44] Furthermore, the withdrawal of K. B. Dutta and his followers from the Congress due to the inclusion of boycott in its programme weakened the organization significantly. Condemning such a split among the Congressmen at the time of crisis, the nationalist *Amrita Bazar Patrika* thus notes that despite the success of the Swadeshi Movement in attaining the goal, it also clearly articulated 'the factional feud within the Congress which was to assume massive proportions in the days to come'.[45]

Although the Swadeshi Movement initiated a novel process in the district that yielded results in a later period, it nonetheless failed to expand the constituency of the nationalist politics beyond students, nationalist lawyers and some zamindars. The reason is not difficult to seek: the Swadeshi Movement was basically an urban movement drawing essentially on the fear of the emergence of the Muslims as a significant political force in Bengal in view of their demographic preponderance. In Midnapur where the overwhelming majority of the population was rural with little or no contact with Calcutta, swadeshi as a political ideology was too distant to attract support among the masses. Besides, Midnapur, a west Bengal district was not affected in any way by Curzon's design and hence the momentum, which the Swadeshi Movement gained elsewhere, was missing; moreover, the fear of Muslim hegemony, that largely determined the nature of the movement in east Bengal, was never considered seriously since the number of Mulsims in the district was too insignificant to merit attention.[46] So, the Swadeshi campaign, though expanded the constituency of nationalist politics as compared with the earlier period, was constrained from the very outset because of its pronounced urban and anti-Muslim bias.

The Swadeshi Movement may not have been effective in Midnapur to the extent it was in east Bengal; it however paved the ground for revolutionary terrorist group which became formidable in 1908. The district was relatively quiet till 1907, but gained notoriety in 1908 with the discovery of a terrorist plot to kill the top British bureaucrats involving Kshudiram and Satyendranath Bose, both from Midnapur. Puzzled by the intensity of the terrorist activity in a district far away from Calcutta and Dhaka, strongholds of revolutionary terrorism, the district administration urged for the appointment of a tough District Collector. Accordingly, Donald Weston was tipped for the post for his ability to contain terrorism,[47] which he proved in the context of the swadeshi upsurge in Calcutta.[48] Weston's appointment was significant from the point of view of the revolutionary terrorists who, so far, were scattered and disorganized, realized the importance of uniting various groups in the face of a superior and well-disciplined British administration.[49]

Although the secret samitis consolidated their strength by 1908-9, their roots can be traced back to 1902 when a society was established by Hemchandra Kanungo and Jnanendranath Basu. Inspired by Aurobindo Ghose, Kanungo and Basu urged the students in particular to participate in the nationalist struggle. Questioning the politics of mendicancy of the moderates, they also popularized the terrorist method which had an appeal given the failure of the Midnapur lawyer politicians to undertake an effective campaign vis-a-vis the British during the Swadeshi Movement. In fact, the inclusion of boycott, which was vehemently opposed by the moderates in the district, was largely the result of Kanungo's insistence in the 1907 district conference.[50]

Although the secret samitis[51] in Midnapur had direct link with the Calcutta Anushilan Samiti,[52] it became strong with the consolidation of different *akhras* which came into being in the district essentially as self-defence organizations of the Hindus following the 1907 Comilla and Jamalpur (east Bengal) riots between Hindus and Muslims.[53] With their consistent effort, Basu and Kanungo built up a strong organization 'with a chain of *akhras*, weaving centres and *chhatra bhandar* branches which served as a cover for revolutionary activity'.[54] According to police reports, four *akhras* were established in Midnapur which, as suggested by their names–Sakti Samiti, Swadeshi Samiti, Santan Samiti and Basanta Malati Akhra–clearly had political objectives, tempered by the then religious nationalism.[55] There were *akhras* in Mahisadal, Tamluk and Contai. Part of the reason for *akhras*' success lay in the financial support of two prominent zamindars of Midnapur–Raja Narendralal Khan of Narajole and Digambar Nanda of Mugberia. In the eyes of the administration, both Khan and Nanda were considered unreliable because of their involvement in revolutionary terrorism.[56] It was not therefore surprising that Weston, after his arrival, left no stone unturned to harass and insult Narendralal Khan. In 1907 he deleted Khan's name from the *Khas Mulakat* list[57] of Midnapur because,

> his manners are very bad; in fact, he seems to me to be deficient in intellect. He is said to be a *ganja* eater which may account for his idiocy. He has mixed himself up with the swadeshi party and I have had frequent complaints of boycotting in his *elaka* [areas], encouraged by his local officers.[58]

Weston brought punitive police into the district and stationed them at all those thanas where the swadeshis were reported to have been active. To keep an eye on the activities of Khan and his followers, he made arrangements for the punitive police to be stationed at the Narajole zamindari. Moreover, after Kshudiram was captured for his involvement in the Muzaffarpur bomb case, Weston engaged police officers specifically to investigate any alleged complicity of the Raja.[59] He, along with 27 others, was arrested for his alleged involvement in hatching a plot to murder the District Collector, Donald Weston.[60] Not only was the government keen to wrap up the so-called trouble makers, it let loose various repressive measures to scare the people away from the Swadeshi campaign. The situation in Midnapur was so panic-stricken that *Bengalee* wrote,

> There is a general sense of insecurity . . . throughout the district. People feel that at any moment their houses may be searched and they may be arrested if only they have incurred the displeasure of the police. . . . The general feeling is that police are masters of the situation and they may do what they please . . . police rule has been substituted in place of the reign of law.[61]

Indiscriminate police repression, unleashed by Weston and his administration, though effective in containing terrorism, had the effect of raising the level of political consciousness in Midnapur. Previously, majority of Midnapur inhabitants were largely indifferent to the activities of the nationalists; repression brought to them the realities of the Swadeshi Movement which provoked the local administration to undertake measures to combat the participants. That the state was unjust gained an easy acceptance once it was announced that the charges against 24 of the 27 arrested in connection with an alleged conspiracy to kill Weston were unfounded given the lack of substantial evidence.[62] In fact, the so-called bomb case appeared flimsy as it was based on the evidence of two police informers and two men who had criminal records.[63] On the whole, Weston's personal vendetta against the Mindapur notables weakened the movement at least temporarily; it nonetheless alienated a large section of the population in the district who were either loyal to the British or indifferent to the nationalist intervention. So, what began by way of organizing the bhadraloks against the British atrocity became formidable as the constituents of nationalist politics gradually expanded. In other words, the so-called elite politics contributed significantly to the freedom struggle though it was constrained from the outset because 'elite action postponed efforts to draw the masses into active political struggle which would have involved conscious [endeavours] to link up national with socio-economic issues through more radical programmes'.[64]

The Partition of Midnapur, 1915-21

Political mobilization in the wake of the Swadeshi Movement exposed, on the one hand, the limitations of an essentially elite revolution and, on the other, crisis of legitimacy of British rule in Midnapur, manifested in the indiscriminate repressive measures applied to the leaders of the movement. Whatever the result of the 1905-9 anti-partition agitation, the

Swadeshi campaign, both in moderate and extremist methods, brought to the forefront of nationalist politics an articulate section of the society which, though had a narrow social basis, put forward an argument championing the nationalist cause against the alien state. Such an attempt is significant because, at one level, it helps develop the logic of countering what is considered as 'unwarranted intervention' of the British state and, at another, it probably paves the ground for other political forces to consolidate which are presently peripheral and insignificant too. In this sense, Swadeshi Movement had played a crucial role in the anti-British mobilization—despite obvious limitations, it provided the future generation with a model. What developed in Midnapur following the announcement of the partition of the district in 1915 merely confirmed that nationalist politics continued to remain elitist at least till the outbreak of the 1920-2 Non-Cooperation Movement.

The partition of Midnapur was justified by the logic of administrative convenience. As the district appeared unmanageable for one district magistrate given its enormous size, the Government of Bengal mooted the idea of the division of the district in 1907. In view of the volatile political situation following the Swadeshi campaign, the Government of India, instead of conceding the demand of partition, recommended the appointment of an Additional District Magistrate to share the burden of the Collector.[65] The arrangement continued till the District Administration Committee recommended the partition of large districts like Midnapur and Mymensingh as an essential part of government's anti-terrorist strategy. Later, in 1915, the Bengal government accepted the suggestion and arrangement was accordingly made to expedite the process.[66] A new district of Hijli was proposed to be created by dividing Midnapur which, as the District Administration Report mentioned, was too big to govern from one centre;[67] such an argument gained currency probably in view of the failure of the local administration to defuse the 'terrorist threat' in the district, especially after abortive attempts on the life of police officers in a couple of thanas in Tamluk.[68]

As soon as the partition plan was made public on 26 January 1915, it provoked widespread resentment among the zamindars and lawyers for reasons connected with their self-interests. The lawyers of Midnapur opposed the partition vehemently as it meant a considerable decline of their income following the creation of two district courts in Midnapur and Hijli. They also apprehended that justice would be denied in the new court because of the reluctance of their expert colleagues to practise in Hijli.[69] Such an argument drew partly upon the fear of the loss of earnings due to a division among the clients who now had the option to try their case in a different court. In fact, while condemning the proposed partition, Upendra Nath Maity, the President of the Midnapur Bar Council, argued that the division of the district would involve tremendous costs since it necessitated the creation of a new set-up–which should be avoided; money, earmarked for the partition, would best be utilized for the development of the district, including road communication which deserved immediate attention to 'contain the terrorist menace'.[70] That the opposition to the partition was determined primarily, if not solely, by material and sectional considerations was evident in the attitude of Biren Sasmol who decided to withdraw from the campaign when there seemed a real possibility of Contai, his residence, being chosen as the headquarters of the proposed district. Insisting that Contai should be made a district town given its literacy rate and particularly literacy in English,[71] Sasmol tried to make a case for the partition.

Similarly, zamindars opposed the partition as it would enhance the cost of running zamindaris if they were located in two different districts. The Tauzi system of revenue collection–which brought non-Khas Mahal lands under a centralized control–necessitated the establishment and maintenance of a new set-up, which meant extra cost. Thus the Nawab of Murshidabad urged the government to abandon the plan by arguing that the location of 20 per cent of his lands in the new district would unnecessarily increase the cost since the rest of landholdings were located in the other district.[72] Likewise, the European-owned Midnapur Zamindari Company (MZC) complained that the proposed division would mean the bifurcation of its landed property in accordance with the jurisdiction of the district; not only would it add to their cost since it would necessitate the establishment of a new set-up, the nature of supervision of the property was likely to be affected, given that it would take a while to develop a disciplined supervisory staff.[73] Though Nawab's request was shelved, the MZC's appeal was accommodated and the district was restructured accordingly.[74]

Finally, there was a small section of Congressmen who found in the partition of Midnapur an imperial design of crushing the nationalist movement. Comparing the scheme with Curzon's 1905 Bengal partition, they underlined the importance of organizing a movement to defeat the plan. As the district played a crucial role during the Swadeshi Movement, the proposed vivisection aimed at crippling the political activities in the district by creating a division among the people.[75] Hence, the nationalist weekly, *Medini Bhandav* exhorted the people to remain united otherwise 'the satanic government' would destroy them:

So, let the people of Midnapur come forward regardless of caste and creed, protest against this terrible scheme of partition. Let them assemble in different places, and in piteous voice make known the anguish of heart, they all feel. Let them unite in their hundreds and . . . [thousands] in towns and in country and set-up a terrible agitation in *a restrained and constitutional way* against this heart rending proposal (emphasis added).[76]

So committed were they to 'a restrained and constitutional way' that the leaders of the agitation condemned those who prepared to adopt the swadeshi techniques of boycott and picketing.[77] Concentrating on the conventional strategy of petition and protest meetings, the *Medini Bhandav* organized meetings of the district notables like the local zamindars, D. N. Hazra and Bhubaneshwar Mitra or lawyers, J. P. Chatterjee and B. N. Sasmol.[78] Not only did they mobilize support through meetings, they also appealed to the Bengal government by sending petitions or memorials to the Governor, Lord Carmichael. Between 1915 and 1919, the government received 18 petitions, signed by the leading men of the district which, though written by different groups, had a remarkable similarities among themselves in terms of the underlying tone essentially of an appeal and not a demand. *Medini Bhandav*, for instance, thus articulated its prayer to Carmichael,

My Lord, Midnapur is an ancient district; do not divide it. O, Lord Charmichael, the sea of compassion and friend of the people, today the 28 lakhs [2.8 million] of your subjects inhabiting in Midnapur are seeking your protection. Grant them again the assurance of safety.[79]

Despite earnest appeals, the government appeared determined to execute the division. In his speech to the protesters in Midnapur, the Bengal Governor defended the decision as the most appropriate step to introduce an effective local self government in India. Insisting that 'a real system of local self government is the greatest need of Bengal', he argued, 'I do not see how, unless you change the whole system of Indian administration–which no one prepares to do . . . I do not see how you can ever get a really effective system of local self government introduced into this country unless you divide up the larger districts.'[80]

Although the government was keen to partition Midnapur for administrative convenience, the scheme was shelved in 1921 due principally to financial reasons. It was thus mentioned in the government communique that 'for financial considerations it has been found necessary to suspend work [for the partition of Midnapur] which, for the present therefore, is in abeyance'.[81] The government decision not to press for division may well have been due to the growing popularity of the B. N.

Sasmol-led Non-Cooperation Movement in the district. As will be shown below, the success of the anti-union board agitation demonstrates the extent to which the anti-state feelings were articulated effectively. The Bengal government was thus probably hesitant to implement the partition scheme that did not appear to have any substantial support from within the district. The movement opposing the partition clearly shows the hegemony of the original moderate techniques which were radically transformed in the 1905-8 Swadeshi campaign by including measures, boycott and picketing in particular, to affect the British commercial interests directly. Since it was confined to those whose material interests were likely to be jeopardized, the movement never became a serious threat to the administration. So, the campaign had no popular basis. And here probably lay the government confidence in challenging the anti-partition movement which lacked any substantial backing from the district.[82]

The anti-partition agitation during 1915-21 is significant for having articulated a process whereby a campaign was organized on the basis of local issues. Though the 1905 Swadeshi Movement provided the basic impetus, the movement against the division of Midnapur was different in its insistence on essentially 'moderate techniques' of 'prayer, protest and petition'. The root of schism between Sasmol and his colleagues that became formidable in the Non-Cooperation Movement lay in the former's endeavour in involving the masses for the first time in political campaign;[83] Sasmol defended the partition as it would allow the people of Contai to enjoy the benefit of a district town. It is however debatable whether the consideration of popular benefit swayed Sasmol especially when 'people' had a very narrow basis; what is significant is that he initiated a process of mobilization whereby people or masses were identified as crucial actors in the freedom struggle. In this sense, Sasmol's intervention, though in a limited way, was certainly a break in the political style that pervaded the anti-British campaign during the period between 1905 and 1919.

The Non-Cooperation Movement, 1921-2

The Non-Cooperation Movement is certainly a break with the past. Gandhi's arrival on the political scene introduced various new dimensions to the nationalist politics. India's freedom struggle was no longer confined to bhadraloks only, but was expanded to incorporate new social groups which so far remained peripheral. Concomitant to the extension of the constituency of nationalist politics was adoption of new slogans which radicalized the Congress to a large extent. Not content with the so-called mendicant politics, the Gandhi-led Congress undertook several measures which created new constituents of support. Gandhi rose to prominence at a time when both the moderate and extremist methods were proved futile given the incessant attampts of the people at the grassroots to challenge the colonial state which allowed vested interests to grow and thrive. So, the involvement of new social groups in the freedom struggle helped crystallize their search for a new order. Not always significant, these forces undoubtedly articulated new socio-political and economic issues which never figured in the pre-1921 Congress agenda presumably because of its narrow social basis. So, a complex interplay of factors involving the state, the Congress and the mass drive for changing the prevalent socio-economic and political order led to the Non-Cooperation Movement which, though essentially an anti-British offensive, laid the foundation of an altogether new movements challenging both the vested interests and the alien state.

Organizationally, the Congress, no longer confined merely to the elites, soon developed into a national movement with agricultural links extending far into the country and its support coming from wide sections of the population. An important reason as to why the Congress became a mass organization probably lay in an effective merger of the Non-Cooperation and Khilafat causes. Recognizing the Muslims as a separate political group in the 1916 Lucknow Pact,[84] the Congress adopted perhaps the most meaningful strategy to build a mass movement by projecting Hindu-Muslim unity. It is however debatable whether only the Khilafat cause which was not at all directly related to India's struggle for freedom, cemented the bond between the Muslims and Hindus in the wake of the Non-Cooperation Movement though the disintegration of the Khaliph was too remote to have an impact on the ordinary Muslims.[85] Whatever the factors that contributed to the expansion of the Congress, the rise of its membership was spectacular, as shown in the table (p. 78).

Although the table is by no means exhaustive, it draws our attention to the gradual increase and decline of the Congress delegates during and after the Non-Cooperation campaign. One is thus inclined to underline the importance primarily of the religious content of the Khilafat in political mobilization during the Non-Cooperation Movement given the sudden increase of the Muslim delegates and their indifference later. Notwithstanding the adverse consequences of articulating the Muslim demands as separate from those of the Indian National Congress in later days, Gandhi's decision to champion the Khilafat cause broaden the social basis of the nationalist movement. Attributing exploitation at different levels to the alien state, the Congress leadership succeeded in infusing popular misery with a political content. It is not therefore surprising that different kinds of political movements were organized during the Non-Cooperation days which though drew upon anti-British feelings,

Year	*Total Number of Delegates*	*Muslims*	*% of Muslims vis-a-vis Total*
1918	4,868	205	4.0%
1919	8,126	314	4.5%
1920	14,582	1,050	7.2%
1921	4,729	–	–
1922	3,248	111	3.6%

Source: Gopal Krishna, The Development of the National Congress as a Mass Organization, *Journal of Asian Studies*, 25, 3, 1966, p. 421.

were basically attacks on the well-entrenched vested interests. As will be shown below, the Non-Cooperation call let loose hitherto unknown socio-economic and political forces that decisively shaped and thus consequently made the nature of the nationalist intervention more complex than ever.

Apart from including boycott of schools, colleges and law courts, the Non-Cooperation campaign adopted a more militant stance concentrating on boycott of foreign clothes (including public bonfires) and boycott of the visit of the Prince of Wales in November 1921. Since the 1920 Calcutta Congress, delegates were reported to have insisted on non-payment of taxes; the administration expressed concern because such an issue was likely to gain an easy acceptance since it was championed by the Bengal contingent comprising principally 'the exdetenus and the intelligentsia which . . . have at their disposal many thousands of men who are available for propaganda amongst the masses of the most unscrupulous, reckless and dangerous character'.[86] Despite Gandhi's reluctance,[87] boycott was included in the Congress agenda in the Bombay AICC meeting of 28-30 July primarily to accommodate the radical elements within the Congress. As Bhattacharyya has shown, the economic boycott though complementary to economic swadeshi, actually enhanced the profit of Indian textile magnates. Before the war, Indian mill-owners, for instance, controlled only 25 per cent of the textile market which expanded to 42 per cent by the end of 1921; the prices also rose by three times.[88]

As regards boycott of schools and colleges, the Non-Cooperation campaign probably attained a dramatic success. Gandhi was convinced that the English education was futile and urged the students to leave the government-controlled educational institutions; the appeal had magnificent results in the context of the opening of a large number of national schools and colleges throughout the country. As the table below shows, though their popularity was not the same, the national schools and colleges attracted a large number of students.

It is true that the number of students enrolled in these schools and colleges was not large enough to cause anxiety. What alarmed the administration was the impact of the boycott slogan on the government institutions as a whole; almost 80 per cent of them were seriously affected between 1919 and 1921. While explaining this phenomenon, the official report thus admitted,

> There was something in the movement that appealed to most diverse types of minds. . . . Imagination has been fired and a spiritual uplift initiated. Something that had been wanting in our college life had been supplied. . . the situation presented possibilities of romance and adventure that irradiated [otherwise sterile] student life. Picketing and procession were [therefore] as irresistible to such minds as a bump supper and a 'rag' to Oxford undergraduates.
>
> [Students] became for the first time conscious that they were wasting time over a kind of education not suited to their needs and leading them to an office stool.[89]

National schools and colleges failed to provide an effective alternative to the prevalent academic institution and by 1923, except in Bengal,[90] the lack of interest in such an experiment was clearly evident.[91] The official explanation is also significant in having brought out the limitations of existing system of education which was at its best tuned to the creation of merely a pool of clerks.[92]

Whatever the reasons, the educational boycott was more effective in contrast with other Non-Cooperation agendas. For instance, the initial appeal for self sacrifice was hardly successful: only 24 titles were

Province	*Institutions*	*Scholars*	*Effect of Non-Cooperation on Certain Institutions up to March 1921*
Madras	92	5,072	1,71,111
Bombay	189	17,100	42,416
Bengal	190	14, 819	1,03,107
United Provinces	137	8,476	49,171
Punjab	69	8,046	1,11,078
Bihar and Orissa	442	17,330	23,190
Central Provinces	86	6,338	71,759
Assam	38	1,908	12,186
NWFP	4	120	41,3432

Source: P. C. Bamford, *Histories of Non-Cooperation and Khilafat Movements, Government of India*, New Delhi, 1925, p. 104.

surrendered out of 5,186, and the number of lawyers giving up practice was 180 in 1921.[93] Polling was low in many places in the 1920 Council elections, falling to 8 per cent in Bombay city and 5 per cent in Lahore; candidates contested in all but six out of 637 seats and council functioning could not be disrupted.[94] Compared with the erstwhile Congress campaign, the Non-Cooperation Movement demonstrated that 'the old closed shop of limited politics had been thrown wide open. Far greater numbers than before were participating in an overt political campaign, using a far wider range of techniques than earlier politicians had ever used simultaneously . . . and participants came from all parts of India.'[95] The political nation was thus expanded to accommodate various kinds of interests, manifested in the type of the movements, organized with a view to redressing local grievances which, on various occasions, were attributed to colonialism. As a consequence, the nation had to confront with various new constituents which were either peripheral or too insignificant to deserve attention in political mobilization.

An important dimension of the nationalist politics unfolded with the incorporation of the working class struggle in its fold. In 1921, there were 396 strikes involving 600,351 workers and a loss of 6,994,426 mandays.[96] What provoked strikes was the recession in the post-war period which forced the factory owners to cut production with a four-day week. The Bengal jute mill workers were hard hit by this new schedule of production which largely accounts for an epidemic of strikes in 1921: a total of 137 strikes affecting 186,479 workers. The leadership was vested in the newly emerged section of 'the Hindu right as well as a number of left groups dedicated to the creation of a socialist movement focused on the grievances of the workers and peasants'.[97] Organizing the workers in trade unions,[98] these labour activists caused alarm to the British administration which by highlighting their bhadralok background strove assiduously to create a fissure between the workers and the leadership.[99] Apart from jute mill towns, the participants in the Non-Cooperation campaign tried to organise a strike in Raniganj-Jharia coal mines. Although both the leaders, Swami Viswanand and Swami Darsananand, were involved in the movement against the mine-owners essentially to ameliorate the conditions of the mine-workers, the strike was reported to have been instigated by the Marwari businessmen who wanted to get into coal business, so far monopolised by the Europeans.[100]

The Chandpur incident of 1921 is probably the most publicized event during the Non-Cooperation Movement showing the appeal of Gandhi as a leader who was acceptable to the Assam tea garden workers regardless of religion, caste and region. Inspired by Gandhi's call for swaraj for the people which meant an end to exploitation, the tea garden workers in Chandpur, mostly from the UP and Bihar, started a long trek without seeking manager's permission for home which brought them to Chandpur in Tippera district on 15 May 1921. Despite adverse consequences, the workers undertook such drastic steps probably in response to the prevalent rumour that 'Gandhi raj has been established [and hence] the exploiters [garden owners] are on the run'.[101] In order to prevent the workers from boarding a steamer for their journey, the local administration employed Gurkha military police who resorted to indiscriminate firing. Such 'an inhuman act'[102] provoked mass resentment which was translated into steamer and rail strikes in east Bengal. The C. R. Das-led Bengal Congress immediately took up the cause of the workers to sharpen its attack on the colonial state. The chain of strikes in Bengal that followed the Chandpur firing was partly attributable to the involvement of the leading Congressmen like C. R. Das and J. M. Sengupta and partly due to a 'spontaneous rising of the entire population especially the lower classes who expressed through the strikes their acute sense of economic exploitation and racial abasement under white rule'.[103] A disturbed Ronaldshay who appeared panic-stricken in view of the widespread nature of the strike wrote,

> The most disquieting feature is the extent of the hold which events have shown they have already acquired over large classes of people. They have been able to call strikes in the inland steamer lines and the Assam-Bengal Railway, and they have been able to call hartals in a number of east Bengal towns simultaneously.[104]

The 'strike fever', as it was characterized in the official discourse,[105] was endemic and affected primarily the industries of eastern India. Part of the reason lay in the fact that the leadership succeeded in attributing workers' misery principally to the European/American ownership that with its association with the colonial state, was naturally insensitive to the grievances of the Indians. Besides, the role of the local Congress leadership appeared crucial in organizing the disparate workers for a cause by providing an ideological direction[106] as well as material help. For leaders, like C. R. Das and J. M. Sengupta labour was increasingly becoming an important constituency of the nationalist politics, recognized later in the 1922 Gaya Congress; and thus by championing the workers' cause, they initiated a process which, though signalled and articulated too various contradictions in the Gandhi-led movement, widened the social base of the freedom struggle. Because strike 'do not fall within the plan of non-violent non-cooperation'[107] Gandhi while condemning the strike fever argued,

In India we want no political strikes . . . we must gain control over the unruly and disturbing elements . . . we seek not to destroy capital or capitalists, but to regulate the relations between capital and labour. We want to harness capital to our side. *It would be folly to encourage sympathetic strikes* (emphasis added).[108]

The Non-Cooperation Movement also brought the peasants to the forefront of the nationalist politics. By according priority to village reconstruction through self-help, Gandhi articulated his plan for an economic revival 'through spinning wheel and hand-woven cloth [*charkha* and *khadi*], panchayats or arbitration courts, national schools and campaign for Hindu-Muslim unity and against the evils of liquor and untouchability'.[109] Although these programmes may not have been uniformly effective as strategies for political mobilization they nonetheless unfolded a new process by involving the hitherto neglected section of society in a struggle which, despite its pronounced political content, was equally a battle against the well-entrenched vested interests in the localities. It was not therefore surprising that peasants of Kanika in Orissa challenged the local zamindars for having demanded an extra rent. Drawing upon Gandhi, the militant section of the Orissa Congress leaders organized 'the peasants for the establishment of Gandhi raj when no one would have to pay rent'; so convinced were the peasants that they 'boycotted and intimidated', on occasions, 'those who were inclined to pay rents to the zamindars'.[110] The movement, though led by the Orissa Congress, did not receive Gandhi's approval, and was later unconditionally revoked. Gandhi was however inclined to encourage a no revenue campaign in a rayatwari settlement area, like Bardoil and not in any zamindari region where it would inevitably involve 'no rent'. By trying to contain 'no rent' campaigns, Gandhi projected a specific type of leadership which mobilized peasants exclusively in its terms and conditions. Peasants were organised and mobilised on the so-called unifying issues which transcend even the well-defined boundaries among the antagonistic classes.[111] So, it was logical when Gandhi 'deprecated all attempts to create a discord between landlords and tenants and advised the tenants to suffer rather than fight for they had to join all forces for fighting the most powerful zamindar, namely the Government'.[112]

Gandhi's political agenda sharpened the division within the nationalist leadership which saw the peasant cause as integral to the anti-imperial struggle. For the Kishan Sabhas, 'no rent' was a logical demand in a vertically-divided society, though it affected adversely the landlords who were Indians; so, the struggle of the peasantry took a different turn in areas where they were pre-dominant. In the Congress-dominated areas, the contradiction that reigned supreme was between imperialism and nationalism and the local leadership therefore succeeded in integrating the movements in the localities with its pan-Indian counterpart on the basis of an anti-imperial logic. Despite surplus extraction, the contradiction between landlords and peasants never became sharp enough to cause a fissure in the multi-class platform which the leadership so carefully nurtured. Midnapur is a glaring example showing the extent to which the Congress leaders effectively tuned the peasant movement to identify imperialism as singularly responsible for severe dislocation in society. Such a correlation gained ground in the peasant mind probably due, *inter alia,* to a peculiar socio-economic and political configuration in Midnapur.

The Non-Cooperation Movement in Midnapur

In the wake of the Non-Cooperation Movement, Midnapur became prominent by confronting the state and thus ushered in a new era in her history. Between 1921 and 1922, political movements in the district underwent radical changes: bhadraloks became marginalized and a wider section of the population participated in the anti-British campaign. Apart from a unique socio-economic environment which largely accounts for a homogeneity among the participants regardless of both horizontal and vertical differentiation, the role of B.N. Sasmol was singularly important in sustaining and directing the popular zeal according to a well-defined programme. It was C.R. Das who brought Sasmol to the provincial politics which was, in the pre-Das period, largely confined to Calcutta. The militancy Das perceived in different movements at the local levels led him to realize the necessity of projecting local political actors to the provincial level so as to widen the organizational base of the Congress.[113] He therefore recruited a group of young leaders like Anil Baran Ray of Bankura, J.M. Sengupta of Chittagong and B.N. Sasmol of Midnapur who already had carved out a position of importance in the nationalist political circles by organizing anti-state campaigns at the grass-roots. Hailed as someone who 'always maintained some links with the district',[114] Sasmol was easily identified with the local people probably because of his Mahishya caste background and the success he attained in transcending simultaneously the limitation of being a bhadralok. He acquired wide public support through extensive social service particularly relief work during the floods between 1913 and 1920. Not only did he publicize the misery of the local people in the press[115] he also single-handedly organized relief works.[116] Sasmol's involvement in flood relief led to a direct confrontation with the district administration which was selective in providing relief to the people, particularly during the 1913 floods.[117] This was significant especially in the context of what was to follow later. On the one hand, by raising voice, Sasmol articulated his opposition to the colonial state which had 'no moral right to rule' because of its failure to 'offer protection to its subject during a severe crisis';[118] on the other, by extending relief to all flood victims irrespective of caste and class, Sasmol also projected his search for a wider constituency beyond the narrow confines of bhadralok-dominated institutional politics. By articulating the local issues which had an important bearing on the all pervasive colonial state, Sasmol represented a new type of Congress leadership that, for the first time, tried to link the grassroots with the organized world of politics. In fact, what was thus initiated made Midnapur distinctly different from the rest of Bengal.

The 1920 Midnapur council election is a significant entry point to unfathom the process that loomed large later. Sasmol's decision to withdraw from voting following the 1920 Nagpur resolution allowed 'various unknown people' to contest the council elections. It was disappointing to the local people as *Nihar* announced, 'people have neither heard of them nor have they done any work for the country . . . there are some candidates about whom people of the district know very little or nothing'.[119] Moreover, a snide remark of A.C. Dutt, a candidate in the fray, in which Midnapur was identified, rather pejoratively *as land of chasas,*[120] ruined his chance in the election. This remark provoked a hostile reaction among the predominantly Mahishya voters who considered it a personal affront on them. *Nihar*, articulating anger sarcastically wrote, 'we are glad to know that many educated local people who hail from the land of peasants . . . we are also glad to know . . . that there are enough qualified peasants among the candidates'.[121]

Although the personality of the candidate continued to play a decisive role the 1920 election brought-out two significant issues: (*a*) the crystallization of peasant pride costed A.C. Dutt his seat in the council for having undermined the *chasa* identity and (*b*) in the campaign, the issue of locals versus outsiders also figured prominently. In fact a majority of the candidates, though hailed from Midnapur but settled elsewhere, advertised in *Nihar* to prove that their roots lay in the district.[122] Such a drive on the part of the candidates show the changing nature of politics in the localities where an identity with the area was important. Also, there was a growing awareness of the need to reach out beyond the bhadralok-dominated coterie politics, particularly in view of the expansion of franchise. For the candidates to win, the newly-enfranchised section of rural population needed to be taken into confidence. The election highlighted another significant dimension of local politics: though Midnapur figured prominently in the 1905 Swadeshi Movement, issues which became important were those related solely to the individual personalities, and the logic of anti-imperial struggle was completely forgotten. At one level, the events, culminated in the 1920 election articulated the distinctiveness of Midnapur as well as its insularity from the national and provincial scene; at another probably significant level, they also demonstrate the mechanics of self-organization at the grassroots where mobilization drew upon completely different sets of ideas and logic in which the characteristically distinct identity of the localities appeared significant. The 1921 anti-Union Board Movement is probably the best example demonstrating the extent to which 'the local pride' was crucial in organizing an effective assault on the colonial state at the grassroots.

The anti-Union Board Agitation, 1921

The introduction of the Union Board as the lowest unit of administration provoked a widespread unrest in the district. Involving various though antagonistic strata of society, the organised thrust of the movement was directed against the colonial state. There the principal organizers came primarily from the Congress, particularly its Gandhian wing. In terms of social background, the leadership was vested in the *jotedar*-rich peasant section, but the movement in some cases, created the possibility of the emergence of the lower peasantry as a political power.

The Union Board was introduced in the 1919 Bengal Village Self Government (BVSG) Act to strengthen administration at the grassroots. Each Union Board consisted of nine members–six elected and three nominated by the government. Since it was the administrative organ 'to ensure justice'[123] the Union Board was vested with power and duties. That the primary objective of the Act was to ascertain the government authority at the grassroots was evident in its emphasis on the appointment of more *dafadars* and chowkidars. In their appointment however, the District Magistrate was given a free hand suggesting the extent to which the elected members were easily bypassed in case of recruiting those who were considered pivots in rural administration. Although the Board members had virtually no power in appointment, the Union Board was required to pay the salaries and the cost of equipment used by the *dafadars* and chowkidars; they are not, however, accountable to the Board but were attached to the police thana within which the union was located. To strengthen the government surveillance, the chowkidars were to report to the officer in charge of the thana 'the movements of all bad characters within the unions' and 'arrival of suspicious character in the neighbourhood'. He was authorized to 'arrest . . . any person who has been concerned in any cognizable offence or against whom a reasonable complaint has been made, or credible information has been received, or a reasonable suspicion exists of his having been so concerned'.[124]

The Union Boards were also expected to contribute to rural development by undertaking public utility services, promoting health, comfort and convenience of the rural masses. Hence the priority was accorded to arrange the supply of potable water and adequate sanitation facilities. As part of public services, the Board was also assigned the task of building and maintenance of roads, bridges and waterways; part of its budget was also earmarked for small irrigation projects, primary schools and dispensaries, public library and reading room. In view of the favourable provisions ensuring public well-being, the Act evoked a mixed response.[125] The loyalist press welcomed the Act while the nationalist newspaper, particularly the *Amrita Bazar Patrika,* qualified its support by underlining that the stipulation would basically be utilized to ensure the government's 'surveillance' in rural areas through a pool of 'loyal dafadars and chowkidars'.[126]

Since the government did not sanction money for the Boards 'to encourage them to undertake taxation for rural improvement',[127] the Union Boards had to raise their resources locally with almost no outside help. The Act thus stipulated,

> The Union Board shall impose yearly on persons who are owners or occupiers of buildings . . . a rate amounting to (a) the sum required . . . for salaries and equipment of the dafadars and chowkidars and salaries of the establishment of the union board , and (b) the sum estimated to be required to meet the expenses of the board in carrying out any of the other purposes of this Act.[128]

The annual assessment on a person might be increased up to Rs. 84. In case of default of payment of union rates, the Board was authorized to

> levy, by the distraint and sale of a sufficient portion of the movable property of the defaulter, the amount of his arrears together with a sum equal to half the amount of such arrears, by way of penalty.[129]

The government reluctance to help the Union Boards financially even at the outset was significant enough to argue that the government was indifferent to the cause of rural development despite its explicit commitment otherwise.

The Union Board was instituted with a 50 per cent increase of the existing chowkidari tax. After meeting the statutory obligations, the Board, as Sanyal has shown, was left with too meagre a sum to undertake its multifarious duties.[130] The severe financial limitations of the Boards caught the loyalist newspaper, *The Statesman* by surprise which consequently made an appeal to the government to allocate funds to enable the Board to function; otherwise, the Congress volunteers would identify the government as an ineffective instrument that tended 'to make verbal assurances without a commitment'.[131]

The decision to introduce the Union Boards did not, at least initially, provoke resentment in Midnapur. *Nihar*, the local weekly, welcomed the government drive as it would ensure the participation of a greater number of educated people in public life.[132] Moreover, a favourable opinion appeared to have been created because of the government propaganda that the Board would eliminate scarcity of water and would also look after the general well-being of the population.[133] The apparent support was however withdrawn once it was widely known that the Board meant a 50 per cent increase in chowkidar tax. By exposing the logical flaws of new taxation in a permanently settled area, B. N. Sasmol, the leader of anti-Union Board agitation, argued,

> One thing absolutely clear now is that new taxation is being imposed under this Act upon our permanently settled lands which must for ever remain immune from fresh taxation of any kind according to the provision of Regulation 1 of 1793. It does not matter by what means they are taking the money from us now, for their demand is based upon the income from permanently settled lands. And therefore they are not only directly taxing our agricultural income, but also indirectly putting a fresh tax upon our lands permanently settled, *in direct violation of the existing provisions of law on the subject* (emphasis added).[134]

Such a meticulous interpretation of BVSG was persuasive enough to articulate the opposition to the state. While explaining the nature of the agitation, A. W. Cook, the District Magistrate of Midnapur had no doubt to concede that 'the subtlety of the whole campaign lay in the fact that Sasmol as a lawyer was interpreting the sections of the act' to the people who were 'convinced that Sasmol was right.' So, 'the principal cause of the discontent was undoubtedly the unscrupulous propaganda carried on by Mr. Sasmol'.[135] Confirming that 'it is abundantly clear that it is impossible to work the Act [in Midnapur]',[136] Cook also underlined the extent to which the administration was defending a weak case in the face of an organized effort of the Congress.

Sasmol's argument drawing out the implications of Act aimed at protecting the landed interests, i.e. the propertied classes which would suffer in view of the proposed taxation. Although it meant eventually the increase of rent and would thus affect the cultivators as a whole, he carefully phrased his speeches in such a way as not to provoke a movement to challenge the vested interests. In his perception, 'people' remain a unified category despite obvious horizontal and vertical differentiation among themselves. Here probably lies, as we will see, an explanation as to why Sasmol was almost indifferent to the Jangal Mahal Santhal Movement as it caused a chasm in the multi-class Congress organization for its insistence on attacking the landed interests.

Apart from the fear of taxation what organized the villagers was the apprehension that through the Union Boards, foreign bureaucracy would penetrate into the rural area and thereby erode the autonomy of village administration. In Sasmol's view, 'the establishment of union boards would not only destroy the villagers' traditional right to settle their internal affairs at the level of the village and on their own initiative', but would also 'intrude into the privacy of their family life'.[137] Through the village chowkidars and *dafadars*, the government would collect information about all the activities in the villages, including the private life of the inhabitants; and thus the village would lose their independent space which they nurtured so carefully to assert their identity vis-a-vis others.

His assertion that the introduction of the Boards would undermine the traditional village life appeared more convincing in his opposition to the construction of privies as part of the proposed sanitation scheme. To him, the plan to build privies in the villages seemed most ridiculous because 'it is not sanitation which is responsible for high death rates, but it is starvation, pure and simple . . . that causes massive deaths in the villages'.[138] Moreover, in such an attempt, Sasmol also found 'an evil design to modernise our village social life which is already in a process of disintegration' and thus 'it is a question of principle [with him] to have anything to do with the Bengal Village Self Government Act'.[139]

The selection of issues shows the leadership's strategic sense. Tax increases would certainly hurt the majority given the bad crop during 1920-1[140] and intrusion into the village administration would also erode the power of the upper strata over the internal affairs of the villages. On these two issues, Sasmol easily built a broad political platform encompassing people from all strata.

So well-entrenched was the feeling of opposition to the Union Boards that the government appeared bewildered. The idea that Mahishyas were threatened seemed to have played a crucial role in defining a particular context in which other probably principal contradictions remained peripheral; and anti-British sentiments gained precedence.

Inspired by 'the strength and combination of the feeling against Union Boards', D. L. Dey, the Sub Divisional Officer of Ghatal in his report to the Midnapur District Magistrate, wrote,

> I am convinced that it is not all shouting, but that the people will resist, to their utmost and in any manner that they can, the establishment of the Boards. There is practically no one in the thana, . . . on whom we can depend for whole-hearted work in connection with the Union Boards. . . . As regards the people themselves I find that they are determined not to pay the union rates . . . unless and until Mr. Sasmol tells them to do so.[141]

Not only did the Union Board members refuse to work, it was also found that very few people paid the tax preferring to hand over, of their own accord, utensils, etc., to the distraining officer.[142] Even after the attachments of the household goods, the government found themselves in a dilemma as to what to do with those attached items as nobody in the villages were willing to help to transfer them. The auction of the attached goods also turned out be a mockery. The following report in the press underlines the extent to which the threat of auction did not work because of the non-cooperation of the local people.

> The goods of Krishna Bhuia were the first to be put to the auction. It was quite a lot of costly valuables but the price which was to set the bidding in motion was Rs. 10 only which however came down to Rs. 4, this again to Re. 1 only. But there was nobody to bid for the things. So the auction had to be postponed.[143]

Such a solidarity among the villagers caused an anxiety to the local administration which tried various methods, including the threat of arrest, to assert its authority. In his tour to the affected areas, S. N. Ray, the Midnapur Joint Magistrate realized the far-reaching impact of the 'poisonous agitation', led by 'the Fact Sasmol' on the villages because 'there is a stubbornness which is unusual and which springs from the belief, however it might have been inspired, that these boards mean extra taxation which they are not prepared to pay'.[144]

Although the anti-Union Board campaign was a direct challenge to the governmental authority, it remained a passive movement. Once the villagers resolved not to pay the tax, there was very little to do except to await the government moves to attach their belongings. The leadership sustained the tempo by holding public meetings in which the principal issues were reiterated. Moreover, by regularly holding 'meetings in private houses', Sasmol and his lieutenants provided an impetus to the movement in two ways: (*a*) since meetings were held in private, women took part in large numbers–which, by itself, was significant in expanding the constituency of the nationalist politics and (*b*) the role of women was also decisive because it was they who contributed significantly to the popularization of the Congress cause by underlining 'the demonic nature' of the government in their private conversations–that gained an easy acceptance probably in view of the decision to increase union rates despite the bad crop during 1920-1.[145]

Social boycott was another strategy which was effective given the village solidarity. In Sasmol's speeches, the threat of social boycott figured prominently. The story of Krishnananda Das, the Panskura Union Board president who was boycotted for having helped the Sub Inspector of Police to attach property, was widely publicised. *Nihar* reported the plight of Das who was identified as 'a traitor' and thus deserved punishment.[146] The reluctance of the chowkidars and *dafadars* to help the administration in removing the attached goods was attributable, to a significant extent, to the consequences of social boycott which became a reality particularly after the Das incident. Thus the helpless Sub Divisional Officer of Ghatal wrote, 'those who have been persuaded [to help] . . . have been effectively muzzled and compelled to change their views by social pressure and boycott and intimidation'.[147]

On the whole, the opposition to the Union Boards was a success as the majority of the people refused to pay tax. Besides boycott, the tehsildars faced an opposition, almost from the outset while collecting the union rates. According to a government report, chowkidars in Tamluk sub-division were willing to assist the tehsildars in attaching the property of the defaulters. They complained that 'they were threatened' but 'they refused to disclose the names of the culprits'. In some cases, tehsildars were abused 'in profane languages' and were denied 'shelter'.[148] In view of the threat of stern action against those helping the government, even the British officer of Contai, for instance, writes Hitesranjan Sanyal, 'declined to proceed to discharge his duties when he became apprehensive at the sight of a group of seemingly refractory villagers making a great noise that he perceived to be their howling at him and quickly returned to the town'.[149]

By November 1921, it was clear that there was no way of avoiding the withdrawal of the Union Boards. The government was also keen not to press for its continuity because 'to delay longer would be to throw [the people of Midnapur] in the arms of the non-cooperators altogether'.[150] Insistence on 'the implementation of the 1919 Bengal Village Self Government Act would [therefore] eventually lead to even greater trouble'.[151] Moreover several officers were also convinced that the revocation of the Union Boards 'will destroy the combination of the villagers and the non-cooperators will not be able to get the handle which they now find in Union Board'.[152] So, in order to take the wind away from their sail, they unanimously recommended the dissolution of the Union Boards.

The withdrawal of the Union Boards in December, 1921[153] was a remarkable success for the nationalists in the sense that the anti-Union Board agitation sustained and probably strengthened the multi-class Congress platform despite the articulation of conflicting interests as well. Here probably lies the importance of the local Congress leadership in effectively mobilizing the people for the nationalist cause. The explanation however remains incomplete if we define the success of the anti-Union Board campaign merely as a product of a mobilization from the top, Instead, it is at these moments that 'peasant consciousness perceives in organized political authority–the formal machinery of the state and its representatives–an external threat to the peasant community and there occurs *this apparently spontaneous collective resistance to authority* (emphasis added).[154]

The campaign against the Union Board expanded the constituency of nationalist politics by incorporating the hitherto marginal social groups. Although the Congress was able to reach out beyond the narrow-confines of bhadraloks it had nonetheless articulated a limited view by championing essentially the landed interests–which kept the movement within conservative, *albeit* relatively militant, parameters. That the agitation aimed at protecting the peasant proprietors was evident in the demand for the withdrawal of union rates which meant a tax increase for them. So the movement was directed against the government which was held responsible for a severe dislocation in rural society. In other words, through its conscious efforts, the leadership succeeded in directing mass energies against the state without necessarily articulating other obvious contradictions in rural society emanating from the vertical and horizontal differentiation among the people. Yet, the campaign against the Union Board enabled the Sasmol-led Congress to carve out a new constituency for itself among that section of the rural population who had been allowed by the 1919 Government of India Act to vote on the basis of property. In this sense, it is plausible to argue that the Non-Cooperation Movement widened the social basis of the nationalist politics in Midnapur.

The anti-Union Board Movement is, as the above discussion shows, certainly a break with the past in the sense that it brought new actors on the political scene; it is also unique because it provoked different kinds of agitation drawing on the popular resentment against the vested interests, particularly the zamindars. The reluctance of the local Congress under Sasmol's stewardship to lead the Santhal agitation against the landlords shows, *inter alia*, the extent to which the Congress was constrained by its well-defined ideological priority. Since an attack on zamindari property had devastating consequences, especially in the context of a carefully nurtured multi-class political movement, neither the Congress nor Sasmol himself allowed agitation which had the potential of disrupting the social equilibrium.

Swapan Dasgupta who has studied the Santhal Movement in the Jungle Mahal area of Midnapur during 1921-3, has analysed the nature of such an intervention and its participants.[155] The Jungle Mahals comprising Jhargram, Binpur, Salbani, Garbetta and Gopiballavpur were divided among the five large landowners including the Andrew Yule-managed MZC; the rest owned by the Indians of whom the Raja of Jhargram came to the limelight during the Non-Cooperation Movement for his reported involvement in the Congress activities.[156] Inhabited by the tribals predominantly Santhals,[157] the area did not receive the Congress attention even as late as 1921 though the district Congress leadership was terribly disturbed, if not scared, by the growing resentment among, particularly the Santhals. In fact, the frequent *haat* (market place) looting in 1918 caused anxiety to *Nihar* which underlined the extent to which the existing government machinery was inadequate vis-a-vis the tribals.[158] Insisting on the police protection of *haats* as the only available way, the bhadralok mouthpiece, *Nihar* exposed the ideological constraint of the Sasmol-led Congress which was ready to mobilize the adivasis so long as they were content merely with an anti-British agenda.

The situation seemed favourable for the anti-British sentiments to grow and consolidate because the European controlled MZC possessed the bulk of the land in the Jungle Mahal area. With the introduction of the railways, the forests of Midnapur acquired a new commercial value. The MZC, with the state power in its side, rushed to lease or buy large tracts of land and restriction were imposed on Santhals' use of the jungles. Accordingly they were denied access to the forests which were so crucial in their survival; not only did the forests supply the means of livelihood, they occupied a significant space in the tribal culture. So, to the adivasis, the denial of access to the jungles was not merely 'a matter of economic deprivation, but an affront on their dignity' [159] It was therefore possible for the Congress to easily organise a movement which could largely be attributed to the prevalent anti-state feeling among the tribals who immediately responded to nationalist call precisely to voice their protest. The 'MZC's European ownership and oppressive landlordism made its holdings the natural focus of agitational activity directed against the

British rule'.[160] Urging the Santhals to fight the zamindars who were responsible for severely dislocating their life, the Congress strategically connected oppression with the British landlords by declarin

> their zamindars were English and Government helped them and did not punish them if they committed any offence, but punished native for petty offences. [Since] Government were oppressive and their enemy and sucked their blood, the tribals by revolting against the state had sought natural justice.[161]

Linked with the drive for natural justice was the tribal perception of 'Diku' who was primarily held responsible for severely disrupting the tribal life. Diku was an outsider who 'personifies all the plagues–the ousting cultivator, the usurer, the policeman, the process server and the rent collector–parasites all'.[162]

Till the early 1921, the Congress appeared indifferent to the Santhal cause. Involved in the anti-Union Board agitation, the local Congress did not also pay an adequate attention to the growing resentment in the Jungle Mahal area. Although Sasmol was aware of the tribal grievances he was however not particularly interested in integrating the tribal agitation with the Congress-launched anti-Union Board Movement probably because of the apprehension that such an agitation would alienate the nationalist zamindars like that of Jhargram who was also a target of the tribal attack for being oppressive.[163] C. R. Das was however quick to respond to the Santhal agitation against the MZC by sending his emissary Satcowripati Roy to Midnapur. Aided by a local lawyer, Sailajananda Sen and his friend M.M. Roy, Satcowripati organized the Santhals on the basis of their specific economic grievances which were rooted, as he convinced them, in the British rule. So, the tribal agitation was geared to the freedom struggle which also aimed at redressing the tribal grievances in the MZC-controlled zamindari area. In other words, the success of Satcowripati Roy in mobilizing the Santhals against the white landed gentry lay in his ability to utilize 'specific economic grievances of the Santhals and harness it to the advantage of the national movement for freedom'.[164]

The C. R. Das-led Congress was always ready to support agitation in the areas where the MZC held property. Such a drive never appeared incongruent with the Congress multi-class ideology because a campaign for economic gain was perfectly in tune with the nationalist movement since the target was an European agency. Linked with this was the firm and open opposition of the Congress to those movements likely to affect the nationalist zamindars adversely. Since Swaraj was defined as freedom from the British rule, such an ideological priority seems obvious. Hence in the Jungle Mahals, the district Congress under Sasmol never encouraged agitation among the Santhal tenants against Indian zamindars precisely because of the implications of offending the patriotic landlords who had always been a significant force in the Bengal Congress.[165] *Nihar,* articulating the Congress position, condemned the tribal effort in extending the campaign beyond the MZC as 'harmful' and therefore 'undesirable' in the context of 'a struggle for freedom from the British rule'.[166] Although the withdrawal of the Congress support largely accounted for the disintegration of the tribal movement, the autonomous Santhal mobilization ushered in a new era by identifying a new constituency which gradually became formidable in the anti-British struggle.

The Civil Disobedience Movement, 1930-2

The Non-Cooperation Movement confirmed the popularity of the Congress and Gandhi's rise as its undisputed leader. By suspending the movement following the Chauri Chaura incident,[167] the Congress Working Committee at Gandhi's behest instructed 'the local Congress committees forthwith to advise the cultivators to pay the land revenue and other taxes due to the Government . . ., and also resolved 'to withdraw from every other preparatory activity of an offensive nature'.[168] Yet in seven years, the Congress changed its stance radically and demanded Purna Swaraj in the 1929 Lahore Congress; with its adoption began the preparation for another civil disobedience.[169] Gandhi's eleven-point ultimatum[170] to the Viceroy however disappointed many leading Congressmen including Nehru since it contained no demand for any change in the political structure, not even the dominion status. 'Bewildered' at Gandhi's charter of demands which ultimately boiled down to a campaign for salt preparation, Nehru thought that 'it was a sad climb down from the Purna Swaraj resolution'.[171] Irwin, the Viceroy was not perturbed at all: in a letter to the Secretary of State, Wedgewood Benn, he wrote, 'at present the prospect of a salt campaign does not keep me awake at night'.[172] Although the eleven points demand appeared an anti-climax to many Congressmen, the Congress Working Committee welcomed 'the proposal of Mahatma Gandhi' and authorized him and those working with him who believed in non-violence as an article of faith 'to start civil disobedience'. Endorsing the campaign for a mass civil disobedience, it emphatically declared,

> in the event of a mass movement taking place, all those who are rendering

voluntary cooperation to the government such as lawyers, and those who are receiving so-called benefits from it, such as students, will withdraw their cooperation or renounce benefits as the case may be, and throw themselves into the final struggle for the freedom.[173]

Gandhi's eleven points incorporated demands of almost every section of Indian society.[174] By choosing salt as the central issue, he strove to organize an anti-British campaign in which the participation of a majority of the people was ensured since salt was essential for everyday survival. The boycott of foreign cloth was also included as a strategy because of its effectiveness in the earlier Congress campaigns. Hence the Civil Disobedience Movement revolved primarily round attacks on the government salt monopoly and the boycott of foreign cloth.

The salt satyagraha affected virtually every province though in some areas, the campaign assumed massive proportions due to the physical proximity with sea. So, Bombay Presidency bore the brunt of the salt campaign. Apart from harming the British economic interests, the salt campaign contributed immensely to political mobilization by generating an atmosphere of contempt for the government which deprived people of a basic necessity of life, viz., salt. By publicizing the government retaliation against the non-violent salt campaign in the press, the Congress sustained the tempo of the movement to such an extent that the Governor-General, not perturbed at all when the movement was launched, appeared panic-stricken and admitted that Gandhi 'planned a fine strategy round the issue of salt [because] salt had value for a broad mass appeal and emotive publicity'.[175]

Similarly, the boycott of foreign cloth was an effective nationwide campaign, organized by the Congress volunteers who perfected this method since the 1905 Swadeshi Movement. Its impact was devastating on the British commercial interests and there was a sharp decline of British cloth imports, 'from £26 million in 1929 to £13.7 million in 1930, and quantity-wise, from 1248 million yards in 1929-30 to only 523 million yards in 1930-1'.[176] It is true that the Great Depression was responsible for a large-scale dislocation in international trade and commerce, yet economic swadeshi helped the Indian mill-owners significantly. Thus in his presidential address to the Bombay mill-owners Association, Homi Modi underlined the Congress contribution by admitting that 'the Swadeshi movement . . . undoubtedly helped the [Indian] industry during a period of grave difficulty [and now] the future may be regarded as full of hope'.[177] Apart from sustaining the traditional constituencies, the Civil Disobedience campaign was remarkable in having extended the Congress influence to women and children. A Home Department report shows that of the 29,054 prisoners on 15 November 1930, no less than 2,050 were below 17 while 359 were women.[178]

As a strategist, Gandhi succeeded in infusing popular misery with a political content by attributing it to the oppressive nature of the Raj. Astonished by the immense popularity of the Civil Disobedience campaign, the moderate Tejbahadur Sapru candidly admitted,

> The Congress has undoubtedly acquired a great hold on popular imaginations. On the roadside stations where until a few months ago I could hardly have suspected that people had any politics. I have seen with my eyes demonstrations and heard with my ears the usual Congress slogans. The popular feeling is one of excitement. It is fed from day to day by continuous and persistent propaganda on the part of the Congressmen–by lectures, delivered by their volunteers in running trains and similar activities . . . there is no doubt whatever in my mind that *there is the most intense distrust of the Government and its professions.* Indeed I have little doubt in my mind that racial feeling has been fanned to a very dangerous extent . . . it seems to me that the Congress is really fighting for its own supremacy in the country (emphasis added).[179]

With a gradual expansion of its organizational network, the Congress certainly became stronger (than before). For Gandhi, the violation of salt law was 'the last throw of a gambler', insisting that even 'the risk of violence was worth it'.[180] The movement appeared inevitable given the government intransigence to concede the most humane demand which was unfortunate, as Gandhi himself articulated, because 'on bended knees I asked for bread and received stones instead'. Hence he repudiated the salt law and regarded it as his 'sacred duty to break the mournful mandatory of compulsory peace that is choking the heart of the nation for want of free vent'.[181]

The Civil Disobedience campaign had galvanized the rural masses into action. Areas like Bardoli and Kheda in Gujarat, Bankura and Arambagh in Bengal, Bihpur in Bihar came to prominence in the first phase of the movement. By resorting to rural constructive work through local ashrams, Gandhians sustained the nationalist spirit which had manifested itself in the form of salt satyagraha during the Civil Disobedience campaign. Salt provided 'the initial catalyst'[182] in the struggle for Purna Swaraj. With the onset of monsoon and also the geographic constraint of its effectiveness as a strategy, the illegal manufacture of salt gradually lost its significance. Hence, the Congress volunteers adopted other techniques to continue with anti-British campaign. In Midnapur, for instance, despite enormous physical coercion and sale of property, the refusal to pay the chowkidari tax instantaneously mobilized the peasants against the state demonstrating the extent to which local grievances gave leverage in the Civil Disobedience Movement. Moreover, as the Bengal Congress was organisationally weak due, *inter alia*, to factional rivalry among its leaders,[183] the province experienced during the Civil Disobedience days a considerable diversity of forms of popular initiative at the grassroots clinging to both Gandhian and revolutionary terrorist tactics.[184]

Civil Disobedience Campaign and the Bengal Congress

Congress in Bengal on the eve of the Civil Disobedience Movement was highly faction-ridden with Subhas Chandra Bose and J.M. Sengupta setting up rival organizations to conduct it. The Bose-controlled Bengal Provincial Congress Committee set up a Civil Disobedience Committee (CDC) in March 1930[185] and Sengupta formed the Bengal Council for Civil Disobedience (BCCD) on the grounds that 'the BPCC did not give any indication that it was organising the province for the ensuing fight'.[186] There was an attempt by the BPCC 'to arrive at a compromise with a view to take a concerted action in the matter of launching Civil Disobedience in Bengal',[187] but it yielded no results and hence two rival committees coexisted until the merger of the two groups in December 1930. The government was relieved because 'the Congress cleavage between J.M. Sengupta and S. Bose meant that the course of the Civil Disobedience Movement in Bengal as a whole was not quite the same intensity as in other provinces'.[188] It acted consciously in perpetuating factional squabbles. In an order issued to the UP government, the Home Department, Government of India, specifically instructed it not to imprison Subhas Bose who was coming to UP to address a meeting of the Naujawan Bharat Sabha because 'owing to Subhas' difference with Sengupta, the Bengal government might prefer him to be out of gaol'.[189] Stanley Jackson, the Bengal Governor, was confident that the factious nature of Congress politics would certainly serve to weaken the Civil Disobedience campaign in Bengal and he too recognized the usefulness of Bose as a divisive force. Writing to Irwin on 9 January 1930, Jackson commented that 'the quarrel between Sengupta and Bose shows no sign of abatement. The result of the trial of Subhas Bose under section 124-A and 120-B will be known in the course of a day or two. I think, it would be unfortunate if he is sentenced to imprisonment.'[190]

Within Congress circles in Bengal, the mutual rivalry even during the Civil Disobedience caused pessimism. For instance, B.C. Roy, a BPCC member, in a letter to Motilal Nehru, expressed the view that 'if Subhas had been out of gaol, or if Sengupta had been working in conjunction with the BPCC, I would have been freer'.[191] A strong anti-faction attitude was evinced. In a letter to the *Amrita Bazar Patrika* editor, A. Chakravarty characterized factional fight as 'nothing but ugly dances of the so-called present day leaders in Bengal'.[192] An appeal was addressed to the contending leaders, Bose and Sengupta, 'to put a stop to these ruinous activities and direct their energy for the good of the country and save Bengal'.[193] But there was no reduction in personal rivalry at the provincial level.

Though Bengal provided the 'largest contingent of arrests [15,000] as well as the highest incidence of violence'[194] the Civil Disobedience campaign never attained its full potential. In terms of actual performance, the Bengal CCD was more successful than its counterparts because Sengupta, its President, had a long-standing alliance with the rural Gandhians of Bengal, most of whom were the core of no-changers who, having shunned legislative politics, had engaged in sustained constructive activities through national schools, khadi centres and ashrams in mufussil areas. These areas, Dhaka, Khulna, Faridpur, Dinajpur, Sylhet, Comilla and Bankura became decisive during the Civil Disobedience campaign.[195] In order to strengthen the bond, Sengupta appointed Prafulla Chandra Ghosh and Kshitish Dasgupta (two prominent Bengal Gandhians) as Secretaries of the BCCD and following his arrest in April 1930, Satish Chandra Dasgupta, who resigned from the CDC, was designated to assume Sengupta's role.[196] Participation of the Bengal Gandhians provided the rare link between the Non-Cooperation and the Civil Disobedience Movements.

Bose's CDC was predominantly urban 'with salt preparation centres in Ghatal (Midnapur) and Twenty-Four Parganas and a few other centres (managed by the local Congress Committees under the general supervision of the BPCC) in Barisal, Noakhali and Howrah'.[197] Of all the centres, Ghatal was most prominent because Congress activities there caused alarm to the district administration. In his letter to W. S. Hopkyns, Chief Secretary to the Government of Bengal, J. Peddie, District Magistrate of Midnapur, corroborated official anxiety by saying that 'I see very little hope of any measure of peace in Ghatal before there are a few more shootings'.[198] The BPCC was extremely successful in mobilizing a large number of urban youths, students and women, but its role in rural Bengal was limited by the fact that the BPCC never realized the importance of espousing the no-tax cause even when the anti-Union Board agitation was endemic in rural Bengal. The CCD, on the contrary, adopted the no-tax resolution in May 1930 long before the Congress mandate was obtained,[199] although the no-tax campaign was never pursued by the

CCD volunteers as whole-heartedly as necessary except in Mahisabathan of Twenty-Four Parganas.[200]

Had it been widespread, the Civil Disobedience campaign would have drawn in the Muslim peasantry as well. Against a conscious policy of promoting 'division within the communities by the administration'[201] the involvement of the Muslim peasantry would certainly have contributed to communal harmony. Neither the BPCC nor the CCD, except for some vague unity calls, took any positive step in this direction. Where there were attempts at the elite level to enlist Muslim support the response was propitious: Moulavi Shamsuddin Ahmed and Moulavi Ashrafuddin Ahmed Chowdhury, two MLCs, for instance, resigned from the Legislative Council and joined the Civil Disobedience campaign.[202] Tanika Sarkar has established that the participation of the educated Muslim middle class in the Civil Disobedience campaign was 'by no means negligible'.[203] Even so, because of the alienation of the vast majority of the Bengal peasantry, the Civil Disobedience campaign never became as effective as the Non-Cooperation and Khilafat Movements had been.

Civil Disobedience in Midnapur, 1930-3

In line with its well-entrenched anti-British tradition, Midnapur witnessed another Congress-led political campaign against the state following the Civil Disobedience call. The Bengal provincial Congres, plagued by factional feud, failed to provide a unified direction to the district though the Bose-controlled CDC and CCD organized salt satyagraha in the Ghatal subdivision of Midnapur. As a result, localities developed, on a large number of occasions, their own forms of resistance. Inspired by the salt campaign, the local activists in the district organized their protests in ways which violated the basic thrust of Gandhian principle, viz., non-violence–demonstrating the growing radicalization of politics at the grassroots. Unlike the Non-Cooperation Movement when Sasmol spearheaded the anti-British offensive in such a way as not to challenge the multi-class alliances, the Civil Disobedience campaign let loose an altogether different and probably threatening (from the Congress point of view) process that was manifested in the movements which had the potentials to disrupt the social order. Though it had never received an adequate attention by the Congress leadership the idea of social revolution, connected integrally with the freedom from the British rule, gained ground in the sharecroppers' agitation against *jotedars* for a better share of crops.[204]

During the Civil Disobedience era, Midnapur saw three different and yet interrelated movements drawing primarily on the local grievances.

Apart from the breaking of salt laws which linked the local Congress volunteers with their pan-Indian counterpart, campaigns against the chowkidari tax and for a better deal for the *bhagchasis* (share-croppers) became formidable too presumably because of the success of the grassroots activists in sustaining the anti-British sentiments since the Non-Cooperation days. Although Civil Disobedience Movement was more effective and complex as well because of the involvement of various sections of society with contradictory ideological implications, its root lay in the Non-Cooperation period. Justifying the preemptive arrests of the Congress volunteers in the district as the only means available to contain the outbreak of the Civil Disobedience campign, F. G. Lowman, the Inspector General of Bengal Police, wrote,

> [The district] appears to have been thoroughly impregnated with the seeds of civil disobedeince and I feel that we shall root out this evil by arresting every single volunteer that we can lay hands in.[205]

Admitting that the Congress organization 'has been extra ordinarily good', he however was stunned as to how 'the Congress organization could enlist such ignorant and uncultivated people'.[206]

Salt Satyagraha in Midnapur

F. G. Lowman's apprehension that the movement would assume devastating proportions was not unfounded and in the first phase of the Civil Disobedeince Movement (April 1930–February 1931), 1,426 persons were arrested in Midnapur in connection with the violation of the salt laws.[207] Besides being a gesture of defiance, the breaking of salt laws had an immediate appeal in the district. Before private salt production was banned in India, Contai and Tamluk in Midnapur, being coastal areas, were two major centres of salt preparation. In fact, its extinction during the colonial deindustrialization 'had left bitter traces in popular memory'.[208] It was not therefore surprising that the inauguration of the salt campaign had aroused popular sympathy so easily in the district. Moreover, since Contai and Tamlu were saline areas the provincial Congress selected them to initiate the Civil Disobedience Movement in the province. The district thus became crucial during the campaign and, as F.W. Kidd, the Superintendent of Police, reminiscensed, 'large number of young volunteers flooded into the district and began to make salt in public places'. While expressing concern as 'nearly half the district became charged with anti-government feelings', he attributed the success of the Congress to the sympathies of the villagers with the salt campaign.[209] Although the BPCC adopted the Civil

Disobedience slogan and accordingly six centres were organised at its behest in Ghatal,[210] most of the 60 illicit salt manufacturing units came into existence due exclusively to local Congress initiative.[211] Not only was the BPCC indifferent to these centres as they were organized and controlled by the Sengupta-led CCD, they were reported to have been denied the AICC funds earmarked for them.[212] Yet, the salt satyagraha attained a dramatic success in the district.

The Civil Disobedience Movement was at its low ebb at the outset and it was largely confined to the Congress volunteers. The police atrocity however changed its character. Guided by J. Peddie, the District Magistrate who always defended 'the mass scale atrocity and torture' to contain seditious attempts, the police force became brutal and unleashed what was identified in the contemporary press as 'the reign of terror'.[213] Attacking the satyagrahees and wrapping up of the youth in prison without valid charges were the government policies followed consistently to quell the anti-government onslaught. Moreover, the authority preferred to recruit Muslim officers to strengthen its attack on the Congress which was essentially a Hindu organization due primarily to Hindu preponderance in the district's population. To cash in on Hindu-Muslim animosity, the District Magistrate thus recommended the appointment of Muslims at the level of Sub Inspector of Police and above.[214] Such a policy may have pleased the administration but alienated a large number of villagers who were either loyalists or indifferent to the Congress. Thus in his report to the District Magistrate, Karunamoy Roy, additional Superintendent of Police, underlined the devastating impact of Peddie's decision on the villagers who expressed disapproval of the government policy of appointing only the Muslims since it was rooted in the perception that the 'Muslims are more loyal than the Hindus'.[215] Moreover, the alleged lenient attitude of the administration towards the Muslim criminals, released primarily to loot the Hindu houses, caused consternation among the villagers. A charge was labelled against the government for being indifferent to the Bhagwanpur *daroga*, Rehamat Bux who was reported to have organized the Muslims 'to loot the villages and terrorise the people'.[216] Besides contributing to communal tension in the district, such an event had also brought different communities together against the state which strove through a policy of divide and rule to create an artificial barrier among them.

The sustained Congress activities since the Non-Cooperation days paid-off during the salt campaign which acquired an altogether different dimension with the mass involvement following the indiscriminate use of violence by police. The 6 April incident appeared to have changed the character of salt satyagraha. In response to the Congress call, the CCD organized centres for manufacturing salt in Contai. The police arrested the leading Congressmen, Prafulla Ghosh, Pramathanath Banerjee and Prafulla Chandra Sen. What triggered off the mass discontent was the reported assault on the women volunteers conducted by the Additional Superintendent of Police. This event had immediately attracted public attention[217] and created a situation in which the villagers regardless of class were drawn to the Congress in its fight against 'a menace'.[218] In another incident, the police had to flee when 'an infuriated mob chased the local daroga and jamadar to a nearby school building'; they were later rescued by the Congress volunteers once 'the building was set on fire'.[219] To settle its score, a well-equipped police contingent arrived on the scene and let loose an indiscriminate wave of repression which though established the British control in the area, strengthened the collective resistance elsewhere.[220] For instance, in Patashpur thana, a crowd of about 200 people attacked the police force following the arrest of the Congress volunteers. Although two villages were killed in police firing, the movement did not seem to have lost momentum at all.[221]

The most remarkable incident, demonstrating on the one hand the fragility of the authority at the grassroots and the relative Congress strength on the other, happened to be the one that unfolded in Chechua hat. Following the killing of two Sub Inspectors of Police for their role in arresting the Congress volunteers, a large contingent of police with both the Additional District Magistrate and Additional Superintendent of Police went to the area to take stock of the situation. What they found was most disconcerting because the Congress had by then mobilized the villagers in case of another British attack on them. The Additional District Magistrate's blow by blow account reveals the extent to which the British authority was significantly eclipsed in the face of a well-thought out plan of action by the Congress. The Additional District Magistrate appeared alarmed because,

> The sight which greeted us was most disagreeable . . . and we found conch-shells and whistles blowing in all the surrounding villages and fields and men running towards us . . . with lathis and taking up their position in the *bundh* (bank of the river) opposite us and shouting and dancing and almost frantic and wild.
>
> . . . I asked these men to disperse within five minutes. They said that they would not disperse but wanted to visit the hat as they had heard that we had arrested some of the villagers and had kept them in the hat. [Later, they conveyed] that the villagers would only retire if we retired with our forces and if we allowed them to see if [the arrested Congress volunteers] were in the hat. I could at once see that from the outset it was only a dodge to take time so that the men could assemble in still larger numbers until complete darkness enveloped them and then to attack us from all sides.

. . . darkness enveloped us and we could hardly see the men except figures moving about in the fields and along the bundh. Whistles and conch-shells began to be blown and men were being rallied . . . there was every reason to think that they were going to rally soon for a night attack. The blowing of conch-shells and whistles could be heard from all the surrounding villages and also loud shouts . . . we decided unanimously that we must move at once to a better position till reinforcement could be received.

. . . we saw a crowd of what looked like 300 to 400 men coming to attack us from the field shouting and running toward us. We left the bundh over which we were proceeding and got into an open space and formed a barricade with our luggage, etc. At this juncture the chowkidars and daffadars who were accompanying us and carrying some of our luggages for want of conveyence threw down the luggages and fled away.[222]

Although eight villagers were killed and twenty-two injured the police lost the battle and were forced to leave Chechua hat. And the panic-stricken Additional District Magistrate admitted,

the whole area of about 10 miles around Chechua hat is absolutely out of control, and is full [of the Congress volunteers]. These volunteers are in constant touch with Calcutta and there is indication that Purna Das of Jugantor Party has been guiding them, as also the other various organizations in Calcutta.[223]

The Additional District Magistate's report has clearly brought out the importance of organization in collective resistance. Aware of the consequence of defiance, the villagers undertook activities to harm the British. Part of the reason for the Congress success in translating the anti-imperial feeling into a movement lay in the sustained activities of the local activists in building an organization for the struggle against the British. In Chechua hat, the police appeared to have been alarmed more probably because of the role of the outsiders including the revolutionary terrorists (Jugantor in particular) who were not averse to combining armed resistance with mass mobilization. It is not therefore surprising for F.G. Lowman, the Inspector General of Police, Bengal, to remark, 'the outbreaks of lawlessness . . . are very likely to recur as soon as [the armed police] are withdrawn, unless we can teach the inhabitants a severe lesson which seems, at present movement, to be an impossibility'.[224] Along with the Congress effort, Lowman's instruction to resort to violence expanded the constituency of nationalist politics almost instantaneously by incorporating these peripheral groups who were not spared by the British police during the operation against 'the lawbreakers'. Forgetting the class differences, the villagers organized themselves against a superior force which appeared to have lost its credibility in view of a near collapse of the collaborative network at the grassroots. So effective was the nationalist campaign that 'all the villages', reported the Midnapur Sadar Sub Divisional Officer, 'had been converted into . . . forts cutting up village paths, filling them with house earth, thorns and rough conch-shells . . . also barricades of huge bamboo trees and houses barricaded with thorns, removal of bamboo bridges and trenches dug in the middle of fields'.[225] Even when the police force managed to get into the villages they found that in many villages the majority of the people had 'absconded leaving their houses locked'.[226] The acting Bengal Governor thus characterized the movement in Midnapur as 'practically a rising'. According to him, the anti-police onslaught was most effective because 'the district was honey-combed with volunteers who had organised the villagers to blow conch-shells whenever a police force appeared'. On hearing conch-shells, 'two villagers from every household were to come out with whatever weapons they could get and attack the police'.[227] In fact, police themselves were held responsible for the movement to strike roots. By an indiscriminate use of violence irrespective of sex they created an atmosphere of terror which was widely publicized by the Congress to gain politically. In order to counter the Congress allegation of severe police brutality, the Bengal government appointed a non-official enquiry committee, headed by J. N. Basu, a member of the Legislative Council which even at the cost of annoying the administration came out heavily against the police by underlining,

> (t)he police generally acted with deliberate and indiscriminate violence for which there was no justification on the ground of upholding law and order or otherwise. The destruction of houses and belongings was wholly unjustiable and showed serious deterioration and degradation in the quality and standard of administration. The acts were such that instead of inspiring respect for law, they brought administration into widespread hatred and contempt.[228]

So, the punitive action by the police instead of undermining, strengthened the Congress morale and the Bengal governor thus admitted, 'I fear that it will be long before that the police regain their ascendancy in the district.'[229]

Anti-chowkidari Tax Campaign

The spirit of salt satyagraha was sustained more vigorously in the anti-chowkidari tax campaign in the district. With the onset of monsoon and return of the cultivators, the backbone of the salt satyagraha, to the fields, the movement seemed to have lost its strength considerably. So far, the Congress built up an anti-British offensive essentially on the anger and spontaneity of the individuals; now, it was necessary to involve the community as a whole to sustain the nationalist spirit. So, the issue was the chowkidari tax which was foricibly imposed in Midnapur to maintain, it was alleged, a constant vigil on its inhabitants; it was considered unjust and the appointment of chowkidar was basically an attempt of the state to intrude into the private life of the villagers. Highlighting the adverse implications of the proposed tax, *Nihar* exhorted the villagers not to pay tax and join the Congress in opposing the government for its evil design.[230] Initially the Congress leaders were hesitant because violation of tax laws would result in the state appropriation of property of those declining to pay.[231] Such a dilemma was shortlived and the movement gradually gained momentum. Part of the reason can be located in the caste solidarity of the Mahishyas who led the earlier anti-British onslaught most successfully. Sasmol's role in evolving the Mahishyas as a community, in the context of the struggle against the state's attempt to introduce Union Boards, was crucial in grasping the importance of caste-solidarity in political mobilization. So, the anti-British sentiments, so carefully nurtured by the post-Sasmol Congress leadership, yielded positive outcomes. Moreover, in the absence of a formidable radical tradition threatening the vested interests, local leadership succeeded in organizing people regardless of class, for the Congress. As seen in the context of the Non-Cooperation Movement, the Congress achievement in Midnapur lay, to a significant extent, in a symbiotic interaction between the prosperous landed gentry and the cultivators. Drawing upon the paternalistic care of the rich and the primordial loyalties of the poor, the local leaders cemented a bond which was otherwise fragile. This peculiar unity between the apparently contradictory social groups was probably at the root of an effective Congress campaign against the chowkidari tax. Moreover, as F.W. Kidd, the Superintendent of Midnapur Police, wrote in his memoirs, 'the political success of the salt campaign . . . enouraged the Congress leaders to try out other means to embarrass the government by action in the district. Hence it was decided to break up the "chowkidari" organization in the areas already affected by anti-government feeling.'[232]

The campaign was, at the outset, directed against the administrative apparatus of the tax collection, managed by the chowkidars and *dafadars*. As a first step, the Congress volunteers asked, and on occasions, forced the villagers to resign from their posts. The result was spectacular and the Congress claimed to have attained widespread success.[233] Admitting that about 1,000 chowkidars resigned,[234] the Midnapur District Magistrate sought another contingent of police to revitalize 'the rural police [which with the resignation of chowkidars and dafadars on a mass scale] was practically crippled'.[235] Despite government's effort to defuse the campaign by punitive measures the anti-chowkidari tax movement assumed alarming proportions and thus a helpless District Magistrate wrote with panic,

> . . . the whole of Tamluk and Contai subdivision plus the thanas of Mohanpur, Danton, Narayangarh and Sabang of Sadar subdivision were out of hand. There were no chaukidars (sic) no dafadars; presidents of panchayats and also the loyalists are scared. . . . In these areas, the district magistrate and additional district magistrate were insulted in the worst possible manners.[236]

While explaining the mass scale resignation, the local authority attributed it to Congress coercion which appeared plausible given the threat of assault and social boycott, the chowkidars were subjected to. The contention was not entirely unfounded and there are innumerable instances showing that not only did the Congress volunteers harass the loyal chowkidars their families were also ill-treated. These incidents culminated in a deplorable outrage in December 1930 when two chowkidars who had been threatened with various penalties on previous occasions 'were murdered by an infuriated mob for having arrested certain volunteers'.[237] Though it was condemned by the Congress categorically, such an extreme case appeared to have contributed immensely to the success of the movement. So far, those sympathetic to the Congress participated wholeheartedly; with the death of the chowkidars, the loyalists realized the adverse consequences of supporting the government which was totally inept in the face of the Congress attack. As a result, '20 per cent of the chowkidars who still remained aloof from the nationalist movement, joined the Congress and thus the movement became not only all-pervasive but most effective too'.[238] The death threat may have played a crucial role in indirectly persuading the chowkidars to appreciate the Congress call; the implications of social boycott were equally disastrous to the villagers. For instance, a loyalist President of a panchayat in Potashpur thana in Tamluk was socially boycotted for his assistance in collecting chowkidari tax: not only was he denied 'the supply of milk and water, the artist of the village declined to make the images of Durga for his puja'.[239] Such a full-proof social boycott was possible largely because of the village solidarity regardless of class which was, most effectively, directed against the state. For the villagers, the state did not seem to be a reliable ally in so far as their daily existence was concerned. And thus, they could not afford to 'risk social ostracism since they are dependent on other villagers for day to day needs'.[240]

Likewise, the movement against the payment of chowkidari tax had resulted in spontaneous outbursts challenging the state. As the proposed tax aimed at strengthening the administration at the grassroots at the cost of the villagers, the Congress easily mobilized support to oppose the government. Highlighting the adverse consequences of chowkidari tax–not only did it entail extra financial burden it was also an attempt to encroach in the private life of the villagers through chowkidars who would be loyal to the authority,[241] the local Congress undertook a campaign for its withdrawal. The response to the Congress call was very impressive. In Sabang, only 432 out of 15,536 paid their chowkidari tax; in Tamluk and Contai 80 per cent of the tax payers declined to pay their contribution 'because chowkidari tax was unjust'.[242] 'Not a single anna of tax' was realized despite severe repression, unleashed by the government.[243] The local administration was in disarray and appeared to have been completely outmanoeuvred by the Congress activists. The authority failed to attach properties to realize the taxes. In a majority of the cases, it was found that 'when the police party was sighted, the entire village was evacuated in minutes with villagers taking their cattle and valuables with them'.[244] The failure of police to preempt such an evacuation was possible due to a round-the-clock vigil by the villagers 'to spot the approaching police contingent'; by 'blowing conch-shells and whistles' the message was put across to the villages and the police attempt to seize property was generally aborted.[245] To streamline the administration, the Bengal government deputed 494 out of 1061 special police officers to combat the Congress onslaught in Midnapur.[246] With extra policemen, the government succeeded in arresting the so-called 'ring leaders'.[247] Despite the incarceration of the leading Congressmen from Tamluk and Contai, it had little impact on the movement which attained the goal as the 1931 Gandhi-Irwin truce halted temporarily the collection of chowkidari tax.

During the Civil Disobedience Movement, the Congress volunteers experimented with parallel arbitration courts which became significant in the 1942 open rebellion. There were 31 parallel courts in Midnapur: 16 were in Tamluk and the rest scattered throughout the district.[248] The jurisdiction of the courts was confined generally to the civil disputes though there are instances in which it was also stretched, on occasions, to criminal cases.[249] According to an official report, the courts were best organized in Mahisadal (Tamluk) where villages had a hierarchy of three courts–*pratham* comprising young men, *madhyam* of elder men and *uttam* of the old men.[250] The Congress had also instituted mobile courts to settle disputes in different locations.[251]

Whatever the impact on the district, these courts articulated popular protests in a novel way. By arbitrating in disputes, the Congressmen strove to create a parallel legal system which, though did not affect the British courts at all, caused alarm to the administration with the rising popularity of these courts in Tamluk and Contai.[252] Apart from the local police, the district Bar Council insisted on an immediate clamp down since the parallel courts were obviously a threat to the lawyers.[253] Moreover, that the Congress-managed courts ran successfully in Contai and Tamluk brings out the significance of caste solidarity in sustaining them. In both these areas, not only were the Mahishyas demographically preponderant they were also economically the dominant class which continued to lead the mulit-class political movements against the British. Although the parallel courts were not particularly decisive elsewhere their success in projecting an effective alternative had exposed the crisis of legitimacy of the British rule at the grassroots. To the local people, the continuity of a different structure of judiciary and its growing popularity was 'a sign of the government weakness'. 'The ordinary cultivator . . . simply squatted on his haunches and laughing sarcastically said', reported the Additional District Magistrate,

> We know how powerful the Sarkar is. Formerly even the zamindar of Narajole had to make an appointment with the District Magistrate and additional District Magistrate before he would find an opportunity to see them. Now, we find the District Magistrate and additional District Magistrate coming round to us, villagers, begging us to pay our taxes. [254]

What is evident is that the governmental authority was significantly undermined in the district despite severe repression. The local Congress, by translating the spontaneous anti-British sentiments into an organized assault, sustained the tempo of the movement long beyond what the Bengal provincial Congress anticipated. It was therefore not surprising that at the height of the Civil Disobedience when the government unleashed several brutal measures, more than 10,000 people were arrested in Midnapur.[255] So alarmed was the Government of India that its Home Secretary frankly admitted, 'I would put Midnapur as the district where the prestige of the government has fallen more than in any other.'[256]

The pre-eminence of Midnapur in the nationalist movement during the Civil Disobedience era was largely due to the ability of the local Congress leadership to take up issues popular with rich peasants.[257] Although the Civil Disobedience campaign attained the goal and the social equilibrium was not generally disrupted, its success provoked other kinds of movements threatening the multi-class platform so assiduously nurtured by the Congress leadership. As was shown earlier, the role of the *bhagchasis* was crucial in the 1921 anti-Union Board Movement; without their active participation it would have been impossible for the local Congress to popularize the nationalist cause at the grassroots. Such efforts linking different layers of society contributed to agrarian movements in which peasant issues figured prominently. For instance, a new feature in the Congress campaign, as the Bengal Chief Secretary reported, 'is the preaching of non-payment of rent [and] volunteers have also been inciting tenants not to pay irrigation dues, but cut the banks when they want water'.[258] These movements though not always properly directed, began to spread steadily from 1922 onwards, and assumed serious proportions after the first phase of Civil Disobedience campaign in 1930-1.[259]

Peasant assertiveness in Midnapur can be traced back to March 1922 when the sharecroppers in an open meeting demanded reduction of 'illegal exaction'. Again in 1928, legislators of Midnapur 'who voted with the Swarajya Party in favour of the privileges of the landlords against attempts to strengthen the rights of the tenants, were subject to strong criticism for their action as soon as they came back to their constituencies'.[260] Though the opposition to those supporting the 1928 Act did not cause panic to the local Congress, it certainly led to a serious debate.

The criticism against the Congress stance in this regard articulated a completely different point of view championing the interests of the middle class tenants against the zamindars. Underlining the adverse impact of the schism within the Congres, *Nihar*, the Congress mouthpiece, apprehended 'whether it is at all possible to have mass civil disobedience where all these mutually contradictory interests will be included'.[261]

The most glaring instance of sharecropper resistance can be found during the second phase of the Civil Disobedience Movement. The clashes between the sharecroppers and *jotedars* led to the intervention of the local Congress leaders to save the multi class political platform of Congress. The terms of the compromise included,

> (*a*) all levies except the charges for preparing the winnowing floor should be abolished with effect from 1931-2, (*b*) the bhagchasis will be required to pay towards the preparation of the winnowing floor only in the areas where this levy is sanctioned by the custom but the rates will be reduced, (*c*) hay should be shared equally between the bhagchasis and the *jotedars*, (*d*) the bhagchasis should not refuse to cultivate the land of their respective *jotedars* and (*e*) the *jotedars* should not evict the bhagchasis unless there are direct charges against them.[262]

The compromise formula, which was certainly more pro-*bhagchasis* than pro-*jotedar,* revealed the organizational gap between the provincial and local leadership. The provincial Congress, as its stand in relation to the 1928 Bengal Tenancy (Amendment) Act shows, was reluctant to protect the tenants against the landlords, while in this case the Midnapur Congress brought about a compromise which undoubtedly ensured the rights of the tenants. This particular stand seemed to be the result of the newly emerged extremist section inside the Congress. According to an official report, 'by the beginning of 1933, Congress organization in Midnapur was very much under the influence of a new radical group which openly denied its connection with the doings of Gandhi'.[263] This was the beginning of a new wave which crystallized by 1939 when an indigenous kishan group 'rose against the local Congress committees because they incorporated the landlords'. The consequence was that 'the kishan organization is slowly but surely cutting itself adrift the Congress'.[264]

Revolutionary Terrorism in Midnapur

Revolutionary terrorism had also played a crucial role in the anti-British struggle. Midnapur hit the headlines often since three District Magistrates were, in succession, murdered between 1930 and 1933. John Hubbeck, an ICS (1902-47) officer, wrote, 'Midnapur district gained an evil notoreity from the assassination of three district magistrates in quick succession'.[265] In view of the well-entrenched anti-British sentiments, accerbated by the indiscriminate police repression, these actions were generally sympathetically received there.[266] Although the local leadership condemned 'terroristic devices'[267] the acts of political assassination were believed to have supplemented other subversive activities, carried out in the name of the Congress. In the Chechua hat incident, as shown above, the role of the Calcutta-based Jugantor Party was significant in both organizing villagers and sustaining the mass zeal for a political goal. Besides, the nature of the seize also shows the extent to which the organizers were not averse to combining armed resistance with mass mobilization. In the context of movements challenging the British rule *en masse,* revolutionary terrorism as a strategy had also articulated an altogether different political process which, by linking the grassroots with the leadership, created new avenues for mobilization from the top. By according primacy to the issues of local interests, those subscribing to violence merely complemented the struggle in the localities for the redressal of local grievances. Initially, the government underestimated the effect of revolutionary terrorism on the district as it was engineered principally by the outsiders.[268] With the murder of J. Peddie, the Midnapur District Magistrate in 1931 by Bimal Dasgupta, a Midnapur Collegiate School student, the authority adopted stern administrative measures 'to clear the educational institutions of pernicious influences [since] there is ample evidence to suspect that revolutionary ideas flourish and are sedulously propagated in the educational institutions in Midnapur'.[269] Any administration which 'believes in itself and is determined to maintain its own integrity and security cannot', the Burdwan Divisional Commissioners declared, 'but accept the challenge implied in the existence of such institutions and refuse to allot for their maintenance such funds as it controls'.[270]

To purge the schools of their 'bad elements', of the four schools in Midnapur, the government of Bengal decided to shut both Hindu School and Collegiate School for a year because 'most of the boys who were associated with the murderers of the district magistrates, Mr. Peddie and Mr. Douglas, were students of this school and the whole institutions is the most dangerous spot in the town'.[271] Midnapur college was also subject to stern action and its government grant was reduced by half.[272] Only the Town School was spared because 'its political activities appear to be rather less than those of other institutions . . . and that the majority of the sons of the local government officials [study] there'.[273] It was also recommended that the district magistrate should be represented on the managing committee of each school and 'no teacher should be appointed without a scrutiny of his previous record and a prior reference to the District Magistrate'.[274] Insisting that participation in political activity should be punishable with dismissal, the Home Department also instructed 'to exclude from Government Service all students and ex-students of Hindu School at Midnapur', in the hope that the action thus taken 'will make clear to the youth themselves and to their guardians that sedition and crime are not profitable'.[275] So alarmed was the administration in view of the reported popularity of the revolutionary groups particularly in Chittagong[276] and Midnapur, a proposal was also initiated to pursue a similar policy against other institutions throughout the province. The government however apprehended that 'such a course may cause intense dissatisfaction all over the province and the blacklisted institutions will eventually turn into ready-made nationalist schools, the formation of which is the objective of the anarchists'[277] and the suggestion was accordingly shelved.

By resorting to terroristic devices revolutionaries caused alarm to the administration; in the process, they however alienated the villagers who disapproved 'the terrorist conspiracy'[278] for two reasons: first, since the Midnapur Congress was associated with the Sengupta-led CCD, they opposed the Karmi Sangha-supported BPCC which was instrumental in heckling its leader, Sasmol in its 1926 annual session. Secondly, the role of 'the outsiders', particularly the Calcutta-based terrorist groups, in fomenting terrorism in the district acted negatively in two ways; (*a*) the idea that Midnapur required outside leaders in organizing anti-British offensive was an insult since the district produced several leaders in the wake of the nationalist movement that began with the 1905 Swadeshi campaign[279] and (*b*) villagers, who suffered terribly for having declined to pay chowkidari tax, were not willing to tolerate repression simply because some outsiders had come and killed the government officers.[280] Revolutionary terrorism had thus failed to expand its constituency beyond the urban bhadralok and was thus constrained from the outset as a political strategy. Its narrow social basis and the lack of support from the local Congress largely accounted for its gradual decline in the context of a larger movement with mass participation.

Concluding Observations

The period, 1921-32, is significant in the history of India's freedom struggle at least in two major ways: first, the emergence of Gandhi as the undisputed leader of the Congress marked a radical break with the past. Almost all the pre-Gandhian Congress leaders were sceptical about Gandhi. By involving the masses in the nationalist movement, Gandhi articulated a qualitatively different ideology which translated the popular grievances into action against the alien state. A new era dawned in Indian politics and N.C. Chaudhuri thus commented,

> The victory of Gandhism which was the victory of a new kind of nationalism over all previous forms of rational nationalism, preached and practised in modern India, forced the men of all schools not only into silence but into incomprehension.[281]

Given the economic crisis following the first world war, one is inclined to attribute Gandhi's success merely to the adverse consequences of the overall deterioration of the economy. In the official report, it was thus confidently argued,

> The success which attended the Non-Cooperation and Khilafat movements . . .

is undoubtedly attributed to the Great War, for neither the agitation could have attained the dimension which it did but for the economic pressure to which the people were subjected to. This pressure aggravated and magnified local grievances and spread the spirit of unrest thus making, for a time, the work of the agitators easy.[282]

Since the masses bore the brunt of the war, the logic drawing on the adverse consequences of war appears plausible. What is however unique is Gandhi's success in infusing a political content with mass suffering by attributing it to the British rule. So, the campaign he launched did not merely aim at the redressal of economic grievances but was also an attack against the alien state which was held responsible for the general decadence of the country. Moreover, the Non-Cooperation Movement succeeded in mobilizing Hindus and Muslims together largely because of an effective merger between the Non-Cooperation and Khilafat causes. Although this was a rare occasion when both the Hindus and Muslims fought the British unitedly the Congress by recognizing the Muslims as separate from the rest strengthened, at least indirectly, a process that culminated in the articulation of the two nation theory in the 1940 Lahore resolution.

Through the salt campaign, Gandhi involved various new social groups, hitherto peripheral, in the nationalist campaign. By selecting salt as the principal issue of the agitation, he proved how effective he was as a strategist in opposition to a ruthless state. In the popular perception, the state was easily identified as a target of attack since salt was the most basic item in daily existence. The salt satyagraha had different kinds of manifestation at the grassroots. Yet, the campaign unleashed a political process whereby the Congress activists at various levels were linked together for a common cause. Despite the expansion of the constituency of nationalist politics, the Civil Disobedience was constrained from the outset as the Muslims generally stayed away from the campaign. Although the Muslim League did not support the Congress there are instances showing that the Muslims appreciated the salt campaign which, if succeeded, would reduce their burden too.[283] Whatever the impact of such stray instances on Hindu-Muslim relations, the schism between the two communities institutionalized first by the 1916 Lucknow Pact was further consolidated in the wake of the Civil Disobedience Movement which despite its success, remained, to the Muslims at least, merely a Congress campaign.

There was a second important significance of the period. No longer confined to the bhadralok, the Congress became a mass organization following the articulation of local issues in political mobilization. What happened in Midnapur between 1921 and 1932 will illustrate the point further. The Sasmol-led local Congress attained a dramatic success largely because of the adoption of those issues which affected the dominant social groups in Midnapur. Not merely tax increase, the apprehension that the 1921 introduction of Union Boards would disrupt the rural order by intruding into the village through its agents, acted favourably in mobilization against the state. Similarly, the violation of salt laws in 1930-1 triggered off an emotional outburst holding the state responsible for a general decadence in the society. Given its proximity to sea, Midnapur had an advantage over other Bengal districts. Raising an emotive issue like salt, the local Congress thus easily organized an effective anti-British campaign involving people from various layers of society. Likewise, the agitation against the chowkidari tax gained momentum precisely because of the success of the local leadership in articulating anti-British sentiments through an opposition to the state which caused devastations in rural society.

The analysis of the role of the Congress in Midnapur reveals the extent to which the leadership was constrained due primarily to its narrow social basis. Both Sasmol and his successors were willing to undertake a no-tax campaign since it affected the state directly; but they were consistently opposed to no rent campaign for its adverse impact on the multi-class platform, so useful in the anti-British movement. As shown above, the Midnapur Congress sanctioned a no rent campaign against the European-owned Midnapur Zamindari Company but expressed annoyance when an attempt was made to extend the campaign against the zamindars as a whole. So strong was the Congress hold in the district that movements with a different perspective never assumed devastating magnitudes. There were sporadic skirmishes between the *bhagchasis* and rich peasants which never became a serious threat to the carefully nurtured social equlibrium with the hegemony of the dominant section of the society. Thus in Midnapur, the contradiction with imperialism continued to remain decisive during the period between 1921 and 1932.

The success of the Midnapur Congress in rallying people around an anti-imperial ideology lay in the peculiar social composition of the district. The district's caste configuration shows the predominance of the Mahishyas who attained a distinctive status by separating from the Kaibartas in the 1921 census. Economically well-placed, the Mahishyas developed as a well-knit social group that became formidable in the context of anti-British struggle. So intimate was the bond among the

Mahishyas that not only had the Mahishya-dominated Congress struck roots in the district, its anti-British programmes were also pursued most consistently by the people at large despite the possible disastrous consequences. Thus while explaining his difficulty in containing the movement in Midnapur, the Commissioner of Burdwan division admitted that the success of the Congress lay in 'the solidarity of the opposition due to the fact that most of the inhabitants are Mahishyas'.[284] Such a unique social structure probably explains why did the Congress concentrate on the non-payment of tax rather than advocate non-payment of rent. Thus in Midnapur, issues mobilizing people against the state were never diluted and the Congress drawing upon the caste solidarity, posed a serious threat to the administration which was significantly undermined in the context of larger movements involving the masses. The trend, thus set, was to loom large in the wake of the 1942 open rebellion by restricting the Congress attack to the British rule itself and not its state structure.

NOTES

1 In his study of Midnapur zamindars, Chitta Panda has argued, 'the notion of the zamindars as permanent collaborators of the Raj is not correct . . . [i]n Midnapur [because] many of them were either the sympathisers of or participants in the national movement'. See Chitta Panda, *The Decline of Bengal Zamindars: Midnapur, 1870-1920*, unpublished D. Phil thesis, Oxford University, 1988, p. 210.

2 L. S. S. O'Malley, *District Gazetteer, Midnapur*, Bengal Secretariat Book Depot, Calcutta, 1911, p. 52.

3 L. S. S. O'Malley wrote, 'A third of the agricultural population are actual workers, and these include 602,000 rent payers and 10,000 rent receivers, while herdsmen number 14,000 and field labourers 98,000'. See L. S. S. O'Malley, *District Gazetteer, Midnapur*, p. 52.

4 Eric Stokes, *The Peasants and the Raj: Studies in Agrarian Society and Peasant Rebellion in Colonial India*, CUP, Cambridge, p. 32.

5 Rajat and Ratna Ray, 'Zamindars and *Jotedars*: A Study of Rural Politics in Bengal', *MAS*, 9, 1, 1975.

6 J. C. Jack, *The Bakarganj District Gazetteer (1900-1908)*, Government of Bengal Press, Calcutta, 1915.

7 Swapan Dasgupta, *Local Politics in Bengal, Midnapur, 1921-32*, unpublished Ph.D. dissertation, University of London, 1980, p. 48.

8 *Ibid.*

9 Report of the Provincial Banking Enquiry Commission, 1929-30, Vol. 1, p. 194. It notes that the evidence before the commission suggests that the

indebtedness of Tamluk subdivision alone was as high as Rs. 2.6 million or Rs. 4,132 per head of the population. See Vol. 3, pp. 171-3.

10 *Ibid.*, Vol. 1, p. 189; Vol. 2, pp. 135, 148-9.

11 *Ibid.*, Vol. 2, p. 129.

12 Loan generally advanced at the beginning of the cultivating session, in May and June, was paid back in December and January after the harvest. In his evidence before the Banking Commission, M. M. Ray of Contai, Secretary to the Agricultural Commission, underlined, 'the raiyats generally sell the crops in hats as necessity arises. They sell a larger portion of them in the Pous and Magh [December and January] at a very low price to pay off rents, to clear the dues which they previously borrowed during the cultivating season and to buy necessary articles such as clothing and to meet other household expenses'. As the cultivating raiyats . . . are mostly poor and indignant and are involved in debt they are unable to hold the crop for a better price'. See Banking Enquiry Commission, Vol. 2, Evidence, Part I, pp. 795 and 802.

13 Swapan Dasgupta, *Local Politics in Bengal*, p. 54.

14 Apart from social ceremonies, the causes of indebtedness also lay in involvement in litigation, high rate interest charged on cash loans and poverty of the rural masses. Thus 'little surplus is left to the Bengal agriculturist after meeting the bare necessities . . . in fact, the conditions are so uncertain that the agriculturist is often compelled to discount his future income on any terms to relieve present necessity'. *Banking Enquiry Commission,* Vol. 1, Bengal Government Press, Calcutta, 1930, p. 72.

15 *Banking Enquiry Commission, Ibid*, Vol. 1, p. 198. The rate of interest depends on the total amount of capital available in the vicinity. If there is no competition, the moneylender can charge what he likes and the borrower has no option but to accept the rate offered. Moreover, rates of interest charged by the moneylenders were always greater in the richer district of east Bengal. In Pabna, for instance, the rate of interest was as high as 300 per cent.

16 *Ibid.*, Vol. 2, p. 818.

17 Corroborating such a symbiotic interaction, Harigopal Das noted, 'in years of failure of crops due to draught or inundation or similar calamities agriculturists generally borrow paddy and sometimes money either from their landlords or *jotedars* for mere survival. They do not grudge advancing the loans even without any security thereupon'. See Banking Enquiry Commission, Vol. 2, Evidence, Part II, Calcutta, 1911, p. 819.

18 *Ibid.*, Vol. 2, p. 180.

19 Sekhar Banerjee, *Caste, Politics and the Raj: Bengal, 1872-1937*, K. P. Bagchi & Co, Calcutta, 1990. Namasudras were untouchable peasants who felt the upper caste gentry exploitation to be nearer enemy than the distant British overlord; Rajat Ray, *Social Unrest in Bengal,* OUP, 1984, pp. 77-9.

20 West Bengal State Archives, (WBSA hereafter), Calcutta, Home-Poll 71/42, District Officer's chronicles, p. 16.
21 Rajat Ray, *Social Unrest in Bengal,* pp. 241-2.
22 *Ibid.*, p. 242.
23 S. Sarkar, *Modern India,* p. 58.
24 *The Census of India*, Bengal, 1931, p. 477.
25 *Ibid.*, 1931, p. 299. The comparable figure is 51.3 per cent of Baidyas who were literate in English.
26 Rajat Ray, *Social Conflict and Political Unrest in Bengal*, p. 77.
27 *The Census of India,* 1921, Bengal, Vol. V, Part I, p. 348. 'They [Mahishyas] are in greatest strength in Midnapur where there are 856,000 of them, and in Howrah, the 24 Parganas and Hooghly'.

VARIATION OF CASTES IN BENGAL, 1901-31

Caste	*1901*	*1911*	*1921*	*1931*
Baidya	81,218	88,796	10,2931	1,10739
Brahman	1,166,919	1,253,838	1,309,539	1,447,691
Kayastha	9,84,443	1,113,684	1,297,736	1,558,475
Mahishya	1,952,794	2,137,948	2,210,684	2,381,266
Namusudra	1,848,483	1,908,728	2,006,259	2,094,957
Rajbanshi	1,898,241	1,808,790	1,727,111	1,806,390

Source: The Census of India, 1931, Vol. V, part I, Statement No. XII, p. 454.

28 *Ibid.,* p. 346.
29 *Ibid.*
30 Bangiya Sahitya Parishad, Calcutta, *The Mahishya Samaj,* (1327 Banga Shakabda), Vol. X, Nos. 5 & 6, pp. 38-41.
31 *Ibid.*, Vol. II, (1322 Banga Shakabda), pp. 49-50.
32 *Ibid.*, Vol. V, 6 (1325 Banga Shakabda), pp. 156-7.
33 *ABP,* 7 September 1921. Babu Ananga Mohan Chakrabarti was hounded out of the meeting because he remarked that Midnapur had no future so long as it remained 'a land of chasas'.
34 S. Dasgupta, *Local Politics in Bengal*, p. 66.
35 S. Sarkar, *The Swadeshi Movement in Bengal, 1905-8*, PPH, Delhi, 1978.
36 Gordon Johnson, 'The partition of Bengal', *MAS*, 7, 3, 1973, p. 571.
37 *Ibid.*, p. 577.
38 N. N. Das, *History of Midnapur,* Part II, Calcutta, 1962, p. 45.
39 *Ibid.*, pp. 50-2.
40 WBSA, Home-Poll (A), note of Risley, 11 December 1905, quoted in Amalesh Tripathy, *History of Indian National Congress,* (Bengali), Ananda, Calcutta, 1990, p. 67.

41 *Ibid.*

42 WBSA, Home-Poll (A), Report of Donald Weston, District Collector of Midnapur, 1 March 1908.

43 *Ibid.*

44 WBSA, Home-Poll (B proceedings), FR (second half) July, Bengal, 9 August 1908.

45 *ABP*, 9 March 1932.

46 Muslims at the 1901 Census numbered 1,84,958 or 7 per cent of the population while Hindus 2,467,047 or 88 per cent. See L. S. S. O'Malley, *District Gazetteer, Midnapur*, p. 55.

47 WBSA, Home-Poll (B proceedings), Government of Bengal's order, 7 November 1907.

48 Benoyjiban Ghose, *Agnijuger Astraguru Hemchandra* (Bengali), Calcutta, 1952, pp. 34-5.

49 Jadugopal Mukherjee, *Biplabi Jibaner Smriti* (Bengali), Academic Publication, Calcutta, 1982.

50 WBSA, Home-Poll (A proceedings), Donald's report, 1 March 1908.

51 For details of the secret societies, see S. Sarkar, *The Swadeshi Movement in Bengal*, pp. 376-404.

52 For details of the revolutionary terrorist activities of both the Anushilan and Jugantor groups, see Amalesh Tripathy, *The Extremist Challenge in Bengal,* Orient Longman, Bombay, 1967; Hiren Chakrabarty, *Bengal Political Unrest, 1905-20 with Special Reference to Terrorism*, unpublished D. Phil. thesis, Oxford University, 1968; David Laushy, *The Bengal Terrorist and their Conversion to Marxism: Aspects of Regional Nationalism in India, 1905-42,* Firma KLM, Calcutta, 1975; Peter Hees, *Bombs in Bengal,* OUP, Delhi, 1994; Peter Hees, 'Foreign influences on Bengali Revolutionary Terrorism, 1902-8', *MAS*, 28, 3, 1994, pp. 533-56; Gopal Halder, *Ekada* (Bengali), Calcutta, 1979.

53 *ABP,* 31 October 1907

54 S. Sarkar, *The Swadeshi Movement in Bengal,* p. 372

55 WBSA Police reports–quoted in S. Dasgupta, Ph.D. thesis, p. 70; for details on the religious basis of extremism, see Amalesh Tripathy, *The Extremist Challenge*, p. 18.

56 Narajole Raja helped raise funds to send Kanungo to Paris to learn the art of bomb making; while, Nanda allowed the revolutionary terrorists to use an isolated part of his zamindari for arms training. See Benoyjiban Ghose, *Agnijuger Ashtraguru, Hemchandra,* pp. 53, 74-5; also S. Sarkar, *The Swadeshi Movement in Bengal,* pp. 478-9.

57 A list of the privileged few zamindars who (a) had free access to the top British/Indian officers and (b) were generally invited during the visits of the dignitaries.

58 WBSA, Home-Poll 126/1912, No. 12, quoted in S. Dasgupta, *Local Politics in Bengal*, p. 71.

59 Diary of Mazhrul Haq (a police officer, posted in Midnapur, 1907-10), p. 62, quoted in S. Dasgupta, *Local Politics in Bengal*, p. 71.

60 WBSA, Home-Poll, 51 (3)/1909: F. W. Duke, the Chief Secretary, Bengal's report of 8 August 1909.

61 *The Bengalee*, 1 September 1908, attached with WBSA, Home-Poll 51/1909.

62 *ABP*, 11 December 1909.

63 Benoyjiban Ghose, *Agnijuger Ashtraguru Hemchandra*, p. 80.

64 S. Sarkar, *Modern India*, Macmillan, Delhi, 1983, p. 125. Sarkar writes, 'the social limitations of Bengal revolutionary terrorism remain obvious. In a 1918 official list of 186 killed or convicted revolutionaries, no less than 165 came from the upper castes, Brahman, Kayastha and Vaidya'.

65 WBSA, Bengal Political Proceedings, Political Department, December 1911, pp. 23-6.

66 WBSA, Home-Poll 11/1915, FR, Bengal (1st half), February 1915.

67 *Ibid.*

68 *ABP*, 7 August 1915; in its edition of 18 August 1915, *The Statesman*, Calcutta, referring to the well-entrenched 'terrorist menace' defended the partition of the district.

69 *ABP*, 17 November 1917.

70 *The Statesman*, Calcutta, 7 July 1920.

71 Bengal Political Proceedings, Political Department, March 1915, quoted in S. Dasgupta, *Local Politics in Bengal*, p. 80.

72 *Ibid.*

73 *Ibid.*

74 *ABP*, 21 May 1915. There was a widespread protest as soon as the MZC's demand was conceded. In a letter to the editor, the decision was identified as one which drew heavily on racial consideration. Attributing the rise of terrorism to the government's discrimination against Indians, the *ABP* held the administration responsible for the growth and consolidation of terrorist organizations.

75 Referring to Sasmol's defence of the partition as it would make Contai the district town, Debdas Karan, the owner of *Medini Bhandav*, a Bengali weekly, warned of the disastrous consequences of a split among the people in the context of the anti-British campaign.

76 *Medini Bhandav*, 14 July 1913; WBSA, Report on Native Newspaper (hereafter RNP), Bengal, 26 July 1913.

77 *Ibid.*

78 *Bengalee*, 21 December 1912, RNP, Bengal, 4 January 1913.

79 *Medini bhandav*, 21 July 1917, RNP, Bengal, 2 August 1917.

80 WBSA, Bengal Political Proceedings, October 1919, No. 44. Carmichael's speech in Midnapur, 17 July 1919; *The Statesman*, 18 July 1919.

81 WBSA, Bengal Political Proceedings, December 1921, Nos. 20-5.

82 Syed Nasim Ali, a non-official member of the Legislative Council, argued,

'by the people do we mean a set of gentlemen sitting one fine morning in the home of another gentleman and passing certain resolutions and publishing them in the newspapers? . . . is it not a fact that the real people were not represented in those proceedings'. See Bengal Legislative Council Proceedings, Vol. III, 1921, p. 519.

83 *Nihar* (a Bengali weekly), 1 September 1915 and 22 September 1915; RNP, 6 September 1915 and 28 September 1915 respectively. Sasmol wrote articles underlining the importance of the people in the campaign supporting the partition.

84 For details, see Hugh Owen, 'Negotiating the Lucknow Pact', *JAS*, 31.3.1972, pp. 561-87.

85 For details of the Khilafat Movement, see Gail Minault, *The Khilafat Movement, Religious Symbolism and Political Mobilization in India*, New York, 1982.

86 NAI, Home-Poll 3/1921 & KW, note by S. P. O'Donnell, Secretary to the Government of India, 14 January 1921.

87 Judith Brown elaborates the story that unfolded between 1919 and 21 over the formulation of the Non-Cooperation agenda. For details, see Judith Brown, *Gandhi's Rise to Power*, Cambridge, CUP, pp. 250-343.

88 S. Bhattacharyya, 'Cotton Mills and Spinning Wheels: Swadeshi and Indian Capitalist Classes, 1920-22', *Economic and Political Weekly*, 20 November 1977.

89 P.C. Bamford, *Histories of the Non-Cooperation and Khilafat Movements*, Government of India Press, Delhi, 1925, pp. 102-3.

90 IOR, MSS. Eur. E 264 (6), Chelmsford to Montague, 23 February 1922. The total number of national schools and colleges rose from 52,879 to 53,968.

91 *ABP*, 9 September, 1923. Referring to the dwindling number of national school and colleges, *The Statesman* ridiculed the idea of having projected 'insanity' of the Congress leadership. See, *The Statesman*, 7 July 1922.

92 What was thus underlined was merely a reiteration of the findings of the *Calcutta University (Sadler) Commission*, 1917-19. Attributing the student resentment to the prevalent system of learning, the Commission warned the government of disastrous consequences unless adequate steps were taken to adapt the university education to the contemporary needs.

93 It upset the nationalist newspaper like the *ABP* which hailed the decision of C.R. Das and Motilal Nehru who, at the height of their career, gave up the lucrative practice to devote wholeheartedly to the national cause. Since such a sacrifice failed to evoke an emotive response from among the lawyers, the *ABP* lamented, 'where are those selfless and devoted sons of India . . . [who] are ready to sacrifice in the service of the motherland'. See *ABP*, 7 April 1921. Ridiculing the *ABP*, *The Statesman* underlined the extent to which the sacrifice for the nation was subordinated

to the selfish consideration of earning money. Identifying the Non-Cooperation as a hoax, *The Statesman* strove to organize public opinion against the Non-Cooperation Movement. See *The Statesman*, 3 July 1920; 4 July 1920 and 18 April 1921.

94 Sumit Sarkar, *Modern India*, p. 206.

95 Judith Brown, *Gandhi's Rise to Power*, p. 317. Some indication of the response to Non-Cooperation Movement is the following list of convictions by province for offences arising from the Non-Cooperation campaign:

Provinces	*Number of convictions (1921-2)*
Madras	617
Bombay	1,041
Bengal	9,163
United Provinces	2,772
Punjab	1,374
Bihar and Orissa	414
Central Provinces	344
Assam	721
North West Frontier Province	68
Coorg	12
Delhi	186

Source: Judith Brown, *Gandhi's Rise to Power*, p. 318.

96 Sumit Sarkar, *Modern India*, p. 208.

97 In a recent study, Subho Basu has shown the extent to which the Non-Cooperation Movement glavanized the workers into action to challenge the industrialists and the state power. See Subho Basu, *Wokers' Politics in Bengal, 1890-1929: Mill Towns, Strikes and Nationalist Agitations*, unpublished Ph.D. dissertation, University of Cambridge, 1994, ch. VI. Basu has graphically illustrated the way the workers' struggle was degenerated into communal fights which, he argued, was rooted in the growing intensification of the communal politics in the decade.

98 WBSA, Home-Poll 18/1922: report on the jute mill situation, Government of Bengal, 9 September 1922. The number of union rose from 40 in 1920 to 75 in 1922.

99 *ABP* wrote with grief that by deliberately attributing motive to the leadership the government gained on various occasions when the Muslim workers both distanced themselves and also attack their Hindu counterparts. See *ABP*, 25 August 1924. This is however not to argue that

the British was solely responsible for a communal flare up. Basu, in fact, has referred to various instances when the Hindu organizers in the jute mill towns fomented communal troubles by exhorting the Hindus to assert themselves against the Muslims as the only available means to reestablish their past glory. See Subho Basu, *Workers' Politics in Bengal,* pp. 198-201.

100 WBSA, Home-Poll 7/1921, Burdwan District Magistrate to the Chief Secretary, Government of Bengal, 18 Septemeber 1921.

101 IOR, MSS. Eur. D, 609. 2, Zetland collections. *My Diary,* 1 June and 6 June 1921.

102 *The Modern Review,* July 1921.

103 Rajat Ray, *Social Conflict and Political Unrest in Bengal,* p. 279.

104 IOR, MSS. Eur. D. 609 (5), Zetland Collection, Ronaldshay to Montague, 15 June 1921.

105 WBSA, Home-Poll 7/1921, Burdwan District Magistrate to the Chief Secretary, Government of Bengal, 18 September 1921.

106 The C. R. Das-led Bengal Congress emphasizing the political aspect of the struggle was in favour of an organized assault on European capital in India through economic boycott of foreign clothes. Das however wanted to organize peasants and workers from the perspective of the propertied elites without allowing workers an independent space. Even 'the special interests of the workers and peasants were to be defined by bhadralok nationalists. Like his opponents in the colonial bureaucracy, Das wanted workers to be represented by their prosperous countrymen denying the workers any independent role in politics. Though Gandhi and Das differed radically on the need to mobilize the workers for the nationalist movement, in terms of their commitment towards avoiding all forms of class conflict, they were not far apart'. See Subho Basu, *Workers' Politics in Bengal,* pp. 186-7.

107 Gandhi, 'Strike', *Young India,* 16 February 1921.

108 Gandhi, 'the lesson of Assam', *Young India,* 15 June 1921. Gandhi reiterated his argument in a meeting in Calcutta on 11 September 1921 by condemning the strike fever which tended to disrupt unnecessarily the amicable relationship between the industrialists and the workers. *The Statesman,* 22 September 1921.

109 Sumit Sarkar, *Modern India,* p. 209.

110 Biswamoy Pati, *Resistance and Domination*, pp. 62-5.

111 Partha Chatterjee captures this phenomenon in his theoretical formulation of 'passive revolution' where peasants are represented in the nation and not mobilized for the nation. See Partha Chatterjee, *National Colonial Thought*, OUP, New Delhi, 1986.

112 *Leader*, 13 February 1921, quoted in S. Sarkar, *Modern India,* p. 209.

113 Das in the wake of the Non-Cooperation-Khilafat Movement skillfully

seized the opportunity to mobilize the new line of Muslim leadership. Men like Abdullahel Baqui of Dinajpur, Maniruzzaman Islamabadi of Chittagong, Akram Khan of 24 Parganas, Shamsuddin Ahmad of Kusthia and Ashrafuddin Ahmad Chowdhury of Tippera were recruited to the provincial Congress hierarchy. See Bidyut Chakrabarty, *Subhas Bose and Middle Class Radicalism*, pp. 8-9; 184.

114 *Nihar*, 22 June 1920.

115 The local newspapers like *Medini Bhandav* and *Nihar* featured Sasmol's appeal almost every week between 1913 and 1915.

116 The Calcutta newspaper *ABP* while appreciating Sasmol's dedication also included signed appeal of Sasmol to help raise money for relief. See *ABP*, 18 October 1919 and 16 January 1914.

117 *Medini Bhandav*, 10 November 1913; *Nihar*, 11 November 1913; *RNP* (B) 1 December 1913.

118 *Nihar*, 16 November 1920.

119 *Ibid.*

120 *Nihar*, 23 November 1920.

121 *Ibid.*

122 *Nihar* in its various editions contained advertisements by the candidates where a short biography emphasizing their linkages with Midnapur was often published.

123 *The Bengal District Administrative Committee Report, 1913-14* which recommended the introduction of the Union Boards. See the Report, Calcutta, 1915, p. 3. The Report recommended the institution of the boards to involve the newly-enfranchised rural population in the administration.

124 Various provisions of the Bengal Village Self Government Act, 1919 were quoted in Hitesranjan Sanyal, 'Congress in South-eastern Bengal: The anti-Union Board Movement in Medinipur, 1921' in R. Sisson and S. Wolpert (eds.), *Congress and Indian Nationalism*, University of California Press, Berkeley, 1988, pp. 359-60.

125 *The Statesman*, 8 September 1920. It hailed the decision to implement the Act which would bring positive influences of the Raj down to the villages.

126 *ABP*, 11 September 1920.

127 WBSA, Local Self Government Files, No. L 2U/5, L. S. S. O'Malley, District Magistrate, Midnapur, to the Commissioner, Burdwan division, 23 May 1921.

128 The provision of the Act, p. 29–as quoted in Hitesranjan Sanyal, 'The anti-Union Board Movement in Medinipur', p. 360.

129 *Ibid.*

130 Hitesranjan Sanyal has substantiated the point with reference to the following table showing the income and expenditure of Kanthi (Contai) Union Board No. 1:

Source	*Income*
Tax	Rs. 1,176,00
District Board Income	Rs. 100,00
TOTAL	Rs. 1,276,00
Expenditure:	
Salary of 10 Chowkidars and 1 *dafadars*	Rs. 672,00
Equipment of chowkidars and *dafadars*	Rs. 62,00
Salary of one clerk	Rs. 100,00
Commission of Tax collector @ 10 per cent	Rs. 117,00
Miscellaneous expenses	Rs. 49,50
TOTAL	Rs. 1,001,50

Note: So, a meagre Rs. 275,00 was left with the board to carry on its developmental task in 26 villages within the union–and thus less than Rs. 11 was allocated per village. See Hitesranjan Sanyal 'The Anti-Union Board Movement', p. 373.

131 *The Statesman,* 9 September 1920.
132 *Nihar*, 23 November 1920.
133 *Ibid.*
134 B. N. Sasmol, 'Beware of Union Boards', *ABP,* 23 October 1921.
135 WBSA, Local Self Government files, No. L/2U 5, A. W. Cook to the Commissioner, Burdwan, 3 November 1921.
136 *Ibid.*
137 Sasmol's speech, quoted in Hitesranjan Sanyal, Dakshin Paschim Bangalay Jatiotavadi Andolan (Bengali), *Chaturanga*, (Bengali) Kartik-Pous, 1383 (Banga Shakabda), pp. 194-5.
138 *Nihar*, 31 May 1921.
139 *Nihar,* 14 June 1921 and also B. N. Sasmol's 'Beware of Union Boards' in *ABP,* 23 October 1921.
140 Hitesranjan Sanyal, 'Congress Movements in the Villages of Eastern Midnapore, 1921-31' in Alic Thorner, et. al, *Asia Du Sud, Traditions et changements*, Paris, 1979, p. 172.
141 WBSA, Local Self Government l/ 2U 5, D. L. Dey, SDO, Ghatal to District Magistrate, Midnapur, 20 October 1921.
142 WBSA, Local Self Government, L /2U 5, A. W. Cook, District Magistrate, Midnapur, to the Commissioner, Burdwan division, 3 November 1921.
143 *ABP*, 2 October 1921.
144 WBSA, Local Self Government, Bengal, L/2U 5, Report of S. N. Ray,

Joint Magistrate, Midnapur, 1 November 1921.

145 Basanta Kumar Das, *Swadhinata Sangrame Medinipur,* (Bengali), Vol. 1, Medinipur Ithihas Samiti, Calcutta, 1982. The point made by Das, though slightly over-stretched, draws our attention to a process (leading to women participation in the freedom struggle) that loomed large in the 1942 movement.

146 *Nihar*, 27 January 1921.

147 WBSA, Local Self Government, Bengal, L/2U 5, Report of S. N. Ray, Joint Magistrate, Midnapur, 1 November 1921.

148 *Ibid.*

149 Hitesranjan Sanyal, 'Anti-Union Board Movement in Medinipur, 1921', p. 367. Sanyal writes, 'The actual incident was entirely different, the noise in fact emanating from the performance of congregational religious singing of *harisankirtan*. The villagers are known to have performed such songfests on the occasion of the visits of the government employees for tax collection or for distraint.'

150 WBSA, Local Self Government, Bengal, L/2U 5, Report of S. N. Ray, Joint Magistrate, Midnapur, 1 November 1921.

151 WBSA, Local Self Government, Bengal, L/2U 5, SDO, Ghatal to the Midnapur District Magistrate, 1 November 1921.

152 *Ibid.*, report of the Sadar Sub-Divisional Officer, to the Midnapur District Magistrate, 1 November 1921.

153 *Ibid.*, Notification no. 5025, 17 December 1921.

154 Partha Chatterjee, *Bengal, 1920-47: The Land Question*, Vol. 1, K. P. Bagchi, Calcutta, 1984, pp. 111-12.

155 Swapan Dasgupta, 'Adivasi Politics in Midnapur, 1760-1924', in Ranajit Guha (ed.), *Subaltern Studies*, Vol. IV, OUP, Delhi, 1985, pp. 101-35

156 WBSA, Home-Poll 295/1921, report by A. W. Cook, District Magistrate, Midnapur, 7 November 1921. The success of the Congress in organizing an anti-British campaign was attributed to the financial assistance rendered by zamindars.

157 The distribution of the population was as follows:

Adivasi	*Jhargram*	*Binpur*	*Salbani*	*Garbeta*	*Gopiballavpur*
Bhumij	5.25%	5.65%	6.74%	0.67%	6.13%
Kurmi	25.52%	8.94%	21.68%	2.86%	8.84%
Santhal	23.88%	31.17%	15.58%	16.92%	21.32%
Others*	45.35%	54.24%	56.00%	79.55%	63.71%

*Predominant in 'others' were Bagdi, Brahman, Sadgope, Tanti and Teli.

Source: Swapan Dasgupta, 'Adivasi Politics in Midnapur,' p. 103.

158 *Nihar*, 22 January 1918.

159 Swapan Dasgupta 'Adivasi Politics in Midnapur', p. 117.

160 *Ibid.*, p. 125

161 WBSA, Home-Poll 181/1923: the case of European versus Sailajananda Sen and M.M. Roy.

162 R. Carstairs, *Human Nature in Rural India,* London, 1915, p. 325, quoted in Swapan Dasgupta, 'Adivasi Politics in Midnapur', p. 119.

163 Sasmol was willing to concede the tribal demands so long as they were confined to the MZC areas. Underlining the importance of the multi-class platform in the anti-British struggle, he thus urged the Santhals not to attack the nationalist zamindars who were as oppressed by the British as the tribals themselves. *Nihar*, 18 July 1923.

164 Amalesh Tripathy, *Swadhinata Sangrame Jatiya Congress* (Bengali), Anand, Calcutta, 1397, p. 109.

165 Partha Chatterjee has shown how the support of the Bengal Congress to the 1928 Bengal Tenancy (Amendment) Act which ensured the pre-emptive right of the landlords in case of land transfers, caused a fissure in the Congress. See Partha Chatterjee, *Bengal , 1920-47: The Land Question*, pp. 88-95.

166 *Nihar,* 25 September 1923.

167 On 5 February, 1922 at Chauri Chaura in the Gorakhpur district of UP, a mob of about 2000 villagers led by the Congress volunteers attacked a police station killing and burning the entire police staff consisting of two Sub Inspectors of Police, eighteen constables and one chawkidar.

168 The Working Committee resolution, adopted at the Bardoli meeting, held on 11 and 12 February 1922, quoted in P. C. bamford, *Histories of Non-Cooperation and Khilafat Movements*, Government of India Press, Delhi 1925, p. 70.

169 Civil disobedience was the only means of challenging both British rule which appeared to Gandhi 'a perfect personification of violence' and the growing hatred towards the agents of this rule which took the form of casual assassination. See S. Gopal, *The Viceroyalty of Lord Irwin, 1926-31*, Clarendon Press, Oxford, 1957, p. 55.

170 The eleven points enumerated by Gandhi are: (1) total prohibition; (2) reduction of the rupee ratio to 1s 4d; (3) reduction of land revenue by at least 50 per cent and making it subject of legislative control; (4) abolition of the salt tax; (5) reduction of the military expenditure by at least 50 per cent; (6) reduction of the salaries of the highest grade service to one half or less so as to suit the reduced revenue; (7) imposition of protective tariff on foreign cloth; (8) passage of the Coastal Tariff Reservation Bill; (9) discharge of all political prisoners save those condemned for murder, withdrawal of all political prosecutions and abrogation of Section 124-A, Regulation III of 1818 and the like and permission of all Indian exiles to return; (10) abolition of the CID or its popular control; and (11) issue of

licences to use firearms for self-defence, subject to popular control. N. Mitra (ed.), *The Annual Registrar,* 1930, Vol. I, p. 24.

171 Jawaharlal Nehru, *An Autobiography*, p. 210.

172 IOR, Halifax Papers, Mss. Eur. C 152 (6), Irwin to Wedgewood Benn, 20 February 1930.

173 NMML, AICC, G-86/1930, the Congress Working Committee resolution adopted at Sabarmati Ashram meeting, held between 14 and 16 February 1930.

174 To Gandhi, it was an attempt to fill out the practical meaning of independence to make it relevant to as many people as possible, from political activists to businessmen, to small peasants. Sumit Sarkar writes, Gandhi's eleven points 'combined issues of general interest (50% cuts in army expenses and civil service salaries, total prohibition, release of political prisoners, reform of the CID, and changes in the Arms Act allowing popular control of issue of firearms licenses) with three specific bourgeois demands (lowering of the rupee-sterling exchange ratio to 1s 4d, textile protection and reservation of coastal shipping for Indians) and two basically peasant themes–50% reduction in land revenue and abolition of the salt tax and government salt monopoly', Sumit Sarkar, *Modern India*, pp. 284-5.

175 IOR, Halifax Papers, MSS. Eur. C 152 (4), Irwin to Gandhi, 29 March 1930.

176 Sumit Sarkar, *Modern India*, p. 293. Apart from cloth-imports which dwindled drastically, the British commercial interests generally suffered a setback, as the following table shows:

Imports from Britain	*1929*	*1930*	*Decrease (in %)*
Cotton Twist and Yarn (million lbs.)	22	12	45
Cigarettes (thousand lbs.)	4926	3471	30
Drugs and Medicines (thousand Rs.)	8,996	7,417	30
Toilet Requisites (thousand Rs.)	2,666	2,152	19

Source: IOR, Halifax Papers, MSS. Eur. C 152 (6), Viceroy's telegrams to the Secretary of State, 24 and 25 March 1931.

177 NMML, P. T. Papers, file no. 99/1931, Homi Modi's presidential address, 18 March 1931.

178 NAI, Home-Poll 257/V and KW/1930. A note by H. Haig, the Home Member, Government of India, 23 December 1930.

179 IOR, Halifax Papers, MSS. Eur. C 152 (25), Tejbahadur Sapru to Irwin, 19 September 1930.

180 IOR, Halifax Papers, MSS. Eur. C 152 (4), Gandhi to Irwin, 12 March 1930.

181 *Ibid.*

182 Sumit Sarkar, *Modern India*, p. 294.

183 See the following section dealing with the nature of the BPCC involvement in the Civil Disobedience Movement.

184 For instance, the violent upsurge organized by the Surya Sen-led revolutionary terrorist group in Chittagong (Bengal) was not Gandhian by any stretch of imagination. Aiming at establishing the Gandhi raj, the Chittagong revolutionaries launched a direct attack on the British in 1931. See Sumit Sarkar, *Modern India,* p. 286-7, also S. Gopal, *The Viceroyalty of Lord Irwin,* pp. 68-9 . Such an instance was not an exception because other areas too experienced movements which, not strictly Gandhian, drew upon Gandhi's call for civil disobedience. Badshah Khan-led Khudai Khidmatgar, for instance, organised a massive movement in Peshawar (NWFP) in 1930, with crowds confronting armoured cars and denying intensive firing for three hours at Kisakahani Bazar. The textile workers of Sholapur (Maharastra) struck following the news of Gandhi's arrest and burnt liquor shops and attacked police outposts, law courts, the municipal buildings and the railway stations. Although Gandhi's eleven-points charter was silent about the labour issues, the workers rose to revolt in response to the Civil Disobedience campaign.

185 NMML, AICC, G-86/KW (1)/1930, Hari Kumar Chakrabarty, Secretary, BPCC to Secretary, AICC, 11 April 1930.

186 *ABP*, 22 April 1931, Kshitish Dasgupta's letter to the editor, *ABP*.

187 *Advance,* 18 March 1930.

188 WBSA, Home-Poll 345/1931, Sl. No. 18/Part II, a report of S. H. H. Mills, Deputy Commissioner of Police, Special Branch, Calcutta, 17 April 1930.

189 NAI, Home-Poll 146/1931, telegram from the Home Department, government of India, to the UP Government, 6 May 1931.

190 IOR, Halifax Papers, MSS. Eur./C 152/24, Stanley Jackson to Lord Irwin, Governor-General, India, 9 January 1930.

191 NMML, AICC P 6-P 12/1927-31, B. C. Roy to Motilal Nehru, 11 April 1930.

192 *ABP*, 7 June 1931, A. Chakravarty's letter to the editor, *ABP*.

193 *ABP,* 31 May 1931, an open letter to Sengupta and Bose.

194 NMML, AICC G1/1931, Jawaharlal Nehru's report on the progress of Civil Disobedience Movement in the provinces.

195 NMML, AICC G 86/1930, Birendranath Guha, Secretary , BCCD to the AICC Secretary, 6 November 1930.

196 *Ibid.*, 'A Brief Account of the Civil Disobedience Movement in Bengal', report from Comilla (salt campaign), part 1, 1930.

197 NMML, AICC G 86/ KW II/1930 Hari Chakravarty, Secretary, BPCC to the AICC Secretary, 11 April 1930.

198 NAI, Home-Poll 248/1930, J. Peddie, District Magistrate, Midnapur to W. S. Hopkyns, Chief Secretary, Government of Bengal, 12 June 1930.

199 NMML, AICC G 86/1930, 'A Brief Account of Civil Disobedience in Bengal, 1930', Part II, p. 1. The underground Congress newspaper, *The Challenge*, contains information relating to no-tax campaign.

200 *Ibid*., *The Challenge*, 15 September 1930.

201 Tanika Sarkar has shown how the government tried to utilize the 'Pirs' to dissociate the Muslim peasantry from the Civil Disobedience campaign'. See, Tanika Sarkar, 'Communal Riots in Bengal', in M. Hasan (ed.), *Communal and Pan-Islamic Trends in Colonial India*, Manohar, Delhi, 1981, p. 289.

202 NMML, AICC G 86/KW II/1930, Hari Chakravarty to the Congress President, 11 April 1930.

203 Tanika Sarkar, 'First Phase of Civil Disobedience in Bengal, 1930-31', *Indian Historical Review*, 4, 1 (July 1977), p. 90.

204 As will be shown below, both the local and provincial leadership felt terribly threatened and consequently undertook several steps to quell the sharecroppers' agitation including an assurance to incorporate their demand in the Congress charter.

205 WBSA, Home-Poll 403/1929, Lowman to the Chief Secretary, Bengal, 30 September 1929.

206 *Ibid.*

207 Of a total of 12,256 convicted during the period, Midnapur contribution (1,426) was significant. Both the figures, taken from the *ABP*, do not however conform to the widely circulated government figures which were likely to be concocted to project the failure of the movement to strike roots. For instance, the Home Department, Government of India calculated that in Bengal there were only 5,253 convicts. See NAI, Home-Poll 14/8/1931, Home Department, Government of India to the viceroy, 11 June 1931. A comparison between the *ABP* figure, published in its edition of 14 August 1931 and the Home Department calculations, demonstrate the apparent incongruity.

208 Tanika Sarkar, *Bengal, 1928-34: The Politics of Protest*, OUP, Delhi, 1987, p. 80.

209 CSAS, F. W. Kidd, Congress-cum-terrorist activities in Midnapur, 1930-31 (TSS), kept with S. G. Taylor Papers (S. G. Taylor, a member of the Indian Police, retired as the Inspector General of Bengal Police).

210 NMML, AICC, G86 KW (1)/1930, BPCC's report, 21 July 1930. Also, IOR, L/PJ/12/13, FR (2), June 1930.

211 *Nihar,* 3 June 1930.

212 NMML, AICC G 86/1930. In his report to the AICC, G. Singha, the

Tamluk CDC dictator, expressed disappointment at the BPCC's indifference to the salt campaign at the grassroots. Deploring factionalism in the Bengal Congress during a nation-wide anti-British campaign, Singha also appealed to the provincial Congress leaders to 'unite for the sake of motherland'. See G. Singha, *Civil Disobedience in Tamluk*, no date ?

213 *ABP,* 18 June 1930.

214 NAI, Home-Poll 248/1930, J. Peddie to W. S. Hopkyns, Chief Secretary, Bengal, 7 May 1930. *Nihar* also reported that in Contai and Tamluk, out of six Sub Inspector of Police four were Muslim and they were appointed after the Civil Disobedience call. See *Nihar*, 4 June 1930.

215 WBSA, Home-Poll 434/1930, Karunamoy Roy to Peddie, 5 June 1930.

216 Prabodh Chandra Basu, *Bhagwanpurer Ittibritta* (Bengali), Calcutta, 1976, pp. 127-8.

217 *ABP,* 19 April 1930; *Liberty*, 20 April 1930.

218 *Nihar*, 6 May 1930.

219 *Ibid.*

220 NMML, AICC G 86/1930; *The Bengal CCD: A Brief Account of its Work*, p. 8.

221 IOR, L/PJ/12/13, FR, Bengal (2), June 1930.

222 WBSA, Home-Poll 430/1930, Md. Karim, Additional District Magistrate to J. Peddie, District Magistrate, 7 June 1930.

223 *Ibid.*

224 WBSA, Home-Poll 434/1930, F. G. Lowman to W. S. Hopkyns, Chief Secretary, Bengal, 12 June 1930.

225 WBSA, Home-Poll 434/1930, Sub Divisonal Officer, Sadar to District Magistrate, Midnapur, 18 August 1930.

226 WBSA, Home-Poll 434/1930, J. Peddie, District Magistrate to W. S. Hopkyns, Chief Secretary, Bengal, 9 June 1930.

227 IOR, MSS. Eur. 152/24, Halifax Papers, Governor (acting), Bengal, to the Viceroy, 25 June 1930.

228 WBSA, Home-Poll, 249/1930, *Law and Order in Midnapur, 1930: The Report of Non-Official Enquiry Committee*, Calcutta, 1930, p. 17

229 The Bengal Governor's statement was quoted in *India in 1930-31: a report prepared for presentation to Parliament,* Government of India, Calcutta, 1932, p. 535. (available in the NMML).

230 *Nihar,* 7 October 1930.

231 Interview with Sushil Dhara at Mahisadal, Midnapur on 11 December 1985.

232 CSAS, F. W. Kidd, Congress-cum-terrorist activities, 1930-1, (TSS), kept with CSAS, S. G. Taylor Papers.

233 NMML, AICC G 86/1930. According to a report, the call had an electrifying effect and in every unions, chowkidars, in large number, resigned to cripple the tax collection effort. The claim is not possibly exaggerated as the following table shows:

RESIGNATION OF CHOWKIDARS IN MIDNAPUR DURING THE CIVIL DISOBEDIENCE MOVEMENT

Thana	*Resignation**	*Total Chowkidars*
Sabang	103	175
Narayangarh	19	174
Contai	56	282
Patashpur	113	200
Danton	41	183
Khejuri	60	125
Bhagwanpur	101	213
Ramgarh	54	137

* These figures are not complete since a majority of the unions did not send their reports to the AICC.

Source: NMML, AICC, G 86/1930: Bengal Satyagraha Reports.

234 WBSA, Home-Poll J. Peddie to the Chief Secretary, Bengal, 10 January 1931.

235 The letter expressing District Magistrate's anxiety was quoted in *India in 1930-31,* p. 537.

236 WBSA, Home-Poll 249/1930, Peddie to the Chief Secretary, Bengal, 10 January 1931.

237 NMML, *India in 1930-31,* p. 537.

238 Interview with Sushil Dhara at Mahisadal on 11 December 1985, who became most prominent during the 1942 open rebellion.

239 WBSA, Home-Poll 249/1930, Sub Divisonal Officer, Tamluk to J. Peddie, 29 December 1930

240 N. N. Das, *History of Midnapur,* Part II, Calcutta, 1962, p. 164.

241 NMML, AICC G 86/1930 KW (1), A Report on the Civil Disobedience in Tamluk, 7 July 1930.

242 The statistics are quoted from *The Challenge,* 11 August 1930.

243 NMML, AICC G 86/1930, *The BCCD: A Brief Report of its Work*, Part II.

244 WBSA, Home-Poll 249/1930, Sub Divisional Officer, Contai to District Magistrate, 28 August 1930.

245 *Ibid.*

246 NMML, *India in 1930-1,* p. 536.

247 IOR, L/PJ/12/25 Bengal, FR (1) September 1931.

248 IOR, L/PJ/12/25, Bengal, FR (1) March 1931, The Government was at a loss because the establishment of arbitration courts was not an offence in itself.

249 WBSA, Home-Poll 335/1931, Commissioner, Burdwan Division to R. N. Reid, Chief Secretary, Bengal, 28 May 1931.

250 *Ibid.*

251 WBSA, Home-Poll 335/1931, District Magistrate, Midnapur to the Commissioner, Burdwan, 26 May 1931.

252 WBSA, Home-Poll 335/1931, F. W. Kidd, Superintendent of Police, Midnapur, to the District Magistrate, 11 June 1931. Kidd sought District Magistrate's permission to close these courts which, he apprehended, would challenge the British authority soon.

253 *Ibid.*

254 WBSA, Home-Poll 249/1930, Additional District Magistrate, Midnapur, to J. Peddie, District Magistrate, 18 July 1930.

255 NMML, AICC 4/1932, a statistical report of the Civil Disobedience in Midnapur, 1931-2.

256 NAI, Home-Poll 14/8/1931, Home Secretary, Government of India to Lord Irwin, Viceroy, 11 June 1931.

257 Thus John Gallagher wrote, 'the power of the rich peasants, Kaibartas transmuted into Mahishyas, could turn the Civil Disobedience into a mass movement'. See John Gallagher, 'Congress in decline, 1930-9', *MAS*, 7, 3, 1973, p. 614.

258 IOR, L/PJ/12/13, Bengal, FR (1), September 1930.

259 For details, see my 'Political Mobilization in the Localities, the 1942 Quit India Movement in Midnapur', *MAS,* 26, 4, 1992, pp. 791-814.

260 Partha Chatterjee, 'some considerations on the making of the 1928 Bengal Tenancy (Amendment) Act', occasional paper, Centre for Studies in Social Sciences, Calcutta, 1980, pp. 40-1.

261 *Nihar*, 19 November 1929.

262 Hitesranjan Sanyal, 'Congress Movements in the Villages of Eastern Midnapur', in Alice Thorner *et. al. Asia du sud, traditon et changements*, Paris, 1979, p. 177.

263 IOR, L/PJ/12/47, Bengal, FR(2), March 1933.

264 IOR, L/PJ/12/44, Bengal, FR (2), April 1939.

265 See CSAS, Hubbeck Papers, Memoirs (TSS), p. 70. Corroborating such a fear, F. O. Bell, ICS (1930-47) reminiscensed, 'the district had an unenviable reputation as three successive District Magistrates had been murdered between April 1931 and September 1933'. See IOR, MSS. Eur F. 180/8, Memoirs (TSS), pp. 77-8.

266 WBSA, Home-Poll 562/1932, District Magistrate, Midnapur, to the Commissioner, Burdwan divison, 17 May 1932.

267 *Nihar*, 7 January 1931. *Nihar* criticised the murder of J. Peddie, the Midnapur District Magistrate as 'an act of cowardice'.

268 WBSA, Home-Poll 434/1930, J. Peddie's report, 'Recent Disturbances in Midnapur', 11 June 1930.

269 WBSA, Home-Poll 562/1932, Commissioner, Burdwan division to the Chief Secretary, Bengal, 25 May 1932.

270 *Ibid.*

271 WBSA, Home-Poll 562/1932, Secretary, Political Department, Government of Bengal, to the Commissioner, Burdwan division, 17 September 1932.

272 *Ibid.*

273 *Ibid.*

274 *Ibid.*

275 WBSA, Home-Poll 562/1932, Under Secretary, Home Department, Government of Bengal to all Commissioners of divisions, 9 September 1932.

276 For details of Chittagong revolutionaries, see Tanika Sarkar, *Bengal, 1928-34,* pp. 97-101.

277 WBSA, Home-Poll, 562/1932, Secretary, Political Department, Government of Bengal, to the Commissioner, Burdwan division, 17 September 1932.

278 Interview with Gopinandan Goswami at Mahisadal on 12 December 1985.

279 *Ibid.*

280 Atulya Ghosh, 'Kastakalpita' (Bengali), *Desh*, Ananda, Calcutta, 31 December 1977, pp. 41-2

281 N. C. Chaudhuri, *The Autobiography of an Unknown Indian,* University of California Press, Berkeley and Los Angles 1968, p. 400.

282 P. C. Bamford, *Histories of Non-Cooperation and Khilafat Movements,* p. xiii.

283 IOR, L/PJ/12/13, Bengal, FR (2), August 1930. W. S. Hopkyns, the Bengal Chief Secretary, wrote that Muslims too took part in picketing the hat selling taxed salt. Abul Mansur Ahmad, a Krishak Praja Party activist, also underlined the popularity of the salt satyagraha among the Mulsim peasants in east Bengal. See his *Amar Dekha Rajnitir Panchhas Bachhar* (Bengali), Vol. 2, (revised edition), Nauraj Kitabistan, Dhaka, 1989, pp. 50-2.

284 IOR, L/PJ/12/13, Bengal, FR (2), July 1930.

CHAPTER 3

The 1942 Open Rebellion in Midnapur

THE 1942 Quit India Movement is the last great nationalist movement in colonial India. Despite the absence of the top Congress leadership, the movement assumed massive proportions to the extent of a civil rebellion. Not constrained by the lack of central leadership, the rebels had built a structure of the led and the leader which sprang-up from within the region in which the local political leadership appropriated mass grievances to organise the last anti-British offensive. However, the movement which rose to prominence affecting the remotest corner of India rapidly degenerated into the activities of a small group of Congress nationalists who sustained its spirit almost till the end of 1944. The overwhelming desire to get rid of the imperial rule at any cost seems to have propelled an unprecedented activity at the grassroots drawing probably on the possibility of the realization of the aim of the movement. Although the open rebellion failed to attain the goal, thus showing the might of the state vis-a-vis the Congress, it nonetheless projected a crucial element in human consciousness which led people to embark on a political campaign in an otherwise adverse situation.

In Midnapur, where the movement continued unabated despite ruthless oppression, it had features corresponding to a classic jacquerie. During the open rebellion, even after the incarceration of the front rank Gandhian leadership of the local Congress, the movement gained momentum demonstrating probably the extent to which the Quit India declaration created new constituencies of the nationalist politics in the face of British atrocity and torture. Initially, the Congress volunteers organized attacks on police stations, post offices and other government offices, thus conforming to the pattern elsewhere. However, with the deployment of military in the area, the movement went underground and assumed the nature of a classic jacquerie with hit and run attack on the troops; the villagers offered the rebels food and shelter as, for them, it meant a contribution to the nationalist cause. In the process, the Congress emerged as a legitimate authority in the locality. With its own institutional structure and procedures, the nationalist government, that came into being in the wake of the Quit India Movement, imposed taxes and administered justice and punishment. Significant here is not merely the institution of a parallel government, but also the success it achieved in conducting the administration according to its preferences despite various odds. What it probably signifies is the extent to which the nationalist ideology, popularized by the local Congress leadership among the masses, prevailed over other considerations.

By concentrating on the August revolution as it developed in Midnapur, the chapter strives to explain the dynamics of the movement in the localities. Along with a chronological sequence, an attempt will also be made to understand the complexity of the situation that culminated in probably the most purposeful political movement since the 1905 Swadeshi campaign. Although there were threats to the Mahishya-dominated Congress leadership, the nationalist movement never suffered possibly due to the Congress success in attributing the mass grievances principally to the alien rule. So, the contradiction with imperialism continued to remain crucial in the last stages of the nationalist intervention. In this chapter, our effort will thus be directed to capture the peculiarities of political mobilization in the district which, with its long anti-imperial tradition, effectively merged the 'organized' with 'unorganized' world of politics.

Preparation for the Open Rebellion

The 8 August Quit India[1] resolution provoked a nationwide movement; in Midnapur, the preparation for the final battle however began in April 1942 with an opposition to the government's 'denial policy'. Apprehending a Japanese attack in India through the coastal areas, the British administration had adopted a drastic denial policy which was rigidly followed in Midnapur probably because of its well-entrenched anti-British tradition. As a first step, most of the motor buses were withdrawn from the district under the government order as 'a precautionary measure'; the working-hours of the few allowed to ply were further curtailed by a restricted supply of petrol in view of the war crisis.[2] Along with the withdrawal of buses, the local authority took ample care to implement 'the boat denial scheme', adopted in April 1942 for fear of a Japanese invasion of Bengal through the coastal areas. The order issued by the Midnapur District Magistrate entailed that 'all types of boats of the entire Contai subdivision and the Nandigram and Mayana thanas must be removed within three hours to Raichak in the Ghatal subdivision'.[3] Since it was not possible to shift the boats within such a short time to a distant area like Raichak, a large number of boats were either destroyed or sunk to avoid the police atrocity.[4] The policy of boat removal was a mild one compared to its original version when it was decided to follow 'a scorched earth policy' underlining 'complete destruction of internal economy, trade and administration'.[5] Since boats were the only means of transport in the estuarial districts of Bengal, the denial of boats were considered most effective for it would severely restrict the movement of the Japanese in these areas. To execute the policy, the government took over more than 18,000 boats and subsequently abandoned or burnt them.[6] Not content with this, the local administration proceeded to confiscate bicycles. Compensation was meagre[7] and denied to a large number of people for their alleged involvement in the anti-British movement. Besides, all sorts of foodgrains, including rice and paddy, were being procured on an extensive scale and exported outside the district as a part of the denial policy at the cost of the local peple. These governmental measures may have been strategically most appropriate; they however served 'to strengthen the determination of the people to do away with the system responsible for their misery'.[8] The withdrawal of boats had, in particular, a devastating impact in the district because the water transport was the only means of communication in the area. For instance, the marketing of paddy and hay, the principal export items, was severely restricted; similarly, the fishermen were also deprived of their means of livelihood once the boats were taken away. Furthermore, with a restricted supply of essential items, like kerosene, medicine and cloth from outside, the district suffered miserably.[9] So, the denial policy, particularly the withdrawal of boats, affected the economic life of the lower delta, including Midnapur, in such an adverse way that an official felt that it had been 'throttled'.[10]

The Quit India Movement started officially with the 8 August resolution; its outbreak in Midnapur was, however, belated. Part of the reason can be located in the dwindling of membership in the district due principally to the factional fight following the emergence of Forward Bloc under Subhas Bose's stewardship. As the table which follows (p. 137) shows, there was a sharp decline of members between 1939 and 1941 that caused consternation among the district Congress leaders.[11]

Although the table (p. 137) is by no means exhaustive, it, nonetheless, highlights the extent to which the district Congress was affected seriously due to the BPCC split in the wake of the historic fight between Gandhi and Bose. In 1939, with 31,223 members, the Midnapur district Congress was reasonably strong; within two years, it suffered a 42 per cent decrease

Sub-divisions	*1939**	*1941***	*1942****
Sadar	2,496	1,132	5,814
Jhargram	2,118	1,171	2,009
Ghatal	1,019	971	3,104
Tamluk	12,819	8,443	22,819
Contai	12,771	7,103	25,117
TOTAL	31,223	18,820	58,863

Sources: * NMML, AICC P5/1939;
** *Swadhin Bharat* (weekly newspaper), Calcutta, 18 July 1941;
*** Tamralipta Itihas Committee, Congress members in Midnapur, 1942. Sushil Dhara, a participant in the Quit India Movement, confirmed that there was a massive increase in the Congress membership in 1942.

of its members though there was an increase of members in 1942.

The dramatic decline of membership between 1939 and 1941 was largely attributed to the division between Bose and the supporters of the Congress High Command within the BPCC.[12] In fact, a sizeable section within the Midnapur Congress supported Bose for his uncompromising stance vis-a-vis the British.[13] Not swayed by the militant Congress, the orthodox Gandhians, opposed to violence, withdrew from political activities in the district as it meant to them a clear violation of Gandhian principle. Similarly, the Krishak Sabha and a majority of communist activists were reluctant to support an anti-British campaign in accordance with the 'people's war strategy'.[14] Unlike the earlier Congress campaigns, the preparation for the Quit India Movement therefore received a severe jolt at the outset. The administration felt at ease and a confident District Magistrate refusing to peep up the police force wrote, 'there is little likelihood for the present at any rate of serious movement developing in the district. It is clear that there is little desire on the part of the orthodox Gandhians to organise or take part in such a movement.'[15] The Government of Bengal did not seem convinced and therefore warned of a sudden attack by the Congress because of Midnapur's well-entrenched anti-British tradition.[16] Moreover, by referring to the role of the revolutionary terrorists in nurturing the nationalist zeal in the district, D. A. Brayden, the Deputy Inspector General of the Intelligence Bureau, Bengal, felt the necessity of revitalizing the police administration in view of the forthcoming movement which would be far more militant with the spontaneous participation of the revolutionary groups. According to him, 'the reasons why [those who] hitherto opposed Gandhi and the AICC would take part in the movement are, (*a*) the attraction of the "Go Out British" slogan; (*b*) the belief this time that there will be no vetting of volunteers and limitation of their numbers or rigid control of the movement; and (*c*) the movement will provide scope for violent activities'.[17] What was apprehended in the official circle came true because not only did a large contingent of revolutionary terrorists join the movement they also undertook violent campaigns which, they believed, would receive Gandhi's approval. As Pulin Sen who gained prominence for his insistence on militant means, defended, 'whatever the people [did] on their own initiative in the absence of Gandhi and other reputed leaders of the Congress [had] to be taken as the programme of the Congress, and the Congress would stand by it'.[18] Alarmed by the growing popularity of revolutionary ideas in the district, the local authority argued for the closure of the schools because 'they lent themselves to the propagation of sedition and terrorism'.[19]

Student activists played a crucial role in popularizing the Quit India cause. In fact, with the shutting down of schools and colleges on 9 August, most of the students were reported to have devoted themselves wholeheartedly to 'the service of the motherland';[20] they went back to the villages to which they belonged to organize the villagers for the ensuing battle; their activities consisted in the preparation of a mass attack on the symbols of British authority following the incarceration of the top Congress leaders in Bombay. In various meetings addressed by the students, two issues figured prominently: (1) Midnapur with its long anti-British tradition should not lag behind other areas in the last Congress offensive against the alien rule and (2) Gandhi's 'do or die' slogan provided the people of Midnapur with an opportunity to contribute to national independence which should not be lost; in so doing, the people would also advance the nationalist cause for which 'thousands of devoted soldiers of motherland sacrificed their lives'.[21]

As the district Congress was divided the students became crucial in organizing the Quit India Movement in Midnapur. Although their efforts had the potential of initiating a dangerous campaign, the district administration was confident in suggesting that 'while the movement has caught the imagination of the students, many of whom have been actuated by a desire not to be lagging behind students in other provinces, it has made little impression on the people'.[22] Not persuaded by such a logic since Midnapur had launched successful political campaigns in the past, the Bengal government insisted on a fresh review of the political scene because 'demonstrations and meetings by students are probably a smoke screen for larger preparations'.[23]

The period between 9 and 21 August, when the Contai Congress leaders were arrested, saw an unprecedented wave of political meetings[24] in which the student activists urged the villagers to take part in the movement which was identified 'as the final battle in the liberation struggle'.[25] With the closure of schools and colleges, the number of students joining the campaign increased enormously. Inspired by the extremist Jugantor Party which had a considerable influence in Midnapur educational institutions,[26] student leaders, like Pulin Sen, Prabhat Giri, Bangabhusan Jana, Prabir Jana and Rabindranath Maiti,[27] appealed to the villagers to participate in the open rebellion as the only means available to them to put 'an end to their misery'.[28] By attributing the precarious economic condition of the people in Midnapur to the British rule, they succeeded in infusing the mass grievances with a political content. On top of the war crisis, the application of a denial policy affected the district adversely since, as shown above, the removal of boats caused severe dislocations in its economy. So important were the student activists during this period that even senior Congress workers felt marginalized.[29] With their initiative, several volunteer corps were organized in the subdivision of Contai and Tamluk;[30] they, in course of time, played decisive roles in both sustaining and expanding the Congress base in the district.[31]

The role of the students was significant in bringing the members of Forward Bloc and Congress together.[32] As its leader, Subhas Chandra Bose joined the Japanese, the Forward Bloc appeared 'unreliable' for its alleged role in paving the ground for a possible Japanese conquest. With repeated bombings by Japanese planes in Calcutta, Chittagong and Feni areas, 'the problem of Japanese invasion came to the forefront'.[33] In a crucial meeting at Contai in the middle of August, the Forward Bloc activists condemned the Japanese for 'an imperialistic design' and announced their opposition to Bose 'if he was found involved in this'.[34] Such an assurance in public acted miraculously. Sushil Dhara, an active student leader and a witness of the meeting, saw in this the beginning of a new era in Midnapur's history. In his words,

> this meeting was significant in two ways: (*a*) the district's nationalist platform became stronger than ever with the coming together of two formidable political organisations, Forward Bloc and Congress; and (*b*) such an effort at unifying various groups for independence unfolded a unique process whereby different political forces, though opposed to the Gandhi-led Congress leadership, were brought together in the district.[35]

The Contai meeting was a watershed as regards mobilization for the open rebellion. Encouraged by its success, several Congress activists undertook steps to associate the All India Krishak Sabha (AIKS) which had a considerable following in the district, with the August revolution. Since it was a struggle against an alien state for freedom, the local Congress appealed to the AIKS members to 'forget the differences to strengthen the anti-imperial platform'; it was also decided to incorporate 'the peasant demands' in the Congress pledges as 'they were complementary to a fight against exploitation of any kind'.[36] Assured by the Congress that peasantry constituted a significant force in the nationalist struggle, the AIKS convened a meeting in which a principal Congress organizer, Ajoy Mukherjee was reported to have persuaded the audience to join the movement.[37] In the meeting, it was resolved that 'the AIKS would cooperate with the Congress in its opposition against the British' which was identified as 'the principal enemy'.[38] There were AIKS members who vehemently opposed such a union as the Congress was politically conservative. Referring to the Congress opposition to the sharecroppers' struggle for a better deal in the distribution of crops, they were reluctant to accept that a united platform 'was adequate to champion the peasant cause' particularly in view of the well-entrenched Congress bias for 'the landlords'.[39] Such an argument caused a schism within the AIKS rank and file which was evident in the anti-Japanese conference, held at Contai in the third week of August;[40] a majority of them agreed to participate in the Quit India Movement since it aimed at liberating India from the British rule which was held responsible for her 'general decadence'.[41]

Whatever the ideological implications, the AIKS decision to join the Congress-led nationalist platform persuaded several CPI activists to take part in the open rebellion despite the people's war strategy.[42] Although CPI was not strong organizationally in Midnapur, its influence was formidable in a number of villages in Tamluk and Contai. As Midnapur was essentially an agricultural district, the communists worked among the peasants and thus, in most cases, complemented the AIKS effort at organizing anti-landlord offensive at the grassroots.[43] Apprehending disastrous consequences of the AIKS-CPI combine in the context of the Quit India Movement, the local authority insisted on arresting the communist activists as they 'have been deliberately inciting the peasantry to commit violent outrages and to interfere with the normal life of the countryside'.[44] As 'peasants were vulnerable' given their lack of interest in politics 'they are [likely] to be misled by the communists' to embark on activities which they would not have otherwise undertaken.[45] The CPI was reported to have organized the peasantry and workers in the anti-British struggle in those districts where it had a strong organizational network even at the cost of deviating from the well-publicized pro-war strategy.[46] John Herbert, the Bengal Governor, was thus opposed to lift the ban on CPI as 'some of the CPI activists have no intention of stopping anti-government subversive activities'.[47]

Contrary to the pro-war strategy, the role of the AIKS and CPI in supporting the Quit India Movement draws our attention to a different process operating at the grassroots. Midnapur with its long anti-British tradition captured the mass militancy articulated through the organization of a larger political mobilization following the adoption of the Quit India slogan. Neither the AIKS nor the CPI could afford to ignore the mass fervour, evinced during the period; as a result, for them, the call to rally by the Congress was defensible for it challenged the alien state which figured prominently in the mass perception than the distant fascist powers. To project unity, it was decided to hoist, wherever possible, both the Congress and communist flags together.[48] Such 'a new form of campaign' caught the District Magistrate by surprise who therefore suggested a fresh review of the government policy towards the communists in view of their 'direct involvement in the anti-government campaign'.[49] Underlying this lies a significant clue as to why the notion of peoples' war fizzled-out at the level of unorganised politics once the Quit India Movement took off. That it caused alarm to the British was well-articulated in an official note by D. A. Brayden, the Central Intelligence Officer, in which he insisted on a ban on the CPI and other communist groups, otherwise, they, he apprehended, 'would turn their anti-British campaign into a civil war'.[50]

Despite its success in expanding the constituency of nationalist politics by incorporating the peasantry, the Quit India Movement was confined primarily to the Hindus. Although as per the 1941 census, Muslims constituted 7.72 per cent of Midnapur population,[51] the Congress largely failed in popularizing the 'do or die' call among the Muslims. According to an AICC estimate, in a total of 31,223 Congress members in the district, only 154 were Muslims (a mere 0.49 per cent).[52] Interestingly, the ratio of Muslims vis-a-vis the total members in the Congress noticeably declined in 1942[53] though the total membership in the district rose by 47 per cent between 1939 and 1942.[54] In this respect, Midnapur was not different from the rest of Bengal where the Congress suffered a major setback more particularly in the Muslim-majority districts with a massive decline of Muslim members.[55] This shows, on the one hand, the consolidation of the Muslim League and probably the popularity of the two nation theory; and, on the other, it also registers the failure of the Congress to undermine the League's campaign for a separate Muslim state.[56] Instead of countering the British propaganda that the August rebellion was essentially a Hindu movement, the Congress in Midnapur fell pray to its anti-Muslim bias. In a public meeting, it was declared,

> In the present struggle for independence, our Muslim brethren in general are not participating. . . . Muslims betrayed their communal sprit and played into the hands of the British at Contai and Tamluk.[57]

With this declaration, not only were the Muslims alienated from the nationalist movement in the district, they were also identified as 'the despised other' in the struggle for independence. Since the Muslims constituted a tiny minority in the district it had virtually no serious implications. But the schism between the Hindus and Muslims was utilized by the administration to its advantage in combating the nationalists. The British government thus appointed Muslims primarily to revitalize the district administration which encouraged (sic) the Congress to grow and consolidate its hold by being 'lenient'.[58] It was not therefore surprising that N. M. Khan was allowed to continue as Midnapur District Magistrate despite opposition from within the British bureaucracy. For instance, A. Gordon, the Inspector General of Bengal Police, was unhappy with Khan for his refusal to cooperate with the military probably due to his fear of being 'marginalized' in the district administration. The army crackdown was 'delayed', as Gordon noted, because the district authority was initially reluctant to provide the army with 'a district's map'. Apart from this serious charge, the Inspector General also requested the Bengal government to transfer Khan elsewhere 'in the interest of the district' because he defended 'a bad Subdivisional Officer, Wazir Ali Shaikh, ICS [who] harassed wrong people and thus antagonising a number of responsible men who would be quite willing to support the government'. Moreover, Shaikh was alleged to have misappropriated money, earmarked for reward to 'the rural police for supplying information about absconders'. Despite the serious nature of these charges, 'Mr Khan . . . refuses to hear a word against Mr. Shaikh apparently merely on the ground that he is a fellow Muslim.'[59] Several ministers of Bengal were reported to have 'protested against Khan's policy of taking the help of Mohammedans on the ground that such a policy would tend to create communal tension and that it would not be possible to protect the Mohammedans subsequently'.[60] The Bengal government however remained unmoved and N. M. Khan continued as the District Magistrate till the end of 1944.

The district Congress thus largely failed to bring the Muslims to its fold. Yet, in three years between 1939 and 1942, its membership registered almost a two-fold increase which, *inter alia*, underlines the popularity of the Congress. Such a dramatic rise in membership also signifies the extent to which the Congress was all-pervasive in the district at least in the context of the open rebellion. With the passage of time, the campaign that began with the opposition to the denial policy became complex with the participation of various social groups. As the movement was still Mahishya-dominated, it had never deviated from the well-defined nationalist ideology in which the contradiction with imperialism reigned supreme probably because of the Congress success in articulating other major contradictions through an anti-imperial agenda.

Development of the Movement

Of the five subdivisions, Contai and Tamluk[61] became prominent during the Quit India Movement. Not only was there a good network of Congress organization in these areas which yielded results; people participated spontaneously in the 'last battle' as well. The popularity of the Congress caused alarm to the district administration which perhaps led to the official decision to encourage Muslims and other splinter groups to counter and defame the party and its volunteers. Despite serious British attempts, the movement gained momentum beyond imagination. While explaining the massive proportions the open rebellion assumed the District Officers attributed it primarily to the 'lack of good means of communication'.[62] Easy and smooth communication would have provided the administration with an adequate logistic support, but that alone would never have controlled the movement as easily as was anticipated, especially when it had percolated down to the grassroots. At the outset, the District Magistrate was confident that he would crush the rebel with the police force at his disposal; in course of time, he however, realized that the task was not so easy because 'the morale of the police is generally very low'; attributing the low morale to the fact that 'a majority of them are Hindus', Khan requested the Bengal government to send Punjabi Muslim or Sikh police to the district.[63] It is however doubtful whether one could explain the low morale of the police solely with reference to religion given the failure of the administration to 'provide protection to the police, particularly from sub-inspector downwards' who were most vulnerable to the Congress attack. It is therefore not surprising that 'a sub-inspector who was asked to go out with the troops fainted and another shed tears profusely'.[64] In his report to the Inspector General of Bengal Police, S. G. Taylor, the Deputy Inspector General of Bengal Police who was deputed to handle the Congress movement in Midnapur, thus admitted that 'we fail to give them [the district police force] encouragement and to impress upon them that drastic action is likely to save many lives and that they will have your full support in everything that they do'.[65] Although the arrival of a corps of Punjabi Muslim police revitalized the district police force, they were reported to have trampled the Hindu temples and desecrated idols indiscriminately[66] which antagonized even the loyalist Hindus of the district. With the publication of such instances in the Calcutta-based newspapers,[67] the Bengal government instructed the District Magistrate not to indulge in activities 'prejudicial to religious faith' as they were likely to provoke communal violence elsewhere which should be avoided at all costs in the context of the war crisis.[68]

The idea of fighting the final battle against the British appears to have acted miraculously in mobilizing people politically. Although the government was reluctant to admit the role of ideology in organizing a massive anti-British onslaught, the District Officer's chronicle dealing with the emergence and progress of the movement in the district referred to it marginally in a small paragraph of a document consisting of 32 pages.

> The people are very demonstrative in character and highly emotional. Nearly all the local bodies in Contai and Tamluk were under the control of the Congress people. The funds of the local bodies were freely used to strengthen the Congress organization.[69]

The movement passed through *three phases* between August 1942 and August 1944.

The first phase, lasting for about a month between 8 August and 27 September, was the preparatory stage. The Congress volunteers exhorted the villagers to get ready for the forthcoming struggle. Their programme included, *inter alia*, the distribution of leaflets and holding meetings in the village huts. As the movement was truly Gandhian the British representatives in the district seemed less perturbed and thus no specific administrative measure was devised to contain the Congress activities.[70] Taking advantage of government indifference, the Congress mobilized volunteers for the final countdown. These volunteers, mostly students, were divided between two groups: (*a*) one, known as the suicide squad, was to lead the mob in attacking the symbol of the British power and (*b*) the messenger groups were to carry the messages from one camp to another.[71] During the first phase of the movement, the Midnapur rebels established contact with the Calcutta-based Khadi group. Anandaprasad Chowdhury, a member of the central directorate of the Quit India Movement, was therefore sent to the district to guide the campaign. Not only did he arrange the BPCC funds for the Congress activities in Midnapur, his presence brought 'new life to the movement as well'.[72] Although the local Congress was being prepared for an imminent confrontation with the British, Chowdhury's arrival in the district accelerated, as it were, the pace of the campaign because 'he encouraged the Congress rebels to push further the wrecking programme of the Congress and to frustrate all government activities for counteracting the progress of the movement'.[73] Apart from his role in galvanizing the Congress volunteers into action, he was reported to have been instrumental in manufacturing crude hand bombs 'which could be used against the police party raiding a Congress camp or village in quest of Congress rebels'.[74]

The movement entered its second phase with the thana attack on 29 September 1942 and with it the movement went underground. Between 28 September and 30 October, the movement saw the most concerted and aggressive Congress action. Notwithstanding a severe cyclone on 16 October 1942 which disrupted human life completely in Tamluk and Contai subdivisions, the open rebellion continued unabated because, as the British officer admitted, 'the cyclone by itself made very little difference in the plans and attitudes of the leaders of the movement'.[75] Moreover, in a revengeful manner, the District Magistrate issued an order insisting that 'relief was a less pressing matter than restoration of law and order. . . and no outsider shall be allowed to do relief work in the district [which] is the abode of the rebels only'.[76] News of the cyclone was also not published immediately 'as the district is important militarily'. The delay of two weeks in releasing the news confirmed the charge that 'the authorities wanted to [take] revenge on the inhabitants for their support to the rebellion'.[77] Shyama Prasad Mookherjee resigned from the ministry because 'the deliberate delay in publishing the news of the havoc caused on 16th October is a criminal offence . . . most valuable time was thus lost and people suffered and died for want of coordinated and organised relief'. Holding the District Magistrate responsible for such a terrible human misery and suffering, he insisted on punishing

> the district officer [who] failed to rise equal to the occasion and his previous prejudice against the people, who were called rebels, prevented him from doing what any responsible officer was bound to do to mitigate the sufferings of the people. . . . His frame of mind was made known to us when he sent his report recommending that *in view of the political misdeeds of the people, not only should Government withhold relief, but it should not permit any non-official organization to conduct relief in the affected area for one month* (emphasis added).[78]

From 1 November 1942 to 29 September 1944 when the movement was officially dissolved,[79] was the third phase during which the Congress through the provisional national government continued anti-British campaign; its attainment may not have been decisive in the broader perspective of nationalist politics, but it was not insignificant either; the fact that the provisional government continued for almost two years is indicative of its strength vis-a-vis the British which itself can be cited as a successful mass initiative to undertake political mobilization in a completely unfavourable situation.

The three phases, as contoured above, demonstrate that the movement assumed the nature of a civil rebellion with the participation of various social groups, including the peasants. Alarmed by the fact that 'a large crowds of peasantry [who were mobilised by the Congress] are roaming all over the countryside and ready to fall on and overpower any small government agency',[80] the district authority invited army to handle the situation.[81] Accordingly, eleven platoon of troops were brought to the district.[82] In fact, here lies a distinctive feature of the Quit India Movement which was there neither in the 1919-22 Non-Cooperation Movement nor in the 1930-2 Civil Disobedience campaign. As Hitesranjan Sanyal, who studied the Congress movements in this area in great detail[83] had shown the extent to which the principles of Gandhian organization were specifically formulated to guard against the sudden outbursts of spontaneous collective violence during the Non-Cooperation and Civil Disobedience Movements: accordingly, the whole thrust of organizational effort was to channel mass mobilization into peaceful resistance to colonial authority. The Quit India Movement however provided an altogether different picture. Although in the first phase the movement was conducted in accordance with the Gandhian form of resistance, in its second phase, especially towards the end of September 1942, the August revolution took a completely different turn with the involvement of a large contingent of peasantry in Contai and Tamluk. What emerged in the process was a new group of leaders from the lower rungs of the local Congress organization who, by resorting to violent attacks on the symbols of British authority and power, questioned the validity of non-violent resistance in the context of mass repression by the alien state. Thus wrote M. M. Basu, the Additional District Magistrate, Midnapur, 'taken as a whole, the disturbance is far more widespread than would seem from the reports. It almost amounts to *an organised rebellion* in the mild sense of the term'. He also thought that 'a few platoons of troops here and there will be far short of what the situation calls for [especially when] the mob . . . is apparently not afraid of firing and seen extremely well-organised' (emphasis added).[84]

On 29 September 1942, six police station headquarters were attacked simultaneously. It was a well-planned design and the Congress volunteers destroyed the entire communication network in and around the district to prevent government forces from moving between thanas. In fact, the mass attack on police stations caught the administration unawares, as M. M. Basu, the Additional District Magistrate, himself reported,

> The attacks took place so suddenly and simultaneously that no preventive action could be taken beforehand. In many places, information about threatened attacks were received extremely late owing to the fact that communications had been seriously sabotaged and information had been sent by special messengers who had to select devious route for avoiding molestation on the way.[85]

The 29 September thana attack is a watershed in the open rebellion. So far, the movement relying on the well-defined principles of non-violent struggle, was primarily Gandhian. By mobilizing people for a direct confrontation with the government, the Congress introduced a new dimension to the nationalist politics in Midnapur which had not been seen in the past. Although six thanas were attacked simultaneously on 29 September 1942 there had been concerted Congress efforts since the beginning of August to make the rebellion a success.[86] So meticulous was the planning for a mass attack on the police stations that the district administration appeared completely marginalized, and a bewildered district magistrate thus wrote,

> these attacks seem determined and deliberate. All possible preparation appeared to have been made. Telegraph wires were cut at various places and poles bent or uprooted. The principal roads were very effectively sabotages by being cut off at various places, by trees being felled and lain across the road and by the obstacles placed on the road. *The idea apparently was to completely isolate each thana to prevent aid being moved from one thana to another* (emphasis added).[87]

To the Bengal Governor, the events in Midnapur caused 'a grave anxiety'. That the present outbreak was carefully planned, argued John Herbert, 'is shown by the synchronisation of a number of attacks in sparsely defended and less accessible areas'. He blamed the district authority for having allowed the movement to grow at the outset since 'a greater initiative and firmer handling of the initial stages of the trouble might have reduced the scope of violence'.[88]

While explaining the nature of the movement which through its success boosted the morale of the rebels, N.M. Khan, the District Magistrate himself admitted the failure of his administration to contain the upsurge at the beginning. With its tentacles scattered around, the August campaign, Khan reported, posed a serious threat to the state. Not merely confined to the Congress strongholds in the district, the rebels, through this well-entrenched organization popularized the Quit India cause in areas which had [so far] remained 'free from the nationalist influence'. He thus stationed troops surrounding Tamluk and Contai to prevent the

'*Badmashes*' (miscreants) of these two subdivisions 'from moving up and creating troubles in the neighbouring thanas of Sabang, Pingla, Debra and Panskura'.[89] According to him, the dramatic success of the Congress was attributed to (*a*) the failure of his administration to gauge the intensity of the movement before it started and (*b*) the breakdown of the loyalist network in the district showing the extent to which the British became unpopular.[90]

With its long anti-imperial tradition, manifested in both the Non-Cooperation and Civil Disobedience Movements, Midnapur was always a forerunner in the freedom struggle. It was also the case that the administration never received cooperation from the local inhabitants to the extent it had elsewhere. Hence, the task of managing affairs especially during a crisis situation was always difficult, if not impossible. In fact, even before the movement was launched, the police and government officials in Midnapur 'found it difficult to obtain supplies of food-stuff, etc., due to the refusal of the people to sell to them. Special arrangements had [therefore] to be made to send down food-stuffs for the government employees . . . from outside. [Moreover], due to the jeering and forms of harassment, subordinate police find it difficult to move about in the *elaka* [area] and to do their work'.[91] During the peak of the movement, the police failed to wrap-up the rebels as the villagers were firmly opposed to the British. On various occasions, the attempts of the police to arrest the Congress volunteers were aborted because the villagers declined to cooperate. In his utter frustration, the District Magistrate thus suggested that 'the villagers sympathetic to the rebels, should be severely punished'.[92] It is not therefore surprising that several innocent villagers, including women, were subject to police torture in thanas and elsewhere for helping the Congress nationalists.[93]

As in the case of a classic jacquerie, there emerged in Midnapur an informal network of communication between the villagers and the participants in the movement. Even with a large force at his disposal, S. G. Taylor, Deputy Inspector General of Bengal Police, expressed his helplessness because 'the area was extensive, communications not very good and *the local populace was either engaged in the revolution or too terrorised to help us*' (emphasis added).[94] As a result, the government drive to arrest the Congress volunteers was, in most cases, aborted[95] because, as the District Magistrate himself confessed, 'as soon as the [armed] forces reach the village, the rebels somehow or the other come to know of it and desert the village'.[96] In his report to J. C. Irwin, Personal Secretary to the Bengal Governor, A. Gordon, the Inspector General of Bengal Police, graphically described the plight of the British army engaged in arresting 'the ring leaders' of the movement in the context of a well-devised communication network in the district.

On one occasion, there was to be an advance on a particular area which was known to be the Congress Headquarters by four detachments from different points of the compass in the hope that they might get into the position secretly before being spotted by the Scouts whom the rebels put out and thus form a cordon around the particular area before the rebels could break out and disperse. Unfortunately, in actual fact, when the plan was put into operation, the British troops engaged made so much noise in getting a boat across the *bundh* [embankment] between the two pieces of water that Scouts became aware of the move, intimation was given and when the formation of troops closed in, nobody was found.[97]

The Congress 'espionage system' was so effective that the military only occasionally succeeded in arresting the Congress rebels. The villagers devised a unique system of communication by utilising conch-shells for 'warning the rebels of the approach of the police'. Whenever any government party moved from one place to another, 'a conch-shell would be blown by someone, and this would be taken by some others until the entire area would resound with sounds of conch-shells'.[98] Such an efficient system of conveying messages largely accounts for the failure of the British to catch 'the ring leaders' of the movement who 'roam free in the villages [and are] fed, clothed and sheltered by the villagers'.[99] In his encounter with the Congress rebels, M. M. Basu, the Additional District Magistrate, Midnapur, experienced the effectiveness of the Congress system of communication:

In late November, the police arranged to raid the village for apprehending the absconding the Congress rebels. . . . As the search party and the military were crossing a canal, conch-shells were thrice blown from the other side of the embankment. The party hurried to the camp but found none. They found rice, vegetables and other food stuff in the camp. [On another occasion], they found cooked food for nearly two hundred persons ready in an open place.[100]

The devastating cyclone and tidal wave that hit the district on the night of 16 October 1942 killing nearly 15,000 people[101] was hardly a deterrent as Khan wrote that 'the view that the political movement had died a natural death following the recent cyclone is incorrect'.[102] Hence, the local administration urged the Bengal government to deny relief to those villages which were suspected of providing 'shelter to the rebel leaders'. The District Magistrate further recommended that the relief be withheld 'from the disaffected villages until the people hand over the stolen guns and give an undertaking that they will take no further [part] in any subversive movement. This is the only way to prevent recrudescence of the trouble'.[103] Not persuaded by the recommendation,

S. G. Taylor, directing the army in the area, argued that 'any delay in giving relief will encourage the people to seek help from the Congress and give the latter ground for spurious argument that they are more powerful than the government'.[104] He thus suggested,

Every attempt will be made to exploit 'the wrath of god' theory and to impress upon the villagers that it is only the Government that can help them and nobody else. . . . if we are to make capital out of cyclone, arrangements should, if possible, be made for the resources of all private associations to be put up at the disposal of Government so that the distribution can be made under the guidance of local officers.[105]

Even as late as 27 October, eleven days after the cyclone, the administration seemed perplexed as to why 'very few persons have come forward to ask for help, though there must be thousands who are homeless and without food and good water'.[106] So, the government relief operation did not seem to have received a favourable response even in the midst of unprecedented suffering. What is however surprising is that though the government expressed grave concern, it took almost two months to devise an elaborate relief operation.[107] The Congress had set up alternative relief camps in some areas which, due to lack of adequate supply of foodstuff and other essential items, were not well-equipped to undertake massive relief operations in the cyclone-hit district. Since the public morale was high 'the cyclone and tidal wave', as it was acknowledged in the official report, 'did not make any difference to the plans of the Congress leaders'.[108] However, by the end of November 1942, in the face of severe military countdown, the movement took the shape of 'a guerrilla warfare . . . with hit and run tactics, [designed] to dissipate and impose an incessant and exasperating strain upon the forces of law and order'.[109] In the following months, trained volunteers were in the forefront of many attacks on the British and their supporters. Despite adequate preparedness, the local administration largely failed to contain the movement as, it was admitted in the official report,

Operations of the rebel indicate considerable care in planning; an effective warning system had been devised; elementary tactical principles were observed by encirclement and flanking movements clearly on pre-arranged signals; the forces of disorder were accompanied by doctors and nursing orderlies to attend to casualties; and the intelligence system is clearly efficient since the movements contemplated by the police and troops are very early known and measures taken to forestall them.[110]

Although the British troops succeeded in destroying several Congress camps most of the leaders escaped arrest. In the middle of December 1942, the Congress set up its own parallel government corresponding in every detail to the structure and procedure of the colonial state. Organized around a President *(sarvadhinayak* in the Congress parlance), council of ministers, court and war council, 'the national government'[111] or the Jatiya Sarkar continued its activities more or less successfully till it was dismantled in August 1944. Despite problems connected with its operation in camera, the administration under the parallel government appeared most effective in a number of police stations in Contai and Tamluk subdivisions where the government outposts were hardly seen.[112] The initial success of the national government was however temporarily marred by indiscriminate military operation in the villages which began by the middle of December 1942. Once the top leaders began to be arrested, it became clear that the villagers were no longer prepared to face the consequences of providing shelter to the Congress rebels. As a result, 'the acts of the rebel authority became more and more terroristic and less symbol of collective popular violence'.[113] In order to advance the nationalist cause in otherwise adverse circumstances, a participant who was in charge of executing the Jatiya Sarkar's decision reminisced that it was essential to resort to the so-called 'terroristic acts' which entailed murder, kidnapping, organised plunder, imprisonment, arson and destruction of government property and communication network.[114] Underlying the terroristic tendencies probably lay the compulsion of the movement which pursued its goal under the most unfavourable situation: on the one hand, there was ruthless military operation striving to crush the August revolution: on the other, the role of the upper strata of Midnapur as a natural ally of the imperial power weakened the fight for freedom to a large extent. So, the Quit India Movement in Midnapur was an unequal struggle which probably accounts for the specific style of functioning of the national government through a centralized authority. Whatever the interpretation of such a deviation from the path of non-violence, the August upsurge proved the extent to which an ideology is important in political mobilization; the Midnapur instance by justifying violent acts also demonstrated the possibility of the emergence of a different kind of movement within the Gandhian fold– thus indicating probably the intimate connection between the prevalent socio-economic compulsion and the struggle of the day.

Jatiya Sarkar: Its Structure and Procedure of Functioning[115]

The inauguration of the provisional government in Tamluk or the Tamralipta Jatiya Sarkar on 17 December 1942 ushered in a new era in the history of India's freedom struggle. Ideologically committed to non-violence, the Congress nationalists favoured the constitution of a parallel government as 'the only way to alleviate the sufferings of the cyclone-hit people'.[116] Jatiya Sarkar was formed as a part of 'the future federal government of independent India'.[117] Encouraged by the prospect of a Japanese invasion under Subhas Chandra Bose's stewardship, the leading Congressmen appeared confident that the Japanese attack would 'liberate Indians and thus their sufferings will end'.[118] In fact, one of the principal Congress organizers, Sushil Dhara believed that 'the forces of liberation led by Subhas Chandra Bose may choose to come by the sea route and may prefer the coastal areas of Midnapur as their landing base. If it so happens, it would be convenient for them to set foot on a free zone, independent of foreign control, wherefrom they may march on their victorious journey.'[119] That the Japanese-sponsored Subhas Bose-led Azad Hind Fauz was a real threat to the British became apparent with the fall of Singapore in April 1942;[120] and the idea gained ground in Midnapur with its regular propagation in the Azad Hind Radio which was arranged to be heard secretly in the Congress camps.[121]

Although the prospect of Bose's arrival was partly significant the deliberate indifference of the British administration to the cyclone-affected people as the district was a Congress stronghold area, also acted most favourably in the formation of the national government which was authorized to undertake relief and rehabilitation of the flood victims in a systematic fashion. Given the devastating nature of the cyclone and the limitations of the Jatiya Sarkar in terms of resources, the relief operations may not have approximated to the expectations, it nonetheless projected the Sarkar as an effective alternative in the popular consciousness. The Mahendra Relief Committee, constituted by the rebels, was all pervasive in the cyclone-hit areas primarily because of 'the spontaneous participation of the people in its relief operation'.[122] So organized was the Congress effort that even as late as 27 October, eleven days after the cyclone, 'very few people came forward to seek help'[123] from the local administration. J. S. Blair, the Bengal Chief Secretary instructed the Midnapur District Magistrate to arrange for an immediate relief to the affected people because any delay in giving relief would mean the failure of the government to help the people in distress and thus allowing the Congress to strike roots.[124] What he apprehended was probably not unfounded at least till December when the government relief was refused in several villages as 'the distressed villagers' believed that 'non-official relief would soon be given to them'.[125] The Mahendra Relief Committee gained remarkably with the arrival of the Hindu Mahasabha Relief Committee which decided to undertake relief and rehabilitation programmes in association with the Congress activists. The District Magistrate however sought to withdraw the government permission to the Hindu Mahasabha

Relief Committee because he thought that 'some of [its] workers who are ostensibly employed on relief work . . . are only secretively maintaining contact with some of the subversive workers [of the provisional government]'.[126] Apart from the political implications as the Congress rebels were reported to have functioned under the cloak of the relief operation, the District Magistrate's statement also underlined the effectiveness of the non-governmental relief operations. Despite the devastating magnitude of the typhoon, the attitude of the administration did not seem to be favourable. The Jatiya Sarkar however bore no vengeance against the government servant and thus it was proclaimed,

> Jatiya Sarkar, based on non-violence, would not put Government servant under duress, but would effectively isolate them so that they would either have to align themselves with the people or be reduced to the necessity of carrying out the foreign government writ through undiluted barbarism of which they would soon [be sick and tired]. Even their relatives and dear ones would desert them.[127]

In terms of structure and procedure of functioning, the Congress parallel government was not different from the colonial state. With a Sarvadhinayak as the head of the Tamralipta Jatiya Sarkar, the entire area was divided into four different thanas and each thana had a *adhinayak* or commander who was accountable to the *sarvadhinayak*. Accordingly, four thana Jatiya Sarkars were founded in Nandigram, Mahisadal, Sutahata and Tamluk thanas; the *adhinayak*, appointed in each thana, was invested with necessary powers and authority to run the administration in their respective areas with the help of ministers to be appointed by them. In its first official proclamation, the Sarkar announced the names of the *sarvadhinayak* and thana *adhinayaks*:

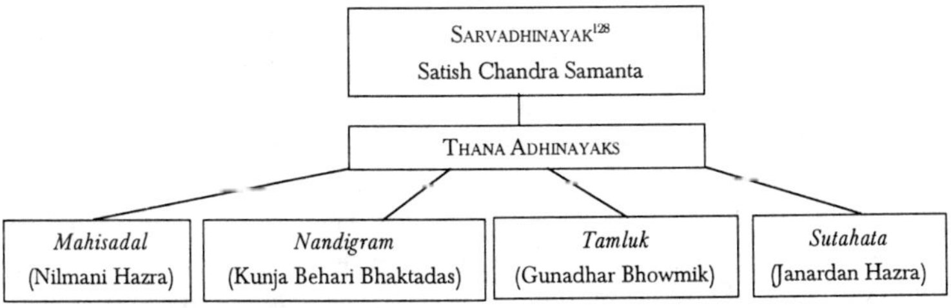

Source: NMML, TICP, Congress Proclamation, 17 December 1942.

According to the proclamation, the volunteer corps 'Vidyut Bahini' (Lightening Brigade) was recognized as the national militia of the provisional government; and *Biplabi* 'will become its mouthpiece'.[129] Four departments were instituted to run the government which are as follows:

(A) The Department of Justice was the most popular department of the

Jatiya Sarkar. Each thana had a department of justice under the control of a full-fledged Minister of Justice. The fee for filing a case was Re. 1– and later increased to Rs. 2. An additional fee of Rs. 2 was levied from 1 January 1944 for emergency cases. Both civil and criminal cases were adjudicated. Against the order and judgement of the thana court, an appeal was always entertained in the sub-divisional court; the final seat of judgement was however the special tribunal consisting of three judges which was authorized to deal with the cases, filed to challenge the judgement of the sub-divisional courts.

The court was not stationary and moved from place to place to suit the convenience of the people. The court proceedings were generally held in public and sometimes as many as 300 people were present. Many long-standing cases of the sub-divisional and district courts were decided by the Jatiya Sarkar courts. In criminal and civil cases, the accused, if found guilty, were subject to various punishments, ranging from warning, whipping, detention and even capital punishment. Property of absconders was attached and sold in public auction where persuasion had failed. Despite obvious odds, the achievement of the Jatiya Sarkar's Justice Department was remarkable and in two years of its existence, it settled 1,681 out of 2,907 cases filed.[130] The courts functioned like a colonial court following its procedures *in toto*, as the following official report shows,

> Ramnath Jana of the Bhagwanpur thana was served with a Congress notice on 21 November by a Congress peon of Lalbazar Sangram Parishad Office [which was created after the Congress was banned in the district] directing him to appear before the said office on 24 November for his trial in the said office against a complaint lodged in the Congress office by Haricharan Jana [of the same area]. Ramnath Jana did not go on the day fixed. On 4 December when Ramnath Jana went to Lalbazar [market] to make some purchases, he was arrested by the Congress volunteers and was taken to the Congress office which directed him to appear before the Congress court. . . . He was taken to a school building and was produced before the socalled judges, Sripati Charan Goswami . . . and Ganesh Pradhan for this trial. The case was decided and he was asked to [give] one-third of homestead land to repay the loan of Rupees forty which he had taken from Haricharan Jana. *The sentence was obeyed by Jana for fear of retaliation* (emphasis added).[131]

So popular were the courts that a large number of cases, withdrawn from the government courts, were filed in the Jatiya Sarkar courts for decision. It was admitted in the government report that as late as June 1944, 'the arbitration courts are gaining popular support owing to the speed with wihich they are said to dispense justice'.[132] Even after its dissolution in September 1944, people were reported to have declined to withdraw the court fees with the hope that their cases would be heard in the Jatiya Sarkar's court.[133]

(B) War Department was mainly concerned with the resistance to the British and their supporters. With the onset of the cyclone however, the War Department devoted wholeheartedly to the relief operation. To carry on its assigned duties, the department depended largely on the Vidyut Bahini which was headed by a GOC (Group Officer in Charge) who was assisted by a commandant. Impressed by Hitler's 'ultra nationalism', Sushil Dhara, the permanent head of the national militia, wanted to organize an army similar to 'the storm troopers in terms of both speed and strength to liberate India'.[134] Apart from a fighting division and an intelligence branch which were useful in anti-British counter offensive, the Bahini had also an ambulance branch consisting of well-trained doctors, paramedics, stretcher-bearers and nurses. It had constituted a *Garam Dal*, a volunteer group, which was put to task under extreme circumstances. The Dal acquired fame by efficiently executing the Sarkar's decision. Innovating a new technique of arresting a loyalist school teacher 'who escaped detention on several occasions, the Dal activists first encircled his house. A Congress volunteer in British police's disguise knocked at the door and told him' that he was called by 'the *bara babu* [officer-in-charge of the police station] in the nearby school building'. As soon as he came out, he was 'lifted away by the volunteers to the Congress court for trial. That he immediately agreed to come in response to a call from the police station confirmed the charge that he was a police informer who never felt hesitant to join the volunteers because they were in police uniform.'[135]

Later in 1943, the Bahini was expanded by creating a separate corps of women volunteers, known as the *Bhagini Sena* (Sisters' army) which played a very useful role in nursing the wounded Congress volunteers in the aftermath of the 29 September thana attack. There was another corps created specifically to guard the prisoners, captured by the Bahini, known as the *Bandi Sena* (soldiers to guard the prisoners), the corps was responsible for shifting the prisoners from the cell to the court. There were about two hundred Bandi Senas[136] though the Congress activists claimed to have recruited more.[137] Since the Senas were trainees to join the Bahini which was to fight the British in a direct confrontation, selection to the corps was made from among those who were not only physically and mentally strong but also below twenty years of age.[138] So strong and organized were the Bandi Senas that they, on a number of occcasions, overpowered the unarmed police trying to rescue 'a kidnapped loyalist'.[139]

(C) Law and Order Department was entrusted with the task of maintaining peace in the Sarkar-administered areas. With assistance from the Intelligence Department, this wing of the Jatiya Sarkar pre-empted military raid on a number of occasions. In wrapping up the criminals, alleged to have been released to sabotage the nationalist movement, the law and order department performed a useful task. With a firm handling by the Sarkar, the number of burglaries and other associated crimes was reduced to a minimum.

(D) Relief and Public Health Department undertook steps to streamline the relief operation in the cyclone and famine-affected areas. Assisted by the non-official relief organizations, the department instituted the Mahendra Relief Committee which, though not properly equipped to handle the devastation of such a magnitude, stood apart in terms of an efficient distribution of limited resources at its disposal. Moreover, given the nature of the disaster, it was not possible to mitigate the human sufferings merely by voluntary help; hence, the Jatiya Sarkar compelled the big landholders who had a surplus stock of foodgrains to distribute them through the Relief Department. Those who did not abide by the Sarkar's order, were subsequently punished and the extra foodstuffs, forcibly taken away, were distributed in accordance with the needs of the villagers. Apprehending a famine situation, the Sarkar adopted a policy to prevent the hoarders from exporting the foodgrains from the district; a close vigil was thus maintained by the Congress volunteers to execute the decision. Furthermore, the nationalist government also sought to find a substitute of rice in other cereals which largely failed primarily because of the age-old rice-dependent food habit.

Besides these major departments, the national government had an Education Department which contributed significantly to the repair of school buildings, severely damaged due to the cyclone and flood. Schools, which were denied government financial grant for their alleged involvement in the nationalist movement, were given monetary help; in view of its meagre resources, the Education Department failed to make a substantial contribution, though its effort was always appreciated and its predicament understood by the villagers. There was a Publicity Department, entrusted with responsibility of publishing bulletins, and propaganda materials and also distributing them outside the sub-division to keep the people informed about the progress of the movement. The national government had also its own postal system through which letters and other items were sent and received.

Apart from the formal structure of governance there existed 'swaraj panchayats', described, in the official report, as 'states in miniature' because 'all the functions, civil and military, are performed by these units'. They administered 'peace and justice, looked to the safety and welfare of the people, guarded the villages from robbers and dacoits, controlled export of food materials and prevented suspected persons from ingressing into villages'. Comprising the chowkidars and dafadars who left the services of the British government, these panchayats caused alarm to the administration which adopted the Essential Service Ordinance Act 'to render chowkidars and dafadars' resignation of services liable to severe punishment'. Nevertheless, the panchayats gained in strength due to 'popular support'.[140]

Although the national government was constrained due to lack of resources[141] and the constant fear of operating in an adverse situation, it alarmed the British administration by being effective longer than anticipated. Not only did Midnapur create a history following the formation of a national government, it also posed a serious threat to the British administration. A. K. Fazlul Haq, the Bengal Chief Minister thus admitted, 'there is no denying the fact that [their] object was to paralyse the civil administration and they succeeded in doing so in at least some areas'.[142]

Women and the August Revolution

Midnapur had a tradition of women's participation in the nationalist struggle. During the Non-Cooperation and Civil Disobedience Movements, women joined the Congress's call for freedom.[143] In most cases, their participation was confined to taking part in the Congress-led processions. It was not a passive involvement, but a fierce commitment to independence. Congress studiously mobilized women politically particularly after the Non Cooperation days. The period, 1939-42, was remarkable because a sizeable section of women joined the Congress, as the following table (p. 158) shows:

There had been a steady increase of women members though the Congress suffered in 1941 due to a sudden decline of its members by 42 per cent (see table on p. 137). What it shows is the growing popularity of the Congress among women who articulated their protest by directly participating in the nationalist movement. Although they carved out a space for themselves their role was to supplement the anti-British campaign within the boundaries, set out by their male colleagues.

There were big names of course, but just as significant was the contribution of the village women who fought spontaneously. Midnapur offers many such examples. During the 1942 movement, women formed

Sub-divisions	*1939**	*1941***	*1942****
Sadar	86	93	181
Jhargram	33	41	41
Ghatal	151	108	208
Tamluk	478	521	903
Contai	538	703	1011
TOTAL	1286 (4.11%)	1466 (8.13%)	2344 (5.52%)

Note: Figures in the parenthesis show the percentage of women members in relation to the total Congress members in the district.

Sources: * NMML, AICC P5/1939;
** *Swadhin Bharat* (weekly newspaper), Calcutta, 18 July 1941;
*** Tamralipta Itihas Committee Papers, Congress members in Midnapur, 1942. Sushil Dhara confirmed that there was a massive increase of women members in 1942.

'a nursing squad', prompted by the local Congress on eve of the 29 September thana attack. This apart, Midnapur Congress leaders raised 'a women corps'; they felt that women should be trained to take up arms for self-defence.[144] *Biplabi*, the Congress propaganda journal reported frequently on rape by the British police for rape was a positive proof of the fundamentally sub human nature of the British and their minions. The nationalists exhorted, 'under no circumstances, can the molestation of women be supported'. Nevertheless, there have been countless instances of soldiers, bestial with lust and fired-up with a victor's boisterousness who molest women in occupied areas. The women were thus instructed to 'carry with them *bati, katari* (different kinds of knife) and daggers, etc. Whenever a police party approaches women, the latter must then and there attack them all together with great force.'[145] They must not let any of 'the man-beasts touch any part of their bodies as long as they are alive'. The very urge for self-defence for women led the Congress leaders to form the Bhagini Sena which also took up arms against the British. Like the Jhansi Brigade of the Subhas Bose-led Indian National Army, the Bhagini Sena spread the message of independence among women. Trained by Sushil Dhara, the Sena acted as an auxiliary to the mainstream Congress platform. According to a participant, the Sena did not exist in the formal sense: it had its representatives in every household who acted as informers and messengers–their services sought extensively since as women they were less open to suspicion.[146]

Organizationally, the Sena was a three tier set-up.[147] At the apex were the leading women cadres who with instructions from the leaders were responsible for implementing the Congress plans and programmes. Driven out of home by scared fathers or husbands, they were subject to severe police torture. The second tier consisted of those women who maintained links between the women leaders and village women, far removed from the nationalist struggle. These efforts yielded results especially after the 29 September thana attack when a large number of women, irrespective of class and creed, pledged to serve the Congress–they knew, this might lead to severe police torture. These women constituted the third tier. While reminiscing, Sushil Dhara admitted that the Congress success in sustaining the movement when its all-India counterpart withered away was principally due to the cooperation of these women–with no political training, no formal education, but inspired. They never came to the forefront but enabled the Congress activists to escape arrest by supplying information.

Why did they join the movement in the first place? Emotionally charged with the spirit of nationalism and convinced by the sacrifices of the Congress nationalists in the district, the Midnapur women felt inspired. To them, the fight for India's freedom was a sacred goal and to attain this, the *mother India* could demand their unalloyed loyalty. The price they had to pay was high. The Sena's women cadres had to sort out their problems within their families; the problem however varied: women those husbands were active Congress members faced less trouble; the unmarried women were discouraged initially but, once convinced, their guardians let them have their way; for the married women, the problem was acute–the Congress leaders had to try hard to win them over. The efforts yielded results and on the thana attack day, 29 September, a large number of women joined the Congress procession and Matangini Hazra, a seventy three year old woman was shot dead while leading to capture the Tamluk thana. Once the movement went underground, the women volunteers played a decisive role in maintaining links among the disparate Congress activists. Without their cooperation, the rebellion, as Dhara confirmed, would have died an early death. Not only did they act behind the scene, the Sena members launched violent campaigns against the British police and soldiers as well. Kumudini Dakua,[148] a participant, reported a number of encounters with the British police.[149] In most cases, they had to be on the offensive for self-defence.

The Congress campaign for freedom and women's participation in it brought about radical social changes in Midnapur. Those who were raped were never ostracised–certainly unthinkable in a society, far-off from Calcutta. Revolutionary terrorism insisting on female education as the first step towards developing the woman's personality, contributed significantly to women's participation in the rebellion. Rejecting the epic-heroine image as ideal for women, it paved the way for women's active role in the battle against the British. Imbibing the sacrifice of Bina Das, Kalpana Dutta, Pritilata Waddedar[150] among others, the Midnapur women plunged into the freedom struggle. Gandhi would not have approved of women resorting to violence. When he wanted to mobilize women, he spoke of the 'great satis' in India's past and of Sita as the ideal women. Kasturba Gandhi, Sarojini Naidu, Maniben Patel, Sushila Nayer,[151] among others were admired because they symbolized, as Gandhi thought, the ideals sacred for Hindus: the mother, the devoted wife and the fellow pilgrim. The Midnapur women activists were Gandhian as well because they resorted to violence if they had to and with Gandhi's approbation since the Mahatma had often argued for the defence of women honour by violent means, if necessary.

Women played, as the above discussion shows, a crucial role in the Indian national movement. Unfortunately, they, like other subordinate groups in society, have been denied their proper recognition. History is about the male. Women are invisible, their identities being negatively portrayed through a vast silence. Neglected in the history in the modern era, women played the principal parts in ancient and medieval India. So, the invisibility of women in history varies. The epic-heroines, Sita and Draupadi, have been discussed as examples of women's capacity to suffer in a situation emphasizing the struggle between 'absolute' and 'relative' *dharma.* Both the *Ramayana* and *Mahabharatha* depict women in relation to their male counterparts as husbands: women undergo suffering and torture for the welfare, long life and good name of the husbands and the couple's offspring, particularly their sons. So, women are indeed projected as powerful creatures but expressing their strength in a different way. There is another image (as the women activists of Midnapur had articulated through their participation in the anti-British struggle)–presenting women as *virangana*, the fighter. Indian history provides countless examples that not only do they suffer for a cause, but also take part in real battle. History and not just folklore and mythology highlights the heroic deeds of these women. What is however *problematique* is that by working from the conventional archives of political history, women appear in the history of nationalism only 'in a contributive role'.[152] The Congress leadership effectively mediated women discontents so that they remained targeted exclusively at imperialism. Gandhi too recognized the power of women and contained it for the cause of independence, uniting the nation behind the freedom struggle at the expense of injustices within caste, class and gender relations.[153] All one can assert here that 'women also took part in nationalist struggle, but one cannot identify any autonomous subjectivity of women'.[154] Midnapur women activists were not different from their counterparts elsewhere: they were brought-in to the Congress fold by their male colleagues. Nonetheless, their involvement in the nationalist movement reflected an awareness of the exploitative colonial system of governance which needed to be replaced by an indigenous one. Committed to liberate the country, the women activists took part in protest which demonstrated, *inter alia*, a will to resist and challenge authority despite adverse consequences.

'Biplabi': The Journal of the Open Rebellion

What is remarkable about the Midnapur rebels is documentary evidence of their activities during the movement. The underground paper dealing with the day-to-day Congress-led anti-British onslaught in the district was *Biplabi*, a Bengali publication that appeared weekly in Tamluk sub-division between September 1942 and late August 1944. Like other propaganda materials for political purposes, *Biplabi* might have exaggerated Congress achievements on occasions. Nonetheless it helped sustain 'the anti-British feelings'[155] by regularly publishing accounts of government brutality in containing the nationalist campaign.

Biplabi was not merely a political pamphlet, it was a serious endeavour at political mobilization as well. The national government appointed a minister for publicity–Prahlad Kumar Pramanik–to supervise the collection of news and production of *Biplabi*. As one goes through this political documentary, one is impressed by the organized effort of the Midnapur rebels to convert suffering into political support. Its arguments were ironic, declamatory, logical, emotional and exhortative in turn. *Biplabi* enabled the nationalists, to a significant extent, to sustain the political support for the movement when it had almost evaporated everywhere. The information available in *Biplabi* may not be authentic, as is true of all propaganda literature, but it is certainly useful for understanding the nature of the nationalist movement organized and controlled solely by the Congress volunteers at the grassroots.

Deconstructing the message *Biplabi* conveyed is a relatively easy task because of its style of presentation in lucid language. Nowhere in the journal does one come across any convoluted statements; its political message was crystal clear: organize for the last battle against the British. By drawing attention to the atrocities committed by the 'British and their minions' on the innocent people, each edition of the journal invariably ends with the slogan 'do or die'. Like any other underground journal investing popular misery and suffering with political content, *Biplabi*, on most occasions, highlighted the heinous crimes like mass rape and other torture inflicted on the local women to incite people against the alien state. Reference was also made to other kinds of atrocities, such as arson and physical assault on men suspected of helping the Congress. The themes that figured in the journal intermittently were selected by the national government in consultation with its editor; with regard to events substantiating a particular theme, the editor had a free hand. The language of the journal varied probably because of the change of the editors due to arrests. With a massive military countdown in Tamluk where the journal was written and cyclostyled, those involved in running the journal were frequently arrested; the national government by constantly providing an alternative set of editors continued to bring out the journal uninterruptedly till it was closed down in August 1944. Apart from the frequent replacement of editors which had an impact on the language and style, the way the journal was produced after March 1943 was likely to contribute to the variation because there were occasions when the journal was first composed separately by two editors in different locations and then compiled by another. *Biplabi* might not have the flair of a literary text; but by addressing its target groups most effectively in their language, it contributed significantly to the continuity of the movement under extremely adverse conditions.

Biplabi resorted to familiar rhetoric to mobilize support in favour of the movement. Two interrelated ideas recur on most occasions: (*a*) the pain and suffering inflicted on the people appeared likely given the reluctance on their part to sacrifice for the cause of the motherland and (*b*) the notion of mother, immensely popularized during the extremist phase of the nationalist movement is frequently invoked in order to draw inspiration. By harping on these ideas which were integrally connected with the Bengali psyche, *Biplabi* succeeded in infusing a new zeal in the movement. So, the choice of ideas was strategically conditioned with a view to preparing and sustaining the ground for the anti-British counter-offensive. Although the movement derived its ideological justification from the creed of non-violence, its mouthpiece, *Biplabi,* however appeared less committed to the professed ideology. For instance, while appreciating the sacrifice of those who fell to the bullet on 29 September 1942, *Biplabi* hailed the acts as nothing but a noble service to the 'Mother with offerings of fresh blood'. In more categorical terms, the journal exhorted,

> The arrival of autumn reminds us that the Mother–she who killed the demon, the *Asura*, she takes the lion as her mount, she who always gives bliss–is coming. The global cry is of death, the earth is shaking. On 12 *Aswin* (29 September)

thousands of her sons in Tamluk and Contai gave their lives as a *puja* sacrifice. They became exalted heroes. Men and women, old and young, chanted Bande Mataram. They succeeded in destroying Satan's den.[156]

On another occasion, *Biplabi* described the devastating cyclone that caused havoc in Midnapur as the destructive dance of nature in the form of *Mahisasura Mardhini* (Goddess Durga). It wrote,

The people's misery has reached the limits of forbearance. It seems as if Mother, *Mahisasura Mardhini* descended to earth as devastation personified. Unlike other occasions, . . . the *naibedya* (alter offerings) offered at the puja this year were lakhs–nay crores (tens of millions) of young lives. Crores of her children were prepared to lay down their lives as lotus offering at her feet. She has manifested herself in the form of devastation because it is her intention to create a new world order after destroying her cowardly children, immersed in sin and battered by poverty and misery. From the ruins of this devastation, there will emerge a new nation that will liberate India after annihilating the British, a people steeped in sins of all description.[157]

The language and idioms that run through the above passage reminds us of Aurobindo's *Jugantor*. Drawing on the mother cult, *Jugantor* urged for supreme sacrifice on the part of those clinging to the extremist ethos as the only method available for wresting freedom from colonialism. Hence, the imagery which is part and parcel of Bankimchandra's *Anadamath* (1882) is recurrent in this newspaper.[158] By playing on the Bengali sentiment, the extremist attack on the alien state built up a strong organizational network which largely accounted for the success of the 1905 anti-partition campaign in Bengal.

Biplabi delved into the extremist spirit by relying a great deal on those songs/poems written by Rabindranath Tagore and Nazrul Islam championing the cause of motherland. Like *Jugantor* which frequently printed Tagore's anti-partition poems to inspire the participants, *Biplabi*, in most of its editions, either began or ended with a revolutionary poem/ song of Tagore or Nazrul. The following poems of Tagore are illustrative here:

At the awakening we hear the message
Fear not! Fear not!
If you sacrifice your life
you will be immortal[159]

On another occasion, the journal concluded,

If you haven't experienced sorrow
how can your sorrows end?

Poison, to be neutralised, must be burned
with the flame of poison.
Let the fire that smoulders within you burn
have no fear of it at all;
when it burns itself to ashes–
No more shall it burn on this earth.
Dying every moment, let Death be
completely drained away.
When it is drained away, life will reappear
and take its rightful place.[160]

(Translation is mine)

The message is clear: in order to generate and sustain the nationalist zeal, Tagore is evoked. Nazrul, unlike Tagore, was a confrontationist and always gave a call to resort to violent means to attain the goal. His insistence on the 'destruction of prison as the only means of saving the nationalist from being tortured'[161] amply demonstrated his preference for means other than non-violence. In its issue of 10 May 1943 Nazrul was again quoted first to inspire the militant section of the Midnapur Congress and secondly to counter the British propaganda that the August revolution was merely a Hindu affair.[162] That Tagore was referred to more often in the journal than Nazrul suggests a specific ideological tilt because the former in his political views was less militant. Whatever the assessment in this regard, by selecting those poems/songs championing, in most cases, ideas other than non-violence, *Biplabi* probably endeavoured to incorporate the spirit of militancy within the Gandhian mould. In other words, despite their declared faith in *ahimsa*, the fact that the Midnapur rebels appreciated means which Gandhi would have never approved[163] indicates the cleavages within the Midnapur Congress.

In terms of its structure, *Biplabi* was a weekly newspaper combining both news and views. In most cases, news items were chosen selectively to highlight the torture and atrocity committed by the British police and its agents. A large contingent of Congressmen and sympathizers were involved in collecting information from different corners of the district; information, thus gathered, was handed over to the district Congress committee through various local Congress committees–the same procedure was more or less followed throughout the period of publication. With the massive military clamp on the movement, it became difficult for the male members to move about openly; housewives in large number came forward to replace them in so far as information-collection was concerned; gradually, the women contingent was brought in as an integral part of the Congress campaign in Midnapur.

With regard to views, the editor of *Biplabi* presented the facts and figures in such a way as to generate maximum hatred and enmity against the British on the part of its readers. Thus, in its 23 November edition, it writes,

> We hear a lot of stories about Japanese barbarism from the lips of British publicists, but can there be anything comprable to such acts as British bestiality? Warring nations have set-up many deplorable acts of barbarism, but the King of Beasts continues to maintain his supremacy in all forms of bestliness . . . But beyond all comparison is the goat-like lust of the British lion, represented in India by Britons who fatten on the food of our own land and who also make proclamation by beat of the drums that they have taken a great vow to defend our freedom from the attacks of an imaginary enemy.[164]

Moreover, by resorting, for instance, to words like bestiality (*poisachiki*), minions (British *kutta*), cannibals (*narakhadak*) to describe the representatives of the alien state, *Biplabi* put forward a specific point of view in presenting the information it collected through the volunteers. Similarly, to convey the message to the villagers, an attempt was constantly made to speak in their idioms. Hence, the idioms like house burner or arsonist (*ghar pora*), hell's doorkeeper (*naraker keet)*, satan's residence (*saitaner basa)* were frequently referred to. As is natural, the journal, the Congress mouthpiece, always appreciated the nationalist activities in superlative terms and the idioms were chosen accordingly.

There are four themes which predominated in *Biplabi*: (*a*) the criminal conduct of security forces; (*b*) the bestiality (*poisachiki*) of the British and their Indian collaborators; (*c*) exhorting and eulogizing sacrifice for the nationalist cause, and (*d*) the artificial or man-made origins of the 1943-4 Bengal famine.

Explaining the purpose of its publication, *Biplabi,* in its first edition, thus declared, '. . . in order to inform the people about this struggle that has been gaining strength despite inhuman torture by the British, we are publishing *Biplabi*. This journal will bring about revolution in our country'.[165] As a propaganda journal with a political goal, *Biplabi* extensively covered the nature of police atrocities in various police stations in Midnapur to generate anti-British sentiments. The rebels were not scared of arrest; they were afraid of police raid on the suspect's house which, in most cases, led to indiscriminate beatings, destruction and loot of property as well. The Congress counter-offensive became effective gradually as people in large numbers participated in the movement. While narrating the inhuman conduct of security forces, the accounts of *Biplabi* run as follows,

. . . the *daroga* (sub inspector of police) sprayed petrol and spirit over the roof with a syringe and set fire to the house of Dr. Janardan Hazra, a Congress volunteer of Sijberya. They allowed no one to come near the house to put out the fire. In cowshed cows started wailing pitifully. Five cows, five goats, two cocks and one cat were burnt alive in the fire.[166]

On 14 October 1942, the senior *daroga* of Mahisadal police station along with ten armed sepoys, raided the house of Sri Mahindra Nath Samanta, a distinguished Congress worker of Chandipur, under the pretext of carrying out a search; they destroyed numerous chests and almirahs and appropriated two ornaments worth of Rupees 25 and 15 respectively.[167]

The bestial activities of the British and Indian police were constantly referred to in *Biplabi.* Police arson of villagers' hut was a terrible aspect of this movement. Nalini Raha, a Sub Inspector of Mahisadal police station who seemed to have enjoyed arson, was identified as *ghar pora* (house burner). In its edition of 6 November 1942, *Biplabi* writes,

On 15 October 1942, Nalini Raha accompanied by 25 armed sepoys and nearly 40 Muslims set fire to the house–under lock–of a distinguished Congressmen, Sri Nilmani Hazra of Rajarampur village. Soon afterwards, the police raided Matakari, an adjacent village, set fire to and looted fourteen houses.

The British bestiality was also demonstrated by 'the frequent report of rape' which was a convincing proof of 'the sub human nature' of the British and their Indian agents. An account in *Biplabi* runs as follows,

. . . police indulged in violations of modesty and searched many houses in Chandipur village. The soldiers finding three solitary women in three different houses, raped all of them successively; each woman was raped by two or three soldiers. The women were found lying unconscious late in the morning.

The soldiers held back two women, aged 18 and 20 years and later raped them. The next morning villagers found [them] lying unconscious near the railway tracks . . . and carried them . . . to the hospital.

. . . a thirty six year old woman was raped by six soldiers of the same group which raped two women elsewhere.[168]

Rape was a deliberate means to cause terror and therefore *Biplabi* gave specific instruction for self-defence to the village women.

. . . four or five women should remain in each room. The women should always carry with them *bati* (a common household knife), *katari* (a thick sickle-shaped knife) daggers etc. Whenever a police party approaches women, the latter must then and there attack the party all together with great force. They must not let any of the man-beasts touch any part of their bodies as long as they are alive.[169]

On another occasion, while elaborating how to defend the women's honour, *Biplabi* in its 25 January edition reiterates,

> Immediately on receipt of information of the enemy's approach, a number of women in your locality must gather together, arm themselves with daggers, knives, batis, katiari, ladles, crowbars, or any other weapon, and go into a room of a house and remain locked there, all in a group. When the villains come, you must strike them with a weapon on any part of their bodies with all your might–only, in this manner, will be human beasts be tamed.[170]

The beastliness of the police and the nationalist counter attack led to a greater awareness among the women of their role in the freedom struggle. The heroic activities of the Bhagini Sena which nursed the wounded and protected village women from physical torture by the police, demonstrated this convincingly.

A special feature of Midnapur was that the village women participated in the nationalist struggle.[171] A continuous effort on the part of the Congress volunteers yielded positive results in the Congress-led raids on the police stations on 29 September 1942. Matangini Hazra of the women volunteers who fell to police bullet was identified in *Biplabi* as 'the most heroic woman [who] deserved praise for her devotion to the cause of freedom, self-sacrifice and zeal to keep the national flag flying'.[172] By referring to her sacrifice for freedom from the British rule, *Biplabi* remembers Matangini's sacrifice in the following way,

> Matangini led one procession from the north of the criminal court building; even after firing commenced, she continued to advance with the tri-colour flag, leaving all the volunteers behind. The police shot her three times. She continued marching despite wounds in the forehead and in both hands. She died chanting 'Bande Mataram'.[173]

The final theme, the 1943-4 Bengal famine, was covered extensively in the journal to prove that 'the famine originated largely because of the government's disruption of the paddy market, and also because of niggardliness of official relief'.[174] The first stage of famine[175] can be said to have begun in Midnapur following the devastating October cyclone when the local crops were substantially destroyed. Before the cyclone, Midnapur had been a surplus district exporting large quantities of rice and paddy. The typhoon however made Midnapur a deficit district ruining, to a significant extent, the local supplies. Such a state of scarcity would have been successfully alleviated, under normal circumstances, by drawing supplies from the unaffected parts of Midnapur and also from other districts. The application of a denial policy however ruled out that possibility. The threat of Japanese invasion led to the denial policy which involved (*a*) the removal from the coastal districts of Midnapur, Bakarganj and Khulna of the rice and paddy estimated to be in excess of local requirements until the end of the next crop year, and (*b*) the withdrawal of all boats capable of carrying ten passangers or more from those parts of the delta considered vulnerable to invasion.[176] Moreover, the Japanese occupation of Burma cut-off about only 5 per cent of the annual import of rice to Bengal.[177] Hence, the practical effect of the loss of Burma rice should not have been severe since only 100,000 tons of it were imported into Bengal; the lack of the availability of Burma rice may not have affected the bhadralok who hardly had fascination for its bad quality. As it was available at a relatively cheaper rate, the Burma rice was consumed largely by the poor who were therefore hard-hit following its disappearance from the market. With a 400 per cent increase in the wholesale price of rice in Bengal between 1942 and 1943[178] the worst sufferers in the whole of Bengal were agricultural labourers who formed the largest group of those who died because 'neither could they afford to buy the rice which was terribly expensive nor were they accustomed to begging for survival'.[179] The crisis appeared to have been aggravated by the series of crop failures that Bengal experienced beginning from 1938[180] and the conditions created by the war made the situation unmanageable.

Rice denial which authorized outside agents to buy surplus grain from cultivators was not very effective in Midnapur which contributed only 6,715 of a total of 40,000 tons of rice acquired (a mere 16.7 per cent).[181] It was widely alleged however that much larger amounts of rice had been bought-up by the denial agents for their personal speculation.[182] The Ispahanis–the leading grain dealers and wholesellers–were reported to have 'made piles of money by hoarding and profiteering in rice, and more particularly by manipulating the price line'.[183] The Bengal Government appeared helpless since the permission to frame the Ispahanis was denied by the government of India probably because 'too many individuals in the Government of India were concerned [and hence] no action should be taken'![184] Apart from hoarding by the big business, the fear that the crisis would loom large 'led those people with money to buy excessively to store for the future'[185] In other words, 'the fear of hunger had seized the whole population and everybody hoarded food with a sort of feverish passion'.[186] A wave of panic therefore swept through Bengal making families which had kept 'one bag of rice for emergency keep four or five instead'.[187] To tackle the crisis, the government undertook relief measures and in particular, had distributed food 'on a generous scale' from the start. After a few months, relief had severely been curtailed 'as lavish expenditure and thus unwarranted in view of the war'.[188] The amount of rice, thus acquired, was utilized 'for the army moving up to defend the Assam Frontier'.[189] On top of these, what caused terrible suffering to the poor in Midnapur was 'the introduction of a most undesirable principle into relief measures, relief according to social class and not entirely in accordance with necessity'. While reminiscing, O.M. Martin, the Bengal Relief Commissioner, elaborated such a peculiar system of relief:

> When I questioned the poor working men in Midnapur about relief operation, I would be told, 'we, poor people, only get the odd handful of millet'. 'What about rice and lentils'. 'These go to the members of the relief committee and to their friends and we get what they cannot eat'.[190]

The situation got out of control by September 1943 when famine reached its height.[191] The starving people began to wander and the hospitals became 'full of famine victims', most of whom suffered from 'the characteristic famine diarrhea'. A new class of patients appeared who were dubbed 'destitutes'.[192] What caused alarm was the outbreak of 'an epidemic of malignant malaria' in Midnapur. The result was that the mortality among the able bodied males was 'twice as heavy as among workers and children'.[193]

The death toll[194] was so severe that in *Biplabi,* the dread image of Bengal as 'a cremation ground' was again and again emphasized,

> Bengal is a vast cremation ground, a meeting place for ghosts and evil spirits, a land so overrun by dogs, jackals and vultures that it make [*sic*] one wonder whether the Bengalis are rally [*sic*] alive or have become ghosts from some distant epoch.

> Bengal today is a vast cremation ground. Her fortune-bestowing sun is on the decline; there are dark storm-clouds hovering on her sky of future; there are signs of destruction on her green horizon. Her sons are deprived of food, clothing and medical care. Who is there to instill in her hope and confidence? Who is there to smear the regal mark of glory on Mother Bengal's golden crown.[195]

In order to highlight the horrifying consequences of famine, *Biplabi* frequently printed accounts of out-migrants, sales of assets, food dacoities and related crimes, hunger suicide, sale of children, abandonment of dependants, etc. Along with a description of the devastating famine, *Biplabi* strove to provide an explanation of its origin and also aimed to convince the reader that only by participating in the open rebellion would there be any hope of a solution. The following extracts articulated the complex arguments highlighting the principal contention,

The extreme misery in the country due to the famine [which was] deliberately created by the British, takes on a more terrible aspect in Midnapur because cyclone and flood joined hands with the British. Yet there is no limit to the devilry of the British. On the one hand, relief is being given in a variety of forms; on the other, four times the amount [of relief] is being collected [as revenue]. Not a single paisa of tax has been remitted in the flood or drought-affected areas of Midnapur–the same Midnapur the occurrence of famine has been communicated right up to England by the beat of drums. The result is that zamindars are filing umpteen suits [for rent] and executing court decrees. How can the tenants contest the cases when they have nothing to eat? The money they get for relief they use to pay their taxes for fear of becoming refugees. In such anarchic conditions, looting is practised with both hands by the police, by soldiers and by all classes of British officials, to the extent of lakhs of rupees.[196]

By September when the famine had reached its height, *Biplabi* attributed its grave nature to the forcible purchase of winter paddy. Criticizing the government's paddy-procurement scheme, *Biplabi* argued,

. . . there is practically no *aus* crop in the district. Little has been cultivated this year while the time for harvesting the *aman* crop is far off. One does not know whether these crops will be snatched away like last year or be harvested and taken home. But at the very moment, a vulture-like glance is being cast on Midnapur by our blood-sucking and ogre-like administration. . . . Can you figure out now the devil's calculated strategy? Do you realise why we are forewarning you? Nearly half the population has died this year; is it your intention–those of you survive–to be wiped out completely in next year's famine by selling your paddy to outsiders? If all of you die, who then will remain to enjoy the benefits of your land, your property and your ancestral homestead? . . . We repeat: inhabitants of Midnapur! Beware! Some few will survive and be spared death till the ripening of the new paddy. Others may [manage to] save their property but only by selling food they require for their daily meals. But for whose enjoyment will they have saved the property if they themselves die? Since death is unavoidable, why this hesitation? Stand up and try to live like a human being in utter disregard of the enemy's devilry. Unite and take courage. Utter the words, 'Bande Mataram' and you shall gather courage.[197]

Biplabi therefore exhorts the people to join the Congress revolt against the British because

. . . it is thousand times better to storm the enemy's camp and drive across the seas than to suffer such unbearable oppression and a slow death. How many people will die of bullets? And how many are on the verge of death from starvation?[198]

In a rather rhetorical way, *Biplabi* strove to rouse the people for an anti-British movement by playing on their sentiments,

Inhabitants of Midnapur! If die you must, then why condemn yourself to a slow death made painful by the pangs of hunger? Instead, let us submerge this develish administration in the sea by facing bullets like heroes. The famine will kill everybody, but how many of us will be killed by bullets? Those who die will be honoured as heroes and those who live will live in independent Midnapur, their bellies stuffed with food. If you fail to do this then there will be not a soul left alive to eat even a single grain of the unripe paddy. . . . How can you live for six months [i.e. until the next winter harvest] when there is not enough rice in the house for six days? . . . The British, who have ruined our villages and converted our golden country into a cremation ground, will then come along with hirelings and loot all the rice paddy that you have cultivated with such labour and care. Just think it over, whether it is better to let this happen or drive off the devil and try to live as a free man with the right to enjoy the fruit of one's labour.[199]

The situation was however no better when a new ministry headed by Nazimuddin took office in October 1943. Blaming Fazlul Haq and his colleagues for the food crisis, the League Ministry resolved

to set up a centrally-controlled trade purchasing organisation for the purchase of marketed surplus through normal trade channels and cooperative societies for building up a provincial reserve providing for deficit areas outside the greater Calcutta.[200]

Despite government's declared objective of achieving 'a complete state monopoly'[201] in the purchase of surplus rice from the denial areas, the official authorization to Ispahani & Co. to buy all the rice and paddy in Midnapur came as a surprise.[202] The government also constituted food committees comprising the local people to assist the denial agent in finding out the surplus rice and paddy in the villages. With the help of the food committee members, Ispahani & Co. succeeded initially in tracking down in Midnapur a large quantity of rice, supposed to be an excess of the requirements. Apprehending the possible disastrous consequences of the purchase of rice, the Jatiya Sarkar issued an order insisting,

(1) Don't sell a single handful of paddy to the firm of Ispahani, to its agents or to anyone else. We also appeal to our coolies, cartmen, boatmen and others not to carry consignments of paddy. If the police resort to firing, then give your lives and not the paddy.

(2) In the name of country, seize the surplus paddy of those among the rich who attempt to sell paddy in disregard of the pleas of the villagers; then arrange for free distribution of the paddy among the destitutes of the village.

(3) Give up completely the idea of paying (*a*) chowkidari tax, (*b*) zamindari

dues and (*c*) government loans till the return of better days when you can provide yourselves with proper food and clothing and live like human beings.

(4) Nobody should accept either the membership or help the food committees which are helping the Ispahanis in snatching the paddy away from our villages and thus are anti-national.

(5) Organize for unity in the village. Make announcement to the effect that nobody will carry rice or paddy that is sold [to an outsider]. Everyone will remain in possession of his traditional property and live off its produce. Sternly punish those who are found guilty of defiance and banish them from the sub-division, if necessary.[203]

The famine was due not to the shortfall in production which had been small, but to hoarding, caused by popular panic and greed as well as government mismanagement.[204] Careful calculations suggest that there was more food in 1943 than in 1941 and thus it seems safe 'to conclude that the disastrous Bengal famine was not the reflection of a remarkable overall shortage of food grains in Bengal'.[205] As A. K. Sen aptly summarizes that in 1943, 'a moderate shortfall in *production* had . . . been translated into an exceptional shortfall in *market release*'[206] (emphasis original). In this sense, the famine was 'man-made'. Since the crisis was not directly caused by a food shortage as such, it was a classic example of what is often termed as 'a classic famine'. Attributing the famine to an enormous rise in price, it was thus stated in *The Report on Bengal*, 'the larger landholders benefitted from the situation, since they could sell most of their rice at an enormous profit . . . the famine thus principally affected one section of the community–the poor classes in rural areas'.[207]

Observations

As an instrument of political propaganda, *Biplabi* capitalizing on anti-British sentiment, played a decisive role in both mobilizing and sustaining support for the open rebellion. That the Jatiya Sarkar continued its operation for two years despite intense police oppression suggests the extent to which the Midnapur rebels successfully utilized this instrument. In the absence of official/non-official records, the information available in *Biplabi* may not be established beyond question, but frequent reference to police atrocity in the district reveals the story of police outrages. An examination of other contemporary sources may provide us with clues to understand the 1942 movement in a broader perspective. *Biplabi*, for instance, refers to the development of the movement elsewhere which indicates the awareness among the Congress activists of the necessity of linking the movement in Midnapur with the rest of India.[208]

The accounts in *Biplabi* are also important in another respect: although the Midnapur Congressmen upheld non-violence throughout the movement, the advocacy of murder when it came to resisting to rape, may sound rather contradictory. *Biplabi's* editor however justified this action as being in tune with Gandhian principle for the Mahatma had often advocated the defence of women's honour by violent means if necessary.[209]

Like *Nildarpan* (1860) of Dinabandhu Mitra and *Anandamath* (1882) of Bankimchandra Chatterjee, *Biplabi* succeeded in investing human misery with political content. Referring to the disastrous consequences of the 1943-4 'man-made' famine, the description in *Biplabi* highlighted the devilish nature of the British administration. Similarly, frequent reference and prominence to rape drew popular attention to 'the British bestiality'. These calculated efforts of the activists sustained and strengthened the Congress organization which added a new chapter of successful popular mobilization by the grassroots political workers to the history of Indian national struggle.

Concluding Comments

The 1942 open rebellion was perhaps the only example showing that the Indians fought the British *en masse* in the absence of top Congress leadership. Apart from projecting mass initiative, the rebellion draws our attention to the autonomy of politics in the unorganized sector. Politics at the grassroots seem different in kind from the politics at the apex. There are reasons to believe that the initiative at the organized level of politics sparked off a monumental movement at the grassroots. It is also true that Gandhi's 'do or die' call acted miraculously and people joined the August revolution 'spontaneously' illustrating peoples' desire to associate with a movement which would force the British to quit India. That the movement began and continued with alarming proportions despite the absence of top leadership seems to suggest that the process of mobilization at the grassroots follows a different logic which may be independent of what happens at the top. This probably demonstrates the autonomy of politics at various levels. Though there should be an underlying thread linking various levels of politics to make it an organic whole, each level has its own dynamics which perhaps explains the continuity of the movement at one level when the all-India counterpart saw its eclipse. The inter level/sector relationships are crucial in understanding why the same movement continued with serious magnitudes at one level and declined at another. For instance, though the Quit India upsurge gained momentum in Midnapur gradually, neither the AICC nor the BPCC provided adequate backing to sustain the popular zeal. Here lies the significance of mass initiative which grew into a monumental movement in a context which seemed otherwise adverse especially after the onset of a devastating cyclone. Although the Midnapur Congress launched the movement in response to the 8 August Quit India resolution, the continuity of the rebellion for almost two years despite severe police and military torture indicates the role of the local people irrespective of caste and class in sustaining the anti-British sentiment.

By championing the open rebellion, the communist organizations–CPI and AIKS–confirmed the extent to which the people's war strategy appeared futile at the grassroots. Ideologically different from the Congress, the communists participated in the nationalist struggle that captured the popular dissent more than anything else. Though the Congress was restrained since it neither organized nor sanctioned movements against vested interests, it articulated and directed the mass fervour most successfully against the imperial authority. In such a situation, political exigency seemed to have considerably influenced the decision to take part in the August upheaval despite violating the people's war line. In fact, the British bureaucracy felt alarmed since the banned Congress operated under the aegis of the communists who escaped government attention for reasons connected with the international scene. For most of the communists, fascism was a distant enemy and hence it was difficult to articulate popular discontent in the district which suffered more due to the British design in the context of cyclone and famine; the Congress endeavour to alleviate human suffering created a space for the nationalists who undertook steps to project that the Congress also fought for the poor. During the famine, by distributing relief materials regardless of class, Congress emerged as an organization, devoted to the popular cause. Anti-imperial sentiments generally remained decisive owing principally to a well-nurtured social homogeneity, explained largely by the predominance of the Mahishyas. And, the communists thus failed, to a significant extent, to draw upon the class schism. Hence, in Midnapur, the popular discontent was translated most effectively in attacks against the Raj which was held responsible for severely dislocating rural society. The communists, by participating in the open rebellion even by challenging the people's war theory, articulated a particular strategy, tuned to a specific configuration of factors at the grassroots.

What is also intriguing is the way the Midnapur rebels resorted to violence and yet remained 'true' Gandhians. Aware of the serious implications of clinging to violence, the nationalists drew upon Gandhi's instruction to defend their action. It was therefore argued in *Biplabi*,

> If there is no alternative, the women's chastity must be protected even it involves killing of human beasts who are madly bent on rape. It is the duty of every man to protect the chastity of women by whatever means available. . . . *Ahimsa* is not equated with cowardice. It is only through the ultimate maturity of courage, valour and self sacrifice that ahimsa is completely manifested.[210]

Gandhi seemed persuaded during his visit to Midnapur in 1945 and supported 'violent acts' in view of the British brutality[211] vis-a-vis women; so, it was ideologically defensible. Such a deviation from non-violence however brings out a distinctive feature of a popular upheaval under extremely adverse circumstances. By directing the masses against the British, the Quit India campaign succeeded in organizing the disparate political forces for a specific cause. In the presence of a strong alien power, what seemed important was to sustain the nationalist zeal by underlining the effectiveness of Jatiya Sarkar which rose as an alternative centre of authority towards the end of 1943 when it stopped, on a number of occasions, exporting of rice from the district. Moreover, by supporting capital punishment for those proved guilty of betraying the nationalist cause, the Sarkar articulated the popular voice reflecting clearly considerations other than non-violence. Shielded by the villagers, not only did the Congress activists roam freely they also succeeded in executing their decision. What it thus reveals is a process at the grassroots which meaningfully explains the apparent incongruity of non-violence, as defined by Gandhi himself with its interpretation in the localities.[212]

The Quit India Movement was primarily a Hindu movement despite Gandhi's urge to create an anti-imperial platform incorporating everybody regardless of religion. Midnapur did not differ much, for though there was a Muslim minority in the district not a single instance of Muslim participation was noticed. During the Danipur Rice Mill Raid (1942), two Muslims were killed; they, however, were criminals serving jail sentences,[213] released ostensibly to sabotage the Congress plan. There are various instances illustrating the government's attempts to utilize the Muslims for an anti-Congress onslaught. Tamluk Police Inspector, Nalini Raha, for instance, undertook several measures with the help of the 'Muslim criminals' to terrorize the villagers. This may have been the reason why the Congress suspected the Muslims which seems irrational since the entire Muslim community in the district was blamed for the deeds of a handful of mischief makers. Whatever the reason, it is plausible to argue that the Hindu-Muslim alienation was evident throughout the Quit India upsurge which otherwise encompassed the entire population of the district. By their phenomenal absence in such a gigantic movement, Midnapur Muslims associated themselves, perhaps unknowingly, with their brethren elsewhere who withdrew participation in the last anti-British offensive with the hope that cooperation with the Raj during the war crisis would ensure Pakistan.

The open rebellion in Midnapur was remarkable in another respect. There was not a single instance of dissent in the administration which thus devoted wholeheartedly to the control of the nationalists in the district. Not only does it point to the Congress' failure to penetrate into the administration, it also highlights the strict discipline of British bureaucracy which, at least, in Midnapur, did not crumble in the face of an unprecedented Congress attack. There are a number of instances of involvement of white police; in most cases, however, the Indians carried out the anti-Congress operation, entailing mass-rape of village women and inflicting inhuman torture on the Congress volunteers. Notwithstanding a strong administration backed by police and military, and the disastrous consequences first of the cyclone and then famine, the movement continued—demonstrating that it was not a handful of Congressmen who upheld the nationalist zeal; instead, the masses who formed the backbone of the movement championed the cause knowing well the adverse consequences of opposition to the British.

Midnapur also offers an example of a successful intermingling of ideology and organization. Nationalism prepared the base and the Congress leadership over time consolidated it through an organizational network in the district which can be traced back to the 1920-2 Non-Cooperation days; having lost the battle to the 'pro-changers', 'no-changers' concentrated on village reconstruction in rural areas as the only means to reach out beyond the world of bhadralok which was necessary in order to organize an effective anti-British campaign. This contributed positively to the building up of a well-knit Congress organization in Midnapur, far removed from Calcutta, the nerve centre of the pre-1947 Bengal politics. So, what became a gigantic movement in 1942 was the result of sincere efforts of Congress volunteers since the beginning of the twentieth century. Not only was the movement remarkable as an instance of successful political mobilization; the 1942 rebellion in Midnapur was perhaps a rare example of active mass involvement which sustained the campaign despite severe British torture—long after the Congress had anticipated. The movement did not succumb to the British counter attack, and was withdrawn only in response to a call from the Mahatma.

NOTES

1 For details, see chapter 1.

2 IOR, R/3/1/358, District Magistrate's instruction to the Sub Divisional Officer, Contai, 27 March 1942.

3 IOR, R/3/1/358 District Magistrate's order, 7 May 1942.

4 Satish Samanta *et al. August Revolution and Two Years' National Government in Midnapur,* Orient Book Co., Calcutta, 1946, p. 7.

5 Paul Greenough, *Prosperity and Misery in Modern Bengal: The famine of 1943-44,* OUP, New York, 1982, p. 89.

6 IOR, L/R/5/297, History of the War Transport Department, p. 42, quoted in I. Kamtekar, *The End of the Colonial State*, unpublished Ph.D. dissertation, University of Cambridge, 1988, p. 34. The figures may not be accurate as Paul Greenough mentions that '66,500 boats were removed from use'. See Paul Greenough, *Prosperity and Misery*, p. 89.

7 The compensation offered was very low: it varied between 8 annas (half a Rupee) and Rs. 10/-. See, Satish Samanta *et al. August Revolution*, p. 8.

8 *Ibid.*

9 In his address to the Bengal Legislative Assembly, on 15 February 1943, Shyama Prasad Mookherjee, a member of the ruling Fazlul Haq ministry, described the plight of the district following the adoption of the denial policy. '. . . nearly 10,000 bicycles were taken away from [the district] and a large number of boats were asked to be surrendered within a very short time and quite a few hundreds were forcibly destroyed by the local authorities because they were not surrendered within the prescribed time. . . . So far as Midnapur was concerned the policy of forcible removal of boats and other conveyance especially bicycles caused severe dislocation in its economy'. See Bengal Legislative Assembly debates, Calcutta, 1943

10 IOR, Eur. D 911/5, Pinnell Papers, Memoirs. (L. G. Pinnell, ICS, Director of Civil Supplies, Bengal, 1942-3 was in charge of boat denial policy in Chittagong).

11 Interview with Gopinandan Goswami (Mahisadal), 15 December 1985 and Ramesh Chandra Kar (Tamluk), 16 December 1985.

12 For details, see my *Subhas Chandra Bose and Middle Class Radicalism*, chapter IV.

13 Interview with Sushil Dhara (Mahisadal), 15 December 1985.

14 The CPI opposed the Quit India Movement which crippled the anti-fascist campaign by challenging the British. See chapter 1, pp. 26-8.

15 WBSA, Home-Poll, 235/42 (1-8), District Magistrate to the Chief Secretary, Bengal, 7 July 1942.

16 *Ibid.,* S. G. Taylor, Inspector General of the Intelligence Bureau, Bengal to the District Magistrate, Midnapur, 18 July 1942.

17 IOR, R/3/1/293, a note by D. A. Brayden, Deputy Inspector General of Police, Bengal, 15 July 1942.

18 IOR, R/3/2/36, M. M. Basu, Additional District Magistrate, Midnapur to J.S. Blair, Chief Secretary, Bengal, 19 July 1942. Basu reporting on series of meetings just before the Quit India Movement was launched sought the Government of Bengal's permission to arrest Pulin Sen for instigating tension in the district.

19 WBSA, Home-Poll 280/42 (collection 2), Superintendent of Police, Midnapur to the Chief Secretary, Bengal, 18 June 1942.

20 Interview with Basantakumar Das, Contai, 16 December 1985. In his *Medinipure Swadhinata Ganasangram* (Bengali), Ajambari, Midnapur, 1975, Das elaborated this point.

21 *Ibid.*

22 WBSA, Home-Poll 235/42 (1-8), District Magistrate, Midnapur to J. S. Blair, Chief Secretary, Bengal, 7 July 1942.

23 IOR, R/3/1/293, Brayden, Deputy Inspector General of Police to the Chief Secretary, Bengal, 16 July 1942.

24 IOR, R/3/2/36, M. M. Basu, Additional District Magistrate, Midnapur to the Chief Secretary, Bengal, 23 August 1942. In his letter to the Chief Secretary, Basu mentioned that there were as many as 28 meetings, organised and addressed by the students within a span of just 12 days.

25 Interview with Billapada Jana of Sutahata, 16 December 1985.

26 See chapter 2 especially the section on revolutionary terrorism in Midnapur. Also significant was the Chechua hat incident in which the revolutionary terrorists participated in a direct battle with the British police.

27 Apart from Pulin Sen, who came from Calcutta, the rest belonged to Midnapur.

28 Sushil Dhara, *Prabaha* (Bengali), p. 113.

29 Interview with Sushi Dhara, Mahisadal, 15 December 1985.

30 Interview with Gopinandan Goswami, Mahisadal, 15 December 1985.

31 IOR, R/3/1/358, intercepted monthly report of the struggle for independence in Bengal, published by the council of action, BPCC, August-September 1942.

32 IOR, R/3/1/358, District Officer's chronicle, p. 17. In this official report it was thus mentioned, 'with students' intervention, the Forward Bloc and the orthodox Congress closed their ranks and agreed to work together for making the movement a success'.

33 IOR, R/3/1/358, intercepted BPCC monthly report, August-September 1942.

34 Basantakumar Das, *A Short History of August Movement in Contai Sub-division*, Contai, 1975, p. 18.

35 Interview with Sushil Dhara, Mahisadal, 15 December 1985. In his report to the Chief Secretary, Bengal, the Sub-divisional Officer, Contai expressed anxiety in view of the merger between Forward Bloc and Congress. See, WBSA, Home-Poll 235/42 (1-2), Sub-divisional Officer to the Chief Secretary, Bengal, 19 August 1942.

36 NMML, Tamralipta Itihas Committee Papers (TICP hereafter), Congress

appeal (unsigned), 11 August 1942.

37 IOR, R/3/2/36, District Magistrate to the Additional Secretary, Home Department, Bengal, 19 August 1942.

38 NMML, TICP, resolution of the meeting, held at Contai on 17 August 1942, signed by Bhupal Panda.

39 Interview with Rashbehari Pal of Contai, 18 December 1985; Sushil Dhara viewed this assumption as 'illogical' since Mahishyas were primarily an agricultural caste and the Congress by championing their demands, actually advanced 'the peasant cause'. Though it is difficult to accept Dhara's argument the message had an electrifying effect and the AIKS was divided and a majority of its members joined the movement.

40 It is difficult to ascertain the date of the meeting as it was not mentioned in the documents; the interviewees gave conflicting dates which fall in the third week of August.

41 Interview with Banshidhar Samanta, Contai and Rashbehari Pal, Contai, 18 December 1985.

42 Interview with Prahlad Pramanik, the Propaganda Minister in the Provisional Government, Calcutta, 21 December 1985.

43 Interview with Rabindranath Mitra, Tamluk, 16 December 1985.

44 IOR, R/3/2/36, District Magistrate to the Additional Secretary, Home Department, Bengal, 19 August 1942.

45 *Ibid.*

46 See chapter 1 (pp. 26-9).

47 WBSA, Home-Poll 235/42, John Herbert, Bengal Governor to Linthgow, the Viceroy, 25 August 1942.

48 Interview with Sushil Dhara, 15 December 1985.

49 IOR, R/3/2/36, N. M. Khan to the Additional Secretary, Home Department, Government of Bengal, 28 August 1942.

50 IOR, R/3/2/47, D. A. Brayden' note, 9 September 1942.

51 *The Census of India*, 1941, Bengal, Vol. IV, Government of India Press, Simla, 1942, p. 77-8. Out of 31,90,647, there were only 24,65,59 Muslims. Apart from Muslims, the following table shows the ratio of other demographically preponderant communities in the district:

Sub Division	*Total Population*	*Hindus*	*Muslims*	*Tribes*
Sadar	96,505	78.01%	8.93%	12.24%
Jhargram	4,26,244	69.09%	1.29%	29.53%
Ghatal	2,94,660	92.49%	5.37%	2.12%
Tamluk	7,53,152	86.75%	12.76%	0.45%
Contai	7,56,085	94.21%	5.72%	0.05%
TOTAL	3,190,647	84.05%	7.72%	7.94%

Note: Sadar: thirteen police stations (Midnapur, Kharagpur, Kharagpur town, Salbani, Keshpur, Debra, Sabang, Pingla, Narayangarh, Keshary, Garbetta, Danton, Mohanpur); *Jhargram*: five police stations (Gopiballavpur, Jhargram, Nayagram, Jambani, Binpur); *Ghatal*: three police stations (Ghatal, Daspur, Chandrakona); *Tamluk*: six police stations (Tamluk, Moyna, Sutahata, Panskura, Nandigram, Mahisadal); and *Contai*: six police stations (Khejuri, Contai, Ramnagar, Bhagwanpur, Egra, Potashpur).

Source: Prepared from *The Census of India*, 1941, Bengal, Vol. IV, Government of India Press, Simla, 1942, pp. 77-8.

52 NMML, AICC P5/1939, defiance and insubordination of the Executive Council, BPCC.

53 Only 264 out of 58,863 were Muslims. So, in absolute numbers, there was an increase between 1939 and 1942; in relative terms, however, a decline (from 0.49 per cent to 0.44 per cent) was noticed.

54 See the table in page 137.

55 NMML, AICC G2/1942: By 1942, only 3 per cent of the Congress members were Muslims. On the whole, there was a staggering decline of 4 per cent of Muslim members between 1939 and 1942.

56 For details, see Joya Chatterjee, *Class, Culture and Conflict: the Second Partition of Bengal, 1937-47,* unpublished Ph.D. dissertation, University of Cambridge, 1990.

57 IOR, R/3/2/38, intercepted BPCC monthly report of the struggle for independence in Bengal, August-September 1942.

58 WBSA, Home-Poll 616/42 (A). In the Commissioners' conference, held on 23 November 1942, the Burdwan Commissioner underlined the role of 'a lenient' district administration in the past in encouraging such a gigantic Congress movement.

59 IOR, R/3/2/36, A. Gordon to J. S. Blair, Chief Secretary, Bengal, 11 February 1943.

60 *Ibid.*, S. G. Taylor, Deputy Inspector General of Police to A. Gordon, Inspector General of Police, Bengal, 2 November 1942.

61 In his letter to the Commissioner of Burdwan division, N. M. Khan, the Midnapur District Magistrate reported that the movement had assumed devastating proportions in all the police stations of Contai and Tamluk subdivisions. There were five police stations in Contai: (1) Potashpur, (2) Contai, (3) Khedgree, (4) Egra, (5) Bhagwanpur; six police stations were in Tamluk: (1) Tamluk, (2) Mahisadal, (3) Nandigram, (4) Moyna, (5) Panskura, (6) Sutahata. Apart from these areas, the Congress rebellion had a significant impact in five police stations in the Sadar subdivisions. See IOR, R/3/2/36, N. M. Khan to the Commissioner, Burdwan division, 23 November 1942.

62 The District Magistrate thus wrote, 'there are no good roads in [these] subdivisions and the country side is mostly under water. Some of the thana Headquarters are practically cut off from the subdivisional

Headquarters'. See IOR, R/3/2/36, N. M. Khan to the Additional Secretary, Home Department, Bengal, 30 September 1942.

63 IOR, R/3/2/36, N. M. Khan to Commissioner, Burdwan division, 5 October 1942.

64 IOR, R/3/2/36, M. M. Basu, Additional District Magistrate, Midnapur, to the Additional Secretary, Home Department, Bengal, 3 September 1942.

65 *Ibid.*, Taylor, the Deputy Inspector General of Police to Gordon, Inspector General of Police, 5 October 1942.

66 NMML, TICP, *Nandigram Bulletin,* 19 October 1942; 27 November 1942 and 30 November 1942.

67 *ABP,* 24 October 1942 and *Anandabazar Patrika*, 27 October 1942.

68 IOR, R/3/2/36, Additional Secretary, Home Department, Bengal to the District Magistrate, 3 November 1942.

69 IOR, R/3/1/358, District Officer's chronicle, Government of Bengal, Calcutta, December 1943, pp. 16-17.

70 The government indifference to the Congress activities was interpreted 'by the villagers as a sign of weakness on the part of the Government'. See IOR, R/3/1/358, District Officer's chronicle, p. 18.

71 IOR, R/3/1/358, District Officer's chronicle, p. 18.

72 Interview with Balailal Das Mahapatra, Contai, 18 December 1985.

73 IOR, R/3/2/36, N. M. Khan to the Commissioner, Burdwan division, 10 September 1942.

74 *Ibid,*. Unlike the earlier campaigns, the Congress rebels in the Quit India Movement threw bombs against the police on several occasions; they prepared hand bombs with explosive substances with the assistance of specialists from Calcutta. Interview with Sushil Dhara, 15 December 1985.

75 IOR, R/3/1/358, District Officer's chronicle, p. 17.

76 IOR, R/3/2/36, Khan to the Chief Secretary, Bengal, 27 September 1942. Unhappy with Khan's remark, his colleague, J. M. Bell, District Magistrate, Burdwan (1942-4) stated, 'whatever may have been the truth of the situation, it is certain that this is not the kind of soothing and placatory remark that district officers are expected to send in to the secretariat, and that it damaged the District Magistrate's reputation with certain ministers whose party affiliations connected them with the groups that were, at any rate, indirectly responsible for the disorder'. See CSAS, J. M. G. Bell Memoirs, pp. 4-5.

77 IOR, R/3/2/55, a report of D. A. Brayden (of the Intelligence Bureau), 11 March 1944.

78 Shyama Prasad Mookherjee's speech in the Bengal Legislative Assembly before his resignation on 12 February 1943. See Bengal Legislative Assembly debate, Calcutta, 1943.

79 Although the Midnapur rebels agreed to stop their activities in response to Gandhi's appeal of 8 August 1944 it took more than six weeks for the movement to withdraw completely since the nationalists found it improper to discontinue all of a sudden when there were pending cases in the

Jatiya Sarkar's courts and other unattended but urgent tasks. So, it was decided in an emergency meeting of the *sarvadhinayak* and other thana *adhinayaks* that the Sarkar would continue till 29 September 1944. See Sushil Dhara, *Prabaha*, p. 176.

80 IOR, R/3/2/36, N. M. Khan to the Additional Secretary, Bengal, 30 September 1942.

81 *Ibid.*, N. M. Khan to the Commissioner, Burdwan Division, 3 October 1942.

82 The following was the distribution of troops in the district:

Contai	two platoon troops
Khejuri	two platoon troops
Ramnagar	two platoon troops
Patashpur	two platoon troops
Egra	one platoon troops
Bhagwanpur	two platoon troops

Source: IOR, R/3/2/36, S. G. Taylor, Deputy Inspector General of Bengal Police to A. Gordon, Inspector General of Bengal Police, 5 October 1942.

83 Hitesranjan Sanyal, 'Dakshin-Paschim Banglay Jatiatabadi Andolon', *Chaturanga*, Calcutta, 38, 1, 1976, 38, 3, 1977 and 39, 1, 1977; 'Congress Movements in the Villages of Eastern Midnapur, 1921-31' in A. Thorner *et al.*, *Asia du sud: traditions et changements,* Paris, Editions du Centre de la Recherche Scientific, 1979, pp. 169-78.

84 IOR, R/3/2/36, M. M. Basu to J. S. Blair, the Chief Secretary, Bengal, 2 October 1942.

85 IOR, R/3/2/36, M. M. Basu, Additional District Magistrate, Midnapur, to J. S. Blair, Chief Secretary, Bengal, 2 October 1942.

86 Interview with Sushil Dhara, Mahisadal, 16 December 1985; interview with Gopinandan Goswami, Mahisadal, 15 December 1942. For details of the preparation for the Quit India Movement, see Satish Samanta, *Sarvadhinayak* (Bengali) Midnapur, 1982, pp. 18-26 and Gopinandan Goswami, *Medinepure Shahid Parichay* (Bengali), Midnapur, 1977.

87 IOR, R/3/2/36, N. M. Khan to the Additional Secretary, Home Department, Bengal, 30 September 1942.

88 IOR, R/3/2/44, John Herbert to Linlithgow, 8 October 1942.

89 IOR, R/3/2/36, Express letter of N.M. Khan to the Commissioner, Burdwan division, 10 October 1942.

90 *Ibid.*, N. M. Khan to the Additional Secretary, Home Department, Bengal, 30 September 1942.

91 *Ibid.*, S. G. Taylor, Deputy Inspector General of Bengal Police to A.Gordon, Inspector General of Bengal Police, 29 September 1942.

92 IOR, R/3/2/36, N. M. Khan's daily report to the Commissioner, Burdwan division, 4 February 1943.

93 *Amrita Bazar Patrika,* 18 July 1943 and *Anandabazar Patrika,* 9 September 1943.

94 IOR, MSS. Eur. F. 161, 5/4, Indian Police collection, S. G. Taylor memoirs (TSS), pp. 3-4.

95 IOR, R/3/2/36, District Magistrate's daily report, 11 October 1942.

96 *Ibid.,* N. M. Khan to the Commissioner, Burdwan division, 13 October 1942.

97 *Ibid.,* A. Gordon to J. C. Irwin, Personal Secretary to the Bengal Governor, 11 November 1942.

98 IOR, R/3/1/358, District Officer's chronicle, p. 20.

99 IOR, R/3/2/36, the daily report (no, 72) of J. E. Adams, Additional Superintendent of Police, Midnapur, 13 November 1942.

100 *Ibid.,* M. M. Basu to the Commissioner, Burdwan division, 30 November 1942.

101 IOR, L/I/1/650/442, According to an official estimate, the damage was 'devastating'. Apart from human casualty, '68,193 heads of cattle had perished or washed away, 1,10,346 houses had collapsed and 76,958 houses were partially damaged. Two steamers, several launches and a large number of boats had capsized. Almost all district board and local board roads were damaged beyond repair and 110 miles of embankment were washed away. 50 percent of the standing crops on 21,511,49 acres of land were damaged'. A report by W. A. Shaikh, Sub-divisional Officer, Tamluk on *Cyclone and Tidal Wave of October 1942*, dated 30 September 1942.

102 IOR, R/3/2/36, N. M. Khan to the Commissioner, Burdwan division, 28 October 1942.

103 *Ibid.,* N. M. Khan to J. S. Blair, Chief Secretary, Bengal, 19 October 1942.

104 *Ibid.,* S. G. Taylor, Deputy Inspector General of Bengal Police to A.Gordon, Inspector General of Bengal Police, 27 October 1942.

105 *Ibid.*

106 *Ibid.*

107 In his letter to the Bengal Governor, A. Gordon, the Inspector General of Bengal Police described in detail the relief operation, to be undertaken in the cyclone-hit areas:

1. Affected areas to be divided into regions; each unit to consist of 2 unions in charge of a selected officer. If necessary, the unit area may have to be reduced further. 2. Nature of relief to be given: (*a*) food (*b*) medicine (*c*) drinking water (*d*) construction of huts (*e*) supply of cattle seeds and agricultural implements (*f*) clothes and (*g*) test relief. 3. Relief should be without any discrimination. 4. Non-official cooperation to be sought for and facilities given for forming relief committees of a representative character. 5. Relaxation of denial policy under suitable conditions regarding use of buses, boats and cycles, increased facilities for transport. 6. Facilities should be given to all persons irrespective of political bias if they express their willingness to devote their time and

energy for relief work and not to participate in a subversive movement. 7. In no circumstances, should anything be done to foment communal tension and one community instigated to act against another. See, IOR, R/3/2/36, A. Gordon to the Governor, Bengal, 1 December 1942.

108 IOR, R/3/1/358, District Officer's chronicle, p. 26.

109 IOR, MSS. Eur. F. 125/42, John Herbert, the Bengal Governor to Linlithgow, the Viceroy, 22 October 1942.

110 IOR, MSS. Eur. F. 125/145, Linlithgow Papers, Quarterly Survey of Political Situation in Bengal (1 August-31 October 1942).

111 For details, see later.

112 IOR, R/3/1/358, District Officer's chronicle, pp. 30-1.

113 Partha Chatterjee, 'spontaneity and organization in peasant movements in Bengal, 1920-47', in *Political violence,* collected seminar papers no. 30, Institute of Commonwealth Studies, University of London, 1987, p. 42.

114 Interview with Sushil Dhara, 15 December 1985.

115 Apart from the interviews, the section below draws upon the following books: Satish Samanta, *Sarvadhinayak*, pp. 36-42; Satish Samanta *et al. August Revolution and two years of national government in Midnapur*, Vol. I, Orient Book Co., Calcutta, 1946, pp. 33-40. *Biplabi*, the official journal of the provisional government, also has details of its operation which has been referred to; official sources, wherever available have also been tapped to build up the argument.

116 Interview with Ramesh Kar, Tamluk, 16 December 1985.

117 It was declared that 'this national government will eventually form a part of the Independent Federal State of India and will introduce a fully democratic administration in future; but due to the present abnormal conditions, all powers and responsibilities of the Government have been vested in a Sarvadhinayak [dictator]'. NMML, TICP, Congress declaration, 17 December 1942.

118 IOR, L/PJ/5/150, J. S. Blair, Chief Secretary's report for the second half of December 1942.

119 Sushil Dhara, 'Ouponibeshikatar Biruddhe Samantaral Sarkar' (Bengali), *Purbadri*, Tamluk, annual number, 1988, pp. 27-8.

120 For details, see my 'Subhas Chandra Bose, Indian National Army and the Axis Strategy, 1941-44', *Modern Asian Studies,* Cambridge (forthcoming)

121 Satish Samanta, *Sarvadhinayak*, p. 37; Sushil Dhara, *Prabaha*, p. 172.

122 IOR, R/3/2/36, S. G. Taylor to A. Gordon, 27 October 1942.

123 *Ibid.*,

124 IOR, R/3/2/36, J. S. Blair to the District Magistrate, 25 October 1942.

125 *Ibid.*, M. M. Basu, Additional District Magistrate to Commissioner, Burdwan division, 7 December 1942.

126 *Ibid.*, N. M. Khan to the Commissioner, Burdwan division, 2 January 1943. He did not allow the Marwari Relief Society to work because of its alleged pro-Congress sympathy. Confiscating the rice and other relief

materials, brought to the district, the District Magistrate also arrested the members of Society which was widely publicised in the Calcutta-based press as an example of British brutality. *ABP*, 18 January 1943; *Swadhinata,* 15 December 1942.

127 NMML, TICP, Congress Proclamation, 17 December 1942.

128 Satish Samanta was the first sarvadhinayak, followed by Ajoy Mookherjee, Satish Sahoo and Baradakanta Kuiti. The procedure of appointing a sarvadhinayak was as follows: with the arrest of the sarvadhinayak, a successor was nominated by the thana adhinayaks after consultation among themselves.

129 NMML, TICP, Congress proclamation, 17 December 1942.

130 *Ibid.*, a review of the Jatiya Sarkar courts, 29 September 1944.

131 IOR, R/3/2/36, Khan to the Commissioner, Burdwan division, 3 January 1943.

132 IOR, L/PJ/5/151, FR (2), June 1944, C. William's, (the Chief Secretary, Bengal) report.

133 Sushil Dhara, *Prabaha,* p. 176, Interview with Ramesh Kar, Tamluk, Sushil Dhara and Gopinandan Goswami, Mahisadal, 15 and 16 December 1985.

134 Sushil Dhara, *Prabaha*, p. 118.

135 As narrated in Sushil Dhara's *Prabaha,* pp. 139-40.

136 NMML, TICP, a note by Bhutnath Samanta who also acted as a Judge in the provisional government at Tamluk, *no date.*

137 Sushil Dhara and Gopinandan Goswami however declined to accept the figure given by Samanta arguing that due to security reasons, it was decided to conceal the names of the Bandi Senas. Interview with Sushil Dhara and Gopinandan Goswami, Mahisadal, 15 and 16 December 1985.

138 Interview with Sushil Dhara, 15 December 1985.

139 IOR, R/3/2/36, a report by M. M. Sanyal, Additional Superintendent of Police, Intelligence Branch, 20 December 1942.

140 IOR, R/3/2/36, the daily report of J. E. Adams, Additional Superintendent of Police, Midnapur, (no. 82), 23 March 1942.

141 It is difficult to estimate the amount of money, the provisional government had possessed given the lack of evidence. Sushil Dhara however mentioned the way, the funds were drawn. Apart from voluntary subscription, collected in village *hats,* money was raised by imposing fines on those alleged to be British informers. Most often, the convicts deposited the fines for fear of retaliation. In the aftermath of the cyclone, the rich in the district donated money and food stuffs liberally to the Mahendra Relief Committee which earned fame for being objective in distributing relief. See, Sushil Dhara, *Prabaha*, pp. 141-2. Amalesh Tripathy (who was kidnapped and later released on payment of ransom because his father's alleged role as a British agent) corroborated Dhara's description. See his,

Swadhinate Sangrame Bharatiya Congress, pp. 317-18.

142 A. K. Fazlul Haq's speech in the Bengal Legislative Assembly on 15 February 1943. See Bengal Legislative Assembly Debates, Calcutta, 1943.

143 NMML, AICC G 86/1930, Contai Civil Disobedience report gives a detail account of women participation in these movements.

144 The table below shows the strength of the Bhagini Sena in numerical terms which cannot be confirmed due to the paucity of other sources.

Sub-divisions	*1942**	*1943*	*1944*
Contai	887	603	607
Tamluk	1119	705	751
TOTAL	2006	1308	1358

*A large number of women were recruited in the Sena on eve of the 29 September thana attack.

Source: NMML, Tamralipta Itihas Committee Papers, file no. 11, the composition of Bhagini Sena.

145 *Biplabi*, 11 October 1942.

146 Interview with Charushila Jana who was actively associated with Bhagini Sena, Sutahata, 16 December 1985.

147 This paragraph draws upon interviews with Sushil Dhara, Gopinandan Goswami and Kumudini Dakua of Mahisadal, 15 and 16 December 1985 and NMML, TICP file numbers 11, 17 and 19.

148 Mahishya herself, Kumudini Dakua who was politically baptised during the open rebellion, played a crucial role in mobilizing women in Midnapur.

149 Interview with Kumudini Dakua, Mahisadal, 15 December 1985.

150 Actively associated with revolutionary activities in Bengal and Maharashtra, they, along with their male colleagues, took a significant part in anti-British Campaign.

151 Apart from Gandhi's wife, Kasturba Gandhi, Naidu, Patel and Nayer who became active in the nationalist politics since the 1930 Salt Satyagraha, rose to prominence in the Quit India Movement.

152 Thus women are mobilized within boundaries laid down by men. The history, articulated in such a way, is a contributive history. See, for details, Kumari Jayawardene, *Feminism and Nationalism in the Third World,* Zed Books, London, 1986, pp. 260-1.

153 The women however gained from the alliance with freedom struggle in that nationalist political activities radicalized them into expressing their own grievances and defused male opposition to the cause, but the nationalist also limited the women's movement in as much as they kept control over the women's activity and could not be relied upon to support the women's demands when male privileges was under threat. For details

of this argument, see Joana Liddle and Roma Joshi, *Daughters of Independence: gender, caste and class in India*, Kali for Women, New Delhi, 1986, pp. 34-8.

154 Partha Chatterjee, *The Nation and its Fragments: Colonial and Post Colonial History*, OUP, Delhi, 1994, p. 137. Chatterjee elaborates the argument with reference to Indian examples. See, for details, chapters VI and VII (pp. 116-57). In her study of the women workers in Bengal's jute industries, Samita Sen has shown how the women workers organized themselves in trade unions championing principally issues other than those concerning gender though women constituted a bulk of the working force. Despite their marginality in organized working class politics, Sen argues, jute mill women have earned and sustained a reputation for militancy. But the expression of their militancy was more in 'the politics of confrontation' rather than in 'organized resistance' on economic and gender issues. See her *Women Workers in the Bengal Jute Industry, 1890-1940: Migration, Motherhood and Militancy*, unpublished Ph.D. dissertation, University of Cambridge, 1992, chapter VI (pp. 218-61).

155 R/3/2/36, a report by S. N. Mitra, Additional Superintendent of Police, Midnapur, 29 March 1943.

156 *Biplabi*, 2 October 1942.

157 *Ibid.*, 26 October 1942.

158 Amalesh Tripathy, *The Extremist Challenge*, Orient Longman, Bombay, 1967, p. 18.

159 *Biplabi*, 24 September 1942.

160 *Ibid.*, 19 February 1944.

161 *Ibid.*, 26 January 1943.

162 Interview with Ramesh Kar, Tamluk, 16 December 1985.

163 In his prayer meeting on 30 December 1945 in Mahisadal Gandhi referred to the subject: 'What you have done is heroic and glorious. However, you have deviated from the path of non-violence'. See *Ananda Bazar Patrika*, 31 December 1945.

164 *Biplabi*, 23 November 1942.

165 *Ibid.*, 24 September 1942.

166 *Ibid.*, 11 October 1942.

167 *Ibid.*, 6 November 1942.

168 *Ibid.*, 23 November 1942.

169 *Ibid.*, 11 October 1942.

170 *Ibid.*, 25 January 1943.

171 For details, see the section on women and the August revolution.

172 *Biplabi*, 2 October 1942.

173 *Ibid.*, 30 September and 2 October 1942.

174 Leaflets circulated in the district harped on this argument. See IOR, L/PJ/5/150, J. S. Blair's FR (1), August 1943.

175 For a general discussion of the Great Bengal Famine, 1943, see A. K. Sen,

Poverty and Famines: An Essay on Entitlement and Deprivation, Clarendon Press, Oxford, 1981 and Paul Greenough, *Prosperity and Misery in Modern Bengal,* OUP, New York,1982. The following section draws on these studies unless otherwise stated.

176 *The Famine Enquiry Commission Report*, p. 25.

177 CSAS, E. W. Holland Papers, Holland, ICS (1930-47) was the secretary, Public Health and Local Government, Bengal (1942-44), pp. 46-7. Confirming that the cessation of normal imports from Burma worsened the crisis, S. G. Taylor, the Private Secretary to the Bengal Governor wrote, 'there was indeed a genuine shortage of rice which is the staple food of the Bengalees. Bengal rice had always been exported to England and other European countries. To compensate for this, it was necessary to import rice from Burma to provide sufficient food for the inhabitants of Bengal. Owing to war, all imports from Burma ceased and when the local crop failed the position became worse'. See CSAS, S. G. Taylor Papers, Memoirs (TSS), p. 12.

178 A. K. Sen, *Poverty and Famines*, pp. 54-5.

179 CSAS, O. M. Martin Papers, Memoirs, p. 251.

180 B. M. Bhatia, *Famines in India: a study in some aspects of the economic history of India (1860-1945)*, Asia Publishing House, London, 1963, p. 321. Also, Arup Maharatna, 'The demography of the Bengal famine of 1943-44: a detailed study', *IESHR*, 31, 2, 1994, pp. 170-215.

181 IOR, Eur D. 911/5, Pinnell Papers, Reply to Questions; statement regarding the movement of rice and paddy from each district of Bengal.

182 Corroborating this allegation, Paul Greenough who has studied the Bengal famine in great length, thus argues, 'Because [the denial agents] were not officials, but employees of large grain firms, because they had been given almost unlimited funds from the exchequer to make purchases, and because their transactions were unsupervised and their accounts never audited, it seems more than likely that the popular suspicion of fraud and rapasity was correct'. See Paul Greenough, *Prosperity and Misery in Modern Bengal,* pp. 94-5.

183 IOR, MSS. Eur. F. 180/10, Memoirs of H. C. Gupta, ICS, Additional Secretary, Public Health and Local Government, Bengal, 1942-4, p. 22.

184 CSAS, S. G. Taylor Papers, Memoirs, p. 13.

185 CSAS, E. W. Holland Papers, Memoirs, p. 47.

186 CSAS, O. M. Martin Papers, Memoirs, p. 251.

187 W. H. J. Christie (of the Food Department) to Abell, 2 September 1943, in *TP,* Vol. IV, No. 95, pp. 117-19.

188 O. M. Martin, the relief Commissioner, Bengal wrote with anguish, 'this was a most unfortunate sequence when scarcity is caused by natural calamity one has to be prepared for a gradually increasing degree of scarcity and expenditure has to be increased in proportion to the increase in distress. But here the relief had been perhaps too generous to start with

and had then been too suddenly curtailed'. See CSAS, O. M. Martin Papers, Memoirs, p. 256.

189 IOR, MSS. Eur. F. 180/9a, Memoirs (TSS) of W. H. J. Christie, ICS, 1934-47, p. 14.

190 CSAS, O. M. Martin Papers, p. 257.

191 For a graphic description of the disastrous impact of famine on the villagers, the following Bengali novels are significant: *Asani Sanket* (by Bibhutibhusan Bandyopadhyay), *Manwantar* (by Tarasankar Bandyopadhyay), *Kaloghora* (by Saroj Roy Chowdhury), *Angar* (by Prabodh Sanyal), *Bahu Galpa* (by Manik Bandyopadhyay); the poems, mentioned below also capture the agony of the famine victims: Janmastami and Padadhawni (by Bishnu Dey), Bivinna Chorus and Timir Hananer Gan (by Jibanananda Das), Anna Dao and Sandip (by Amiya Chakraborti), Poromati and Kranti (by Samar Sen), Swagata (by Subhas Mukhopadhyay); and a play *Navanna* (by the left-influenced Indian Peoples' Theatre Group). For an eye-witness account of the famine, see CSAS, J. Mottram Papers, especially his memoirs (TSS.). Mottram took part in relief operation. Wavell, the Viceroy characterized the Bengal famine as 'one of the greatest disasters that has befallen any people under the British rule'. See IOR, R/3/2/49, Wavell to the Secretary of State, 9 February 1944.

192 CSAS, O. M. Martin Papers, Memoirs, p. 251.

193 *Ibid.*, p. 260. The malaria epidemic caused maximum number of deaths in Bengal in 1943 as the following table shows:

DEATHS DUE TO THE EPIDEMICS, 1943.

Months Deaths	*Total*	*Malaria*	*Cholera*	*Small Pox*
July	100,006	44,046 (44.04%) *	939(0.93%)	5911 (5.91%)
August	105,046	43,536 (41.44%)	837 (0.79%)	2519 (2.39%)
September	106,373	50,824 (47.77%)	924 (0.86%)	1348 (1.26%)
October	123,007	62,515 (50.82%)	1401 (1.31%)	893 (0.72%)
November	144,259	75,216 (52.13%)	2700 (1.87%)	1137 (0.78%)
December	178,231	101,103 (56.72%)	3018 (1.69%)	1636 (0.91%)

*Figures in the parenthesis show the percentage in relation to the total number of deaths.

Note: Deaths of cholera were highest in November and December; small pox in July and August, while malarea continued to be severe throughout 1943 and later, causing maximum number of deaths in December. Thus writes A. K. Sen, 'The starvation of the famine had given way to the epidemic phase.' See, A. K. Sen, *Poverty and Famine*, p. 203.

Source: Adapted from the table in IOR, L/PJ/5/152, Casey, the Bengal Governor to Wavell, Viceroy, 2 January 1946.

194 According to the Famine Enquiry Commission, 1.5 million people died in the 1943-4 famine. See the *famine enquiry commission report*, pp. 109-10. The figure seems to be an underestimate as M.O. Carter, the Chittagong District Collector (1940-7) mentions in his memoirs, 'I do not believe that even today there exists an accurate estimate of the number of people who died as the result of famine in Bengal. See CSAS, M.O. Carter Papers, Memoirs, p. 18. W. R. Aykroyd, a member of Famine Enquiry Commission and also responsible for the estimation, too expressed doubt at the figures given in the report. In his view, 'I now think, it was an underestimate, especially in that it took little account of roadside deaths, but not as gross an underestimate as some critics of the Commission's report who preferred three to four million, declared it to be.' See W. R. Aykroyd, *The Conquest of Famine*, Chatto and Windus, London, 1974, p. 77.

195 *Biplabi*, 7 November 1943.

196 *Ibid.*, 15 May 1943.

197 *Ibid.*, 11 September 1942.

198 *Ibid.*, 15 May 1943.

199 *Ibid.*, 5 July 1943.

200 IOR, R/3/2/49, Government resolution on the food situation in Bengal, adopted in the Bengal Cabinet with the Chief Minister, Nazimuddin on the chair, 4 November 1943.

201 *Ibid.*

202 The opposition from the bureaucrats notwithstanding, Ispahani was tipped for the job by the Chief Minister himself who appeared impressed by his efficiency during the execution of the rice denial policy in 1941-2. See, CSAS, S. G. Taylor Papers, Memoirs, p. 15. Though Ispahani was favoured by Nazimuddin, the Viceroy, Linlithgow held him responsible for creating an artificial scarcity of rice in Bengal which led to the outbreak of famine in 1943. Linlithgow to Amery, 10 August 1943, in *TP*, Vol. IV, pp. 208-9.

203 NMML, TICP File No. 13, the provisional government's order of 7 November 1943. The order, issued in the name of Baradakanto Kuiti, the sarvadhinayak.

204 Even the pro-government *The Statesman* described the government measures to tackle the famine 'as belated'. See *The Statesman*, 8 May 1945.

205 A. K. Sen, *Poverty and Famines*, p. 63.

206 *Ibid.*, p. 76. Explaining the phenomenon in terms of a theory of entitlement, Sen argues that the famine in 1943 was not due to an absolute decline in food availability (FAD) but due to difference in entitlements to it.

207 *The Report on Bengal*, Government of India Press, Delhi, 1945, pp. 67-8. As the famine continued due largely to the government procrastination in undertaking relief operation on a priority basis, David Arnold labels it

as 'a political famine'. David Arnold, *Famine Social Crisis and Historical Change,* OUP, New Delhi, 1988, p. 97.

208 In its various editions, *Biplabi* narrated in detail the progress of the movement and the nature of police brutality in different provinces. Orissa (*Biplabi*, 27 September 1942), Gujrat and Maharastra (*Biplabi*, 30 May 1943), Frontier Province (*Biplabi*, 19 June 1943), Karnataka and Mysore (*Biplabi*, 7 July 1943).

209 *Biplabi,* 25 January 1943.

210 *Ibid.,* 25 January 1943.

211 *Ananda Bazar Patrika,* 30 December 1945.

212 The orthodox Gandhians however never approved the activities of the Congress rebels for 'having clung to violence so often'. After his release from jail, Manmatha Nath Das criticised the Jatiya Sarkar since it deviated from the basic principles of Gandhi's instructions, i.e. non-violence. Urging the Congress members to dissociate from the Jatiya Sarkar, Das strove to organise those opposing the rebels. He however failed because 'except one or two' a majority of them declined to support him. For the text of Das' letter, see IOR, R/3/1/352, T. Wickenden's report on *the Congress disturbances*, pp. 5-6.

213 IOR, R/3/2/36, Khan to John Blair, Chief Secretary, Bengal, 3 December 1942.

Conclusion

THE STUDY has two major components: first, it dwells on the rise and growth of nationalism in Midnapur where the Congress-led anti-British offensive struck deep roots between 1905 and 1944. Although the precise nature of opposition to the foreign rule varied over time the importance of the local leadership in Midnapur made local issues significant in political mobilization. Secondly, by focusing on the Quit India Movement, the study has also underlined the unique features of the open rebellion in which the participants adhered to violent action ignoring its incongruity with the basic tenets of Gandhi's instruction. Such a deviation never appeared serious presumably because a radical Congress became genuinely a political platform representing the multifaceted dimensions of the nationalist struggle. In other words, with Gandhi's arrival, the Congress base was expanded to incorporate hitherto peripheral social groups which often militated against the conservative character of the organization. The articulation of different ideological stands involved in this expansion enlarged the constituency of the national politics. By bringing the masses to the Congress fold, not only did Gandhi radically transform its nature, he also created a substantial space for other political views to evolve and thrive. So, the Congress that emerged in the 1940s, became an expression of various contradictory social forces constituting a united front against the alien state. Left with no alternative, the Congress accommodated radical demands seeking to do away with the structural impediments to social progress. Given the peculiar nature of the Congress which was a product of both the British constitutional initiatives and the mass struggles of the period, it is difficult to describe the Gandhi-led freedom struggle in a unilinear fashion.

This study is about Midnapur and its involvement in the nationalist politics in which Gandhi and his ideology of 'non-violence' generally reigned supreme. Apart from the role of the local Congress in organizing the masses for political action, colonial rule itself was a major factor that forced Indians to reflect on their political subjugation. The nationalist response was, in other words, the collective voice of a subject nation against the colonial rule. A shared context of colonial domination did not however mean that the nature of opposition would be the same everywhere. Here lay the importance of the social and cultural milieus of the participants and also the specificities of the context in shaping the pattern of anti-colonial intervention. Hence, of all Bengal districts, Midnapur continued to play a decisive role in the freedom struggle due primarily to its pronounced anti-imperial sentiments, articulated by the local leadership in movements against the British rule.

II

An attempt has been made in this work to demonstrate that the complexity of the nationalist movement can be gauged through an in-depth study of the localities. Of all the districts of Bengal, Midnapur both sustained the anti-British sentiments and translated them into movements against the colonial state. What inspired the people to participate in the nationalist campaign was the ideology of nationalism; the success of the local Congress however lay more particularly in its ability to nurture the nationalist spirit by attributing the local grievances to the presence of a foreign authority. The Non-Cooperation Movement thus became a campaign against the introduction of the Union Boards which not only meant an extra financial burden on the rural masses but was also a device to strengthen government control over the villages. Tax increase would certainly affect the majority, while the intrusion into the village administration through the Union Boards would erode the power of the upper strata over the internal affairs of the villages. On these two issues, the local Congress easily mobilized people, regardless of class, for the withdrawal of union boards.

The Congress success in the anti-Union Board agitation created a space for itself in Midnapur which largely accounts for its effectiveness as a political organization in the district. During the 1930-2 Civil Disobedience Movement, by selecting salt as the principal issue of the agitation, Gandhi built a broad political platform encompassing people from all strata since salt was a basic necessity of daily existence. In Midnapur, Civil Disobedience was undertaken through a violation of salt laws. Gradually, the movement acquired new dimensions in retaliation against British retaliation. As the Chechua hat incident shows, the Civil Disobedience campaign was no longer confined to 'non-violence' becoming, instead, a mass movement in which the well-publicized Congress instructions were often ignored. Other groups with different ideological persuasions also participated in the Civil Disobedience campaign unleashing a political process through which the constituency of nationalist politics was largely expanded. It is not therefore surprising that the campaign against the British was manifested in different forms, demonstrating probably the growing radicalization of the nationalist movement which, on a large number of occasions, hardly remained Gandhian.

What held the participants together were local issues, strategically nurtured to gain maximum mileage by relating them to imperialism. During the Non-Cooperation Movement, the introduction of the Union Boards was identified as an imperial design to ruin the rural masses; in the Civil Disobedience agitation, it was the imposition of the chowkidari tax that caused alarm. With the withdrawal of the Union Boards and chowkidari tax, the Congress rose as an alternative centre of power in the district. Although both the movements were launched by the Congress, the success in the anti-chowkidari tax campaign during the Civil Disobedience upsurge was attributed, as shown in Chapter 2, to the radical section within the Congress which often clung to violence to attain the goal. Such a deviation did not appear to be disastrous to the local Congress leadership as long as it was directed against the alien authority. So, the B.N. Sasmol-led Midnapur Congress conceded the no-rent campaign against the European-owned Midnapur Zamindari Company in 1932, but opposed vehemently the attempt to extend the same demand to other areas of the district. By declining to support the no-rent campaign as it would harm the landed interests the Midnapur Congress, despite being militant, fitted perfectly well into the Congress ethos.

Drawing principally upon anti-imperial sentiments, the 1942 Quit India Movement became probably the most effective campaign during the freedom struggle. Ideologically Gandhian, the open rebellion however manifested itself in forms which the Mahatma would never have approved. Various social groups, regardless of class, challenged the state despite severe consequences, bringing about a situation in which the British rule temporarily broke down. The success of the Quit India Movement lay, *inter alia,* in the Congress ability to build a united front against the British which was held responsible for dislocation in the rural society. The emergence of Mahishyas as a solid caste group also strengthened the nationalist intervention because Mahishyas, despite class differences among themselves, generally acted as a block in the anti-British campaign. By articulating the contradiction with the Raj as the principal one, the Mahishya-dominated Congress largely succeeded in containing radical tendencies, potentially harmful to the broad political platform. Not only did the leadership attribute local grievances to the foreign rule, it also translated them in a movement which struck at the foundation of the British power in the district. So, apart from social cohesion in caste terms, what brought the people initially to the nationalist movement was: loyalty to the Congress, sympathy with nationalism, antagonism to the police and the feeling that the collapse of the British rule was imminent.[1]

Anti-British sentiments were further consolidated in the wake of the 1943-4 famine in which the government failure to provide an adequate relief was interpreted as a deliberate design to make the people of Midnapur suffer because of their involvement in the freedom struggle. Politically defensible, such an argument was most effective too since besides non-official agencies, the Congress was all-pervasive in the district, especially in the worst-affected areas. With a well-entrenched organization, not only did the nationalists foil various attempts at exporting foodstuff outside the district, they also succeeded in distributing the relief materials most equitably. In popular perception, the Congress therefore emerged as a politically viable alternative in a context when the erosion of imperial legitimacy and popular anti-colonial unrest was making the Raj more dependent on its coercive apparatus. An extensive use of force by the local authority in 1942 was clearly suicidal in view of the growing discontent at the grassroots and consequently the breakdown of the informal network of support to the British. What therefore explains the alarming magnitude of the open rebellion was partly the Congress's success in translating the general popular discontent into a movement against the alien authority and partly the Congress's ability to project itself as an alternative to the British state.

III

The Congress success in sustaining and extending its base in Midnapur can largely be attributed to the peculiar land relations. Unlike other parts of Bengal where the permanent settlement had created the zamindars of 'high landlordism' Midnapur had, as was shown in Chapter 2, a few large zamindars, more than 3000 petty zamindars and a large contingent of tenure holding *ryots* varying in size and influence. Known as *jotedars,* these tenure holders held the key to rural power through their control of rent, credit and marketing operations; their power increased in the first two decades of the century through the Mahishya caste movement. As argued in Chapter 2, this movement inculcated a spirit of peasant pride among the Mahishyas and fostered a sense of fraternity tempered by caste and occupation. The political impact of the rise of Mahishyas as a homogeneous social group was profound and significant for the future Congress campaign against the alien state: it glossed over the real class differences in the countryside and instead developed a vertical peasant identity. Given the existent rural power structure in Midnapur, the caste movement further consolidated the *jotedar's* hold; and it also damaged the possibility of the rise of a political movement along class lines.

Although the *jotedars* had created a space for themselves in rural society, their political potential was not incorporated in the pre-1920 nationalist agitation principally because of the bhadralok hegemony. So, the Swadeshi campaign never provoked an effective movement in the district. Limited to a handful of Congressmen, both the 1905 anti-partition upsurge and the movement against the division of the district in 1915 never assumed serious proportions and it was thus possible for the District Collector to dismiss the Congress as merely 'a talking shop.'[2] In other words, the failure of the local Congress to mobilize the *jotedars,* the most powerful section within the indigenous power structure, largely accounts for a lukewarm nationalist response to the anti-British movement before the 1920-2 Non-Cooperation campaign.

The British constitutional initiatives however brought about decisive changes in rural society. With the expansion of the electorate following the adoption of the 1919 Government of India Act and the Bengal Village Self-Government Act, the right to vote was extended to the 'well-to-do cultivators' who were now constitutionally recognized as a significant section in rural society; with a numerical preponderance, they were a solid block of votes which could sway the balance of rural power in accordance with their predilections. The expansion of suffrage also corresponded with the arrival of Gandhi who radically transformed the nationalist politics by linking 'the masses' with this campaign against the British. By bringing 'new actors' on the political scene, not only did the Mahatma enlarge the constituency of the freedom struggle, he had also initiated a process whereby local issues figured significantly in the nationalist agenda. Thus, B.N. Sasmol successfully mobilized people against the introduction of the Union Boards in Midnapur which by increasing taxation affected the rural people adversely. The anticipated economic hardship as a result of new taxation was clearly attributed to the imperial power and the Sasmol-led local Congress could easily direct mass discontent against the foreign state. That the same Congress was not prepared to pursue a movement challenging the prevalent socio-economic structure in which the hegemony of the well-to-do-cultivators was not contested, was evident in its refusal to undertake a campaign against the Congress-minded local zamindars in the Jungle Mahal areas. Even at the cost of a split within the organization, not only did the Congress oppose agrarian radicalism, but also expelled those responsible for 'instigating the innocent tribals' to attack the zamindari property for fear of diluting the freedom struggle and to counter the threat to vested interests. Furthermore, since moral bonds of patronage were a principal mechanism of cohesion in rural society, there developed a symbiotic relationships between the wealthy and poor which largely contributed to the Congress strength.[3]

Between 1920 and 1944, the Congress played decisive roles in articulating anti-British sentiments because the Congress's political basis had been consolidated with the incorporation of a large section of tenure holders who articulated their anti-British role through participation in the institutions of colonial governance in the localities. The fact that these institutions lacked both resources and substantial power meant that the Congress despite being willing could not execute programmes benefiting the people. In other words, since the livelihood of the people was controlled by forces and powers beyond the reach of the district Congress, the local political activists could easily channellize the popular grievances against colonial power by highlighting its exploitative nature. By articulating the class interests of the broad range of tenure holders or *jotedars,* the Midnapur Congress postulated its own version of political struggle which, though militant vis-a-vis imperialism, opposed movements potentially harmful to the existing socio-economic order. This phenomenon accorded the Midnapur Congress a special characteristic which was well-articulated in its stance towards the 1928 Bengal Tenancy (Amendment) Act. All this also gave the Midnapur Congress a definite ideological orientation distinguishing from the dominant tendency within the Bengal Congress; such a feature largely accounts for its success in avoiding the highly personalized factionalism that crippled the Bengal Congress.[4] As a result, the local Congress based on rural property successfully conducted anti-British movements that displayed considerable militancy without correspondingly upsetting the existent pattern of class relationships in rural society. Interpreted thus, the Midnapur Congress did not deviate from the basic tenets of Gandhism or what the Congress stood for during the freedom struggle which while gradually expanding its political audience never allowed movements challenging the ideological hegemony of indigenous capital and the landed interests.

IV

The Gandhi of the 1942 Quit India Movement seemed to have paid less attention to the question of means especially in his passionate 'do or die' speech. Although the need for non-violence was reiterated, the famous 8 August resolution espoused the call for 'a mass struggle on the widest possible scale' under Gandhi's leadership with the instruction that if the Congress leadership was removed by arrest 'every man and woman who is participating in this movement must function for himself or herself.'[5] Apart from the resolution, Gandhi's statement urging the people to fight till death inspired them to resort to means other than *ahimsa* in the last battle against the Raj. In his public utterances too, the Mahatma appeared to have appreciated violence if circumstances so demanded. For instance, in a press interview, he exhorted, 'this clearly disciplined anarchy (in the shape of the British administration) should be removed at any cost and if as a result, there is a complete lawlessness, I would risk it'[6] On another occasion, he defended a general strike by arguing that 'if a general strike becomes a dire necessity, I shall not flinch'[7] thus undermining his own concept of trusteeship.

The open rebellion though assumed massive proportions waned quickly at the all-India level; it however continued unabated for almost two years in Midnapur where violence too was resorted to in the name of Gandhi. As shown in Chapter 3, the Congress volunteers drew upon Gandhi to justify violence as it meant a significant contribution to the cause of freedom. *Biplabi,* the Congress journal, declared that the Mahatma would have approved violence in the name of serving the motherland.[8] There are instances of the inflicting of death penalty on those who committed a heinous crime like raping the village women to terrorize the participants; though the Congress decision ran counter to Gandhi's *ahimsa,* it was nonetheless justified by drawing attention to his writings in which he was reported to have conceded violence for protecting the honour of women.[9]

Whatever the attainment of the Congress in the open rebellion, 'the location of the Mahatma image' within the existing pattern of popular beliefs and the way it informed direct action, was 'often at variance with the standard interpretation of the Congress creed'.[10] The events during the Quit India Movement demonstrate that on various occasions, Gandhi, the person, appeared insignificant in comparison with 'the image of Mahatma' which was constantly reworked in popular vision in a completely different way which neither Gandhi nor the Congress High Command would have approved. For instance, during the height of the

Quit India Movement, several images of Gandhi gained currency. To the people of Contai, the Mahatma, endowed with divine power, could never be killed; people believed that Gandhi was not 'hurt' even when the British police fired bullets at him. Gandhi could not be kept in jail since, according to a rumour, he, with his power, could escape the prison as soon as he wanted.[11] In Tamluk, the participants believed that 'if you uttered the name, Gandhi, before the British police they would lose the capacity to fire'.[12] Thus it was not merely coincidental that the slogan–*Gandhiji ki joy*–became very popular in the course of the movement. The British administration taking note of the tremendous influence of Gandhi in shaping the popular psyche seemed perplexed at the rapid dissemination of his ideas in remote areas of the district. What probably drew people to Gandhi's ideas was his image as 'a saviour' of the poverty-stricken masses. In a contemporary police report, it was mentioned that 'the real power of [Gandhi's] name is perhaps to be traced back to the ideal' that the Mahatma devoted his life to the cause of the poor Indians.[13] The Congress mobilization for the thana attacks on 29 September 1942 demonstrated the effectiveness of the image of Gandhi which significantly contributed to popularizing the August campaign at the grassroots. Behind its success thus lay the ability of the local Congress to meaningfully explain and translate Gandhi's agenda.

Although the movement was launched by the Congress, its success can be attributed largely to the role of a new group of political activists. As was shown in Chapter 3, with the arrest of the established district Congress leaders, the organization was controlled largely by men and women who rose to prominence only during the open rebellion.

So, there were several Gandhis–each being interpreted differently reflecting the priorities of the participants. Translating Gandhism in such a way as to gain maximum mileage, the local leaders articulated the political agenda by attributing the popular grievances to imperialism. Furthermore, the interpretation of Gandhi's ideas also varied in accordance with the preferences of the leadership involved in the mobilization for anti-British offensive. Thus, for instance, one type of the leadership exemplified in Swami Prajnananda in Bengal, Swami Darshanananda in Bihar or Baba Ramchandra in Pratapgarh, invested the Gandhian message with particularly strong religious overtones. The participation of such outsiders also points to the fact that the peasants still needed an outsider to organize themselves in a society going through a period of acute strain and tension due to peculiar circumstances. This argument, if pursued a litter further, is likely to identify significant gaps in the analyses of some of the early writings of the subaltern historians which in challenging the so-called elitist historiography tended to somewhat romanticize the revolutionary potential of the rural masses.

NOTES

1 In the popular perception, the open rebellion was predicated on a breakdown or the threat of breakdown of the incumbent regime's authority. The situation can be explained in accordance with Gramsci's formulation of 'the crisis of authority' where Gramsci argued, 'If the ruling class has lost its consensus, i.e. is no longer leading but only "dominant", exercising coercive force alone, this means precisely that . . . masses have become detached from their traditional ideologies, and no longer believe what they used to believe previously.' The crisis consists 'precisely in the fact that the old is dying and new cannot be born'. See, Quinton Hoare and G.N. Smith (translated and edited), *Selections from the Prison Notebooks of Antonio Gramsci,* Lawrence and Wishart, London, 1986, pp. 275-6.

2 WBSA, Home-Poll (A), report of Donald Weston, District Collector, Midnapur, 1 March 1908.

3 This symbiotic interaction was completely disrupted in the course of the 1943 Bengal famine when, as Paul Greenough writes, '[r]esource controlling males–landlords, cultivators, heads of the households–declared their inability to feed all those who habitually depended upon them for food and for protection from danger. Patterns of abandonment began to emerge, marked by snapping the moral and economic bonds upon which the rural society had hitherto been erected and leading inevitably to starvation, sickness and the death of million.' Paul Greenough, *Prosperity and Misery in Modern Bengal: The Bengal Famine, 1943-44,* OUP, New York, 1982, p. 138.

4 Jack Gallagher graphically portrays the nature of factional politics in Bengal during 1930-9. See his 'The Congress in Decline', *MAS,* 7, 3, 1973.

5 N. Mitra (ed), *The Indian Annual Register,* July-December 1942, Vol. II, p. 251.

6 Gandhi's interview of 16 May, 1942 in *TP,* Vol. 2, London, 1982, p. 96.

7 *Ibid.,* p. 388.

8 *Biplabi,* 9 July 1943.

9 *Ibid.,* 5 August 1943.

10 Shahid Amin, 'Gandhi as Mahatma: Gorakhpur District, Eastern Uttar Pradesh' in R. Guha (ed.), *Subaltern Studies,* Vol. III, OUP, Delhi, 1984, p. 2. While explaining the role of Gandhi in galvanizing the masses into action in the 1920-2 Non-Cooperation campaign Amin also argues that 'there was no single authorised version of the Mahatma to which [the

participants of the Non-Cooperation Movement] may be said to have subscribed in 1921. Indeed, their ideas about Gandhi's "orders" and "powers" were often at variance with those of the local Congress-Khilafat leadership and clashed with the basic tenets of Gandhism itself. The violence of Chauri Chaura was rooted in this paradox.' See Amin, 'Gandhi as Mahatma', p. 55.

11 Interview with Kumudini Dakua, Mahisadal, 16 December 1985.

12 Interview with Ramesh Kar, Tamluk, 17 December 1985.

13 IOR, R/3/2/36, S. J. Taylor to J. S. Blair, Chief Secretary, Bengal, 3 October 1942.

Glossary

adhinayak	commander
ahimsa	non-violence
Baidya	name of a caste associated with the medical profession
bati	a common household knife
bargadar	share-cropper
bhagchasis	share-cropper
bhagini sena	sisters' brigade
bhadralok	gentleman
caliph	ruler of Turkey and religious leader
chasa	peasant/cultivator
Chasi-mula	peasant-worker combination
Chitapavan Brahman	a type of Brahman in Maharastra
dafadar	village watchman
elaka	area
ganja	intoxicating substance
hartal	strike
Jatiya Sarkar	national government
jotedar	large landowner, holding rights of either intermediate tenure or mere tenancy, sometimes having tenants under him and often engaging in money-lending or grain trading
katari	a thick sickle-shaped knife
Kayastha	writer caste
khas mahals	government estate
kisan	peasant
krishak samitis	peasant organizations
madhyabitta sreni	middle class
madrassah	a school of Islamic learning
mahajan	money-lender
mantra	national pledge

maulana	a title given to a person respected for learning in Islamic theology
maulvi	a learned man in Islam
paikar	local merchant
panchayats	lowest unit of local government in rural areas, composed of a small number of villages
praja	tenant
raiyat or ryot	cultivator who holds lands from landlords subject to certain conditions
ryotwari	land revenue system under which assessments are made on individual holdings
samiti	organization
samya	equality
samyabada	eagalitarianism
samyabadi	one who believes in equality
shardh	Hindu rituals performed following death
swadeshi	indigenous
sikhshitya madhyabitta sreni	educated middle class
talims	wrestling clubs
taluk	a local administrative unit; a revenue subdivision of a district
thana	police station
sarvadhinayak	dictator
ulema	expert in Islamic training
vidyut bahini	lightening brigade
vishayi bhadralok	those having income from a profession

Select Bibliography

PRIVATE PAPERS

INDIA OFFICE RECORDS, LONDON

Anderson (Bengal Governor, 1932-37) Papers, MSS Eur. F 207 and MSS Eur. D 806.
Bell F. C (ICS, Bengal) Papers MSS Eur. F 180/8.
Christie W. H. J (ICS, Bengal) Papers MSS Eur. F 180/9.
Gupta H. C (ICS, Bengal) Papers MSS Eur. F 180/10.
Halifax (Viceroy of India) Papers, MSS Eur. C 152.
Linlithgow (Viceroy of India, 1936-43) Papers, MSS Eur. F 125.
Pinnell L. G. (ICS, Bengal) Papers, MSS Eur. D 911/5.
Templewood (Secretary of State for India, 1931-35) Papers, MSS Eur. E 240.
Willingdon (Governor-General of India, 1931-36) Papers, MSS Eur. F 93.
Brabourne (Bengal Governor, 1937-39) Papers, MSS Eur. F 97.
Zetland (Secretary of State for India, 1935-40), Papers, MSS Eur. D 609.
Reid (acting Bengal Governor, 1938-39) Papers, MSS Eur. E 278.

NEHRU MEMORIAL MUSEUM AND LIBRARY, NEW DELHI

All India Congress Committee Papers, 1920-47.
All India Hindu Mahasabha Papers, 1926-47.
All India Trade Union Congress Papers, 1928-47.
S. P. Mookherjee Papers.
Jawaharlal Nehru Papers.
B. C. Roy Papers.
M. N. Roy Papers.
N. R. Sarkar Papers.
Purshottamdas Thakurdas Papers.
Sahajanand Sarswati Papers.
Tamralipta Itihas Committee Papers.

CENTRE FOR SOUTH ASIAN STUDIES, CAMBRIDGE

Bell Papers.
Cumming Papers.
Donaldson Papers.

Ewing Papers.
Bayley Papers.
Benthall Papers.
Dash Papers.
Holland Papers.
Lloyd Jones Papers.
Ross Papers.
Martin Papers.
Carter Papers.
Hubback Papers.
Maxwell Papers.
Mottram Papers.
Stuart Papers.
Taylor Papers.
Tottenham Papers.
Wiles Papers.

NATIONAL ARCHIVES OF INDIA, NEW DELHI

V. J. Patel Papers.
Rajendra Prasad Papers.
Bholanath Roy Papers.
Wood Collection.

GOVERNMENT RECORDS

INDIA OFFICE LIBRARY, LONDON

Files of Bengal Governor's Secretariat, R/3/2.
Private Office Papers, L/PO.
Records of Information Department, L/I/1.
Records of Public and Judicial Department,L/PJ.
Records of War Department, L/WS.
Indian Police Collection, Mss Eur 161/20.

NATIONAL ARCHIVES OF INDIA

Records of Home Political (Confidential) Department, 1920-47.

WEST BENGAL STATE ARCHIVES, CALCUTTA

Records of Home Political (Confidential) Department, 1920-47.

BANGLADESH SECRETARIAT RECORD ROOM, DHAKA

Police Department 'B' Proceedings, 1921-45.
Home Political (Confidential) 'B' Proceedings, 1921-45.
Revenue Department 'B' Proceedings, 1921-45.

ORAL TRANSCRIPT

INDIA OFFICE LIBRARY

Claude Auchinleck (1904-47) Eur. T/3, Perceival Griffiths (1922-47) Eur. T/31, Philip Mason (1928-47) Eur. T/43, R. Mayne (1910-47) Eur. T/65, I. M. Stephens Eur. T/63, G. Laithwaite (1919-43) Eur. T/69, Paul Benthall Eur R/139.

NEHRU MEMORIAL MUSEUM AND LIBRARY

Satis Dasgupta, R. P. Dutt, S. M. Ghosh, Padam Kant Malviya, Bhupati Majumdar, Anil Baran Roy, Neillie Sengupta, Promode Sengupta.

CENTRE FOR SOUTH ASIAN STUDIES

D. N. Pai, I. Patel, D. Naik, P. B. Patwari, K. G. Prabhu, K. B. Lall, Usha Mehta, Anant Kanekar, K. A. Abbas, T. R. Deogirikan, D. R. Gole, Baburao Chavan.

PUBLISHED RECORDS

REPORTS

Sedition Committee (Rowlatt), 1918.
Calcutta University (Sadler) Commission, 1917-19.
Bengal Unemployment Enquiry (Meek) Committee, 1922-24.
Proceedings of All Parties Conferences, 1928.
Proceedings of the Bengal Legislative Council, 1928-44.
Bengal Provincial Banking Enquiry (De) Committee, 1929-30.
Royal (Whitley) Commission of Labour, 1929-31.
Indian Franchise (Lothian) Committee, 1931-32.
Bengal Jute Enquiry (Finlow) Committee, 1933.
Bengal Jute Enquiry (Fawcus) Committee, 1938-39.
Bengal Land Revenue (Floud) Commission, 1938-40.
Famine Enquiry (Woodhead) Commission, 1944-45.
Census of India, 1901, 1911, 1921, 1931, 1941 and 1951.
Census of Bengal, 1901, 1911, 1921, 1931, 1941 and 1951.
The Transfer of Power, Vols. 1, 2, 3, and 4.

NEWSPAPERS

Advance (English), Calcutta.
Amrita Bazar Patrika (English), Calcutta.
Ananda Bazar Patrika (Bengali), Calcutta.
Azad (Bengali), Calcutta.
Bengalee (English), Calcutta.
Dhaka Prakash (Bengali), Dhaka.

Forward (English), Calcutta.
Ganavani (Bengali), Calcutta.
Harijan (English), Delhi.
The Hindu (English), Madras.
Hindustan Times (English), Delhi.
Langal (Bengali), Calcutta.
The Mussalman (English), Calcutta.
Medini Bhandav (Bengali), Midnapur.
Nandigram Bulletin (Bengali), Midnapur.
Nihar (Bengali), Midnapur.
The Statesman (English), Calcutta.
Swadhinata (Bengali), Calcutta.
The Times (English), London.
The Times of India (English), Bombay.

UNPUBLISHED DOCTORAL THESES

Basu, Subho. 'Workers' Politics in Bengal, 1890-1929: Mill Towns, Strikes and Nationalist Agitations', University of Cambridge, 1994.

Bandopadhyay, Gitasree. 'Constraints in Bengal Politics, 1921-41: Gandhian Leadership', Univertsity of Calcutta, 1980.

Chakravarti, Hiren. 'Bengal Political Unrest, 1905-8 with special reference to terrorism', University of Oxford, 1968.

Chatterjee, Joya. 'Class Culture and Conflict: the second partition of Bengal, 1937-47', University of Cambridge, 1990.

Dasgupta, Swapan. 'Local Politics in Bengal: Midnapur, 1921-24', University of London, 1980.

De, Jatindra Nath. 'The History of the KPP of Bengal, 1929-47: A Study of Changes in Class and Inter-Community Relations in the Agrarian Bengal', University of Delhi, 1977.

Kamtekar, Indivar. 'The End of the Colonial State, 1940-1947', University of Cambridge, 1988.

Karim, A. K. M. 'The Modern Muslim Political Elite in Bengal', University of London, 1964.

Khan, Bazlur Rahaman. 'Some Aspects of Society and Politics in Bengal, 1927-36', University of London, 1979.

Mitra, S. Chandan. 'Political Mobilization and the Nationalist Movement in Eastern Uttar Pradesh and Bihar, 1937-42', University of Oxford, 1983.

Norruzzaman, A. H. M. 'Rise of Muslim Middle Class as a Political Force', University of London, 1964.

Panda, Chitta. 'The Decline of Bengal Zamindars: Midnapur, 1870-1920', University of Oxford, 1988.

Park, R. L. 'The Rise of Militant Nationalism in Bengal: A Regional Study of Indian Nationalism', University of Harvard, 1951.

Rodrigues, Livi. 'Rural Protest and Politics: A Study of Peasant Movement in

Maharastra', University of London, 1984.

Sen, Samita. 'Women Workers in the Bengal Jute Industry, 1890-1940: Migration, Motherhood and Militancy', University of Cambridge, 1992.

ARTICLES

Addy, Premen and Azad, Ibne, 'Politics and Culture in Bengal', *New Left Review*, 79, May-June 1973.

Alavi, Hamza. 'Peasant Classes and Primordial Loyalties', *Journal of Peasant Studies* (hereafter *JPS*), 11, 4, December 1974.

Amin, Shahid. 'Gandhi as Mahatma: Gorakhpur district, Eastern UP [Uttar Pradesh], 1921-1922', in Ranajit Guha (ed.), *Subaltern Studies*, Vol. III, Oxford University Press, Delhi, 1984.

Argov, Daniel. 'Moderates and Extremists: Two Attitudes Towards British Rule in India', St. Antony's (Oxford) paper no. 18, no date.

Arnold, David, 'Gramsci and Peasant Subalternity in India', *JPS*, 2, 4, July 1984.

Awwal-ul, Ifthikar. 'The problem of Middle class educated unemployment in Bengal, 1912-42', *Indian Economic and Social History Review* (hereafter *IESHR*), 19, 1, 1982.

Bagchi, Amiya, 'Reflection on patterns of regional growth in India during the period of British rule', *Bengal Past and Present*, 1, 2, 1976.

Baker, C. J. 'The Congress at the 1937 elections at Madras', *Modern Asian Studies* (hereafter *MAS*), 10, 4, 1976.

Bayly, C. A. 'The Pre-history of communalism? Religious conflict in India, 1700-1860', *MAS*, 19, 2, 1985.

Bhaduri, Amit. 'The evolution of land relations in eastern India under British rule', *IESHR*, 17, 1, 1976

Brenan Lance, 'The illusion of security: the background of separatism in Uttar Pradesh', *MAS*, 18,2, 1984.

Broomfield, J. H. 'The regional elite: a theory of Modern Indian history', *IESHR*, 3, 3, 1966.

——.'The forgotten majority: the Bengali Muslims', in D. A. Low (ed.), *Soundings in Modern South Asian History*, London, 1968.

Chakravarti, Hiren. 'Government and Bengal terrorism, 1912-18', *Bengal Past and Present, July-December*, 1971.

Chakrabarty, Bidyut. 'Bengal Congress and the Peasantry, 1928-38', *South Asia Resarch*, 5, 1, 1985.

——.'Subaltern militancy, 1928-31 and the Indian National Congress: an argument in Bengal working class movement', in Zillur Khan *et al.*, *Tradition and Individual Talent*, Wisconsin, USA, 1988.

——.'The 1932 communal award and its implications in Bengal', *MAS*, 23, 3, 1989.

——.'Jawaharlal Nehru and planning, 1938-41: India at the crossroads', *MAS*, 26, 2, 1992.

——.'Political Mobilization in the localities: the 1942 Quit India Movement in Midnapur', *MAS*, 26, 4, 1992.
——.'Foundations of Indian political thought: a review', *MAS*, 28, 2, 1994
——. 'Defiance and confrontation: the 1942 Quit India Movement in Midnapur', *Social Scientist*, 20 (7 and 8), 1992.
——.'Religion and Indian Nationalism', *Economic and Political Weekly*, June 1993
——.'The 1947 united Bengal movement: a thesis without a synthesis', *IESHR*, 30, 4, 1993.
——.'Gandhi and non-violence', *MAS* (forthcoming).
——.'Subhas Chandra Bose, Indian National Army and the axis strategy', *MAS* (forthcoming).
——.'Intellectual imbroglio and the 1947 Great divide of the subcontinent of India', *MAS* (forthcoming).
Chakrabarty, Dipesh. 'Conditions for knowledge of working class conditions: employers, government and the jute workers of Calcutta, 1890-1940', in Ranajit Guha (ed.), *Subaltern Studies*, Vol. II, Oxford University Press, Delhi, 1983.
——.'On deifying and defying authority: managers and workers in the jute mills of Calcutta, circa 1890-1940', *Past and Present*, 100, August, 1983.
Chatterjee, Partha. 'Bengal: rise and growth of a nationality', *Social Scientist*, 4, 1, 1975.
——.'Agrarian relations and communalism in Bengal, 1926-35', in Ranajit Guha (ed.) *Subaltern Studies*, Vol. 1, Oxford University Press, 1982.
——.'Bengal politics and Muslim masses, 1920-47', *Journal of Commonwealth and Comparative Politics*, 20, 1, 1982.
——.'Spontaneity and Organization in Peasant Movement in Bengal', in W. H. Morris-Jones *et al. Political Violence*, Institute of Commonwealth Studies, London, 1982.
——.'The colonial state and peasant resistance in Bengal', Occasional Paper, 55, Centre of Studies in Social Sciences, Calcutta, January 1983.
——.'Caste and subaltern consciousness', in Ranajit Guha (ed.), *Subaltern Studies*, Vol. VII, Oxford University Press, Delhi, 1989.
——.'History and the nationalisation of Hinduism', *Social Research*, 59, 1, Spring, 1992.
Chatterjee, R. 'C. R. Das and the Chandpur strike of 1921', *Bengal Past and Present*, May-August and September-December 1974.
Chaudhuri, Benoy. 'The process of depeasantization in Bengal and Bihar', *Indian Historical Review* (hereafter *IHR*), 2, 1, 1975.
Damodaran, Vinita. 'Azad Dastas and Dacoit Gangs: the Congress underground movement, 1942-1944', *MAS*, 26, 3, 1992.
Dasgupta, Swapan. 'Adivasi politics in Midnapur, 1760-1924' in R. Guha, *Subaltern Studies*, Vol. IV, Oxford University Press, Delhi, 1985.
De, Amalendu. 'Fazlul Haq and his reaction to the two nation theory', *Bengal Past and Present*, January-April 1974.
Gallagher, John. 'Congress in decline: Bengal 1930-39', *MAS*, 7, 3, 1973.

Ghosh, Pradyut. 'Organizational structure of a revolutionary secret society: Anushilan Samiti, 1901-18', *Bengal Past and Present*, July-December 1978.

Gordon, Leonard. 'Bengal's Gandhi: a study of regionalism, politics and thought', in D. Kopf (ed.), *Bengal Regional Identity*, Asian Studies Centre, Michigan State University, Michigan, East lansing, 1969.

Gordon, Richard. 'Non-cooperation and council entry, 1919-1920', *MAS*, 7, 3, 1973.

Greenough, Paul, 'Indulgence and abundance as an Asian peasant values: a Bengali case in point', *Journal of Asian Studies* (hereafter *JAS*), 42, 4, 1983.

Hardiman, David. 'The Indian faction: a political theory examined', in Ranajit Guha (ed.), *Subaltern Studies*, Vol. 1, Oxford University Press, 1982.

Jalal, Ayesha and Anil Seal. 'Alternative to partition: Muslim politics between the wars', *MAS*, 15, 3, 1981.

Johnson, Gordon. 'Partition, agitation and Congress: Bengal 1904-8', *MAS*, 7, 3, 1973.

Krishna, Gopal. 'The development of Indian National Congress as a mass organization, 1918-23', *JAS*, 25, 3, 1966.

Maharatna, Arup. 'The demography of Bengal famine, 1943-44: a detailed study', *IESHR*, 31, 2, 1994.

Mahatab, P. C. 'Bengal's nobles in politics, 1911-19', *Bengal Past and Present*, July-December 1977.

Mcpherson, K. 'The Muslim of Madras and Calcutta: agitational politics in the early 1920s', *South Asia*, 5 December 1975.

Mukherjee, S. N. 'Class, Caste and Politics in Calcutta, 1815-38', in E. Leach *et al. Elites in South Asia*, Cambridge University Press, Cambridge, 1975.

——.'*Bhadralok* in Bengali language and literature', *Bengal Past and Present*, 95, 181, July-December 1976.

Parekh, Bhikhu. 'Nationalism in a comparative perspective', *Politisches Denken Jahrbuch* (The Yearbook of Germany), Stuttgart, Germany, 1994.

Pati, Biswamoy. 'Storm over Malkangiri: a note of Laxman Naiko's revolt in 1942', in Gyanendra Pandey (ed.), *The Indian Nation in* 1942, K. P. Bagchi, Calcutta, 1988.

——.'The climax of popular protest: the Quit India Movement in Orissa', *IESHR*, 29, 1, 1992.

Potter, David. 'Manpower shortage and the end of colonialism: the case of the ICS' [Indian Civil Services], *MAS*, 7, 2, 1973.

Ray, Rajat. 'The crisis of Bengal agriculture, 1870-1937', *IESHR*, 10, 3, 1973.

——.'The dynamics of continuity in rural Bengal under British imperialism', *IESHR*, 10, 2, 1973.

——.'Masses in politics: the non-cooperation movement in Bengal, 1920-22', *IESHR*, 11, 4, 1974.

——.'Political change in British India', *IESHR*, 14, 4, October-December 1977.

Ray, Rajat and Ratna Ray, 'Zamindars and *jotedars*: study of rural politics in Bengal', *MAS*, 9, 1, 1975.

Ray, Ratna. 'Landlords and peasants: a historiographical view of rural Bengal from pre-colonial to colonial times', *Peasant Studies*, 11, 4, 1984.

Raychaudhuri, Tapan. 'Indian nationalism as animal politics', *The Historical Journal*, 22, 3, 1979.

Rothermund, D. 'Constitutional reforms and national agitation in India, 1900-50', *JAS*, 21, 4, 1962.

——.'Depression of the 1930s', *IESHR*, 18, 1, 1981.

Rizvi, Gowhar. 'The Congress revolt of 1942: a historical revision', *Indo-British Review*, XI, December, 1984.

Sanyal, Hitesranjan. 'Arambager jatiatabadi andolon, 1921-27' (Bengali), *Anya Artha*, 6 and 7, 1974.

——.'Social mobility in Bengal; its sources and constraints', *IESHR*, 2, 1, 1975.

——.'Dakshin-paschim Banglay jatiatabadi andolon' (Bengali), *Chaturanga*, 38 (1 and 3) and 39 (1), 1976-77 and 1977-78.

——.'Congress movements in the villages of southwest Bengal', in Alice Thorner *et al. Asie du Sud: Traditions et Changements*, Paris, 1979.

——.'Congress in south-eastern Bengal: the anti-union board movement in Medinipur, 1921', in R. Sisson and S. Wolpert (ed.) *Congress and Indian Nationalism*, University of California Press, Berkeley, 1988.

Sarkar, Sumit. 'Logic of Gandhian Nationalism: Civil Disobedience and Gandhi-Irwin pact, 1930-31', *IHR*, July 1976.

——.'The conditions and nature of subaltern militancy; Bengal from Swadeshi to Non-Cooperation', Occasional Paper on History and Society, Nehru Memorial Museum and Library, New Delhi, 1983.

Sarkar, Tanika. 'The first phase of Civil Disobedience Movement in Bengal, 1930-31', *IHR*, July 1977.

——.'A study of three communal riots in Bengal, 1930-31', in Mushirul Hasan (ed.), *Communal and Pan Islamic Trends in Colonial India*, Delhi, 1981.

Seal, Anil. 'Imperialism and nationalism in India', *MAS*, 7, 3, 1973.

Smalley, Alan. 'The colonial state and agrarian structure in Bengal', *Journal of Contemporary Asia*, 13, 2, 1983.

Taylor, David. 'The crisis of authority in the Indian National Congress, 1936-39', in B. N Pandey (ed.), *Leadership in South Asia*, Delhi, 1977.

BOOKS

Ahmad, Abul Mansur. *Amar Dekha Rajnitir Panchas Bachhar* (Bengali), Nowroje Kitabistan, Dhaka, 1968.

——.*Atmakatha*, (Bengali), Khosroj Kitabmahal, Dhaka, 1978.

Ahmad, Mazaffar. *Prabandha Sankolon*, (Bengali) National Book Agency, Calcutta, 1970.

——.*Amar Jiban O Bharater Communist Party*, (Bengali), National Book Agency, Calcutta, 1971.

Ahmad, Rafiuddin. *The Bengal Muslims 1871-1906: A Quest for Identity*, Oxford University Press, Delhi, 1981.

Ambedkar, B. R. *Pakistan or partition of India*, Thacker & Co, Bombay, 1945.

Anderson, Benedict. *Imagined Communities: reflections on the origin and spread of nationalism*, Verso, London, 1983.

Annonymous. *Swadhinata Sangrame Midnapur*, (Bengali), Calcutta, 1973.

Argov, Daniel. *Moderates and Extremists in the Indian National Movement, 1883-1920*, London, 1967.

Aykroyd, A. K. *The conquest of famine, Chatto and Windus*, London, 1974.

David, Arnold. *Famine, Social Crisis and Historical Change*, Oxford University Press, Delhi, 1988.

Azad, Maulana. *India Wins Freedom*, Orient Longman, Calcutta, 1959.

Bagchi, Amiya Kumar, *Private Investment in India*, Cambridge University Press, Cambridge, 1972.

Bamford, P. C.*History of the Non-Cooperation and Khilafat Movements*, Government of India Press, Calcutta, 1925.

Bandyopadhyay, Sekhar. *Caste, Politics and the Raj: Bengal*, 1872-1937, K. P. Bagchi, Calcutta, 1990.

Barrier, Gerald N. *Banned: Controversial Literature and Political Control in British India, 1907-1947*, Missouri University Press, Columbia, 1974.

Bayly, C. A. *The Local Roots of Indian Politics, Allahabad, 1880-1920*, Clarendon Press, Oxford, 1975.

——.*Indian Society and the Making of the British Empire*, Cambridge University Press, Cambridge, 1988.

Bhatia, B. M. *Famines in India: a study in some aspects of the economic history of India, 1860-1940*, Asia Publishing House, London, 1963.

Bhattacharyya, Buddhadeva. *et al. Satyagrahas in Bengal, 1921-39*, Minerva Publications, Calcutta, 1977.

——.*Origins of the RSP: From National Revolutionary to Non-Conformist Marxism*, Publicity Concern, Calcutta, 1982.

Bhuyan, A.C. *The Quit India Movement, the Second World War and Indian Nationalism*, Manas, New Delhi, 1975.

Birla, G. D. *In the Shadow of Mahatma: a Personal Memoir*, Orient Longman, Calcutta, 1953.

Biswas, Kalipada. *Jukta Banglar Sesh Adhyay* (Bengali), Orient Book Company, Calcutta, 1966.

Bose, Nirmal Kumar. *The Structure of Hindu Society*, Sangam, New Delhi, 1976.

——.*Bialliser Bangla* (Bengali), Sarswat Library, Calcutta, 1971.

Breuilly, John. *Nationalism and the State*, Manchester University Press, Manchester, 1982.

Broomfield, J. H. *Elite Conflict in a Plural Society: Twentieth Century Bengal*, University of California Press, Berkeley, 1968.

Brown, Judith. *Gandhi's rise to power: Indian politics, 1915-1922*, Cambridge University Press, Cambridge, 1972.

——.*Gandhi and Civil Disobedience: the Mahatma in Indian politics*, Cambridge University Press, Cambridge, 1976.

——.*Modern India: the Origins of an Asian Democracy*, Oxford University Press, Delhi, 1985.

——.*Gandhi: the prisoner of hope*, Yale University Press, New Haven, 1991.

Chakrabarty, Bidyut. *Subhas Chandra Bose and Middle Class Radicalism: a Study in Indian Nationalism, 1928-40*, London, 1990 and Oxford University Press, Delhi, 1990.

——.*Biplabi: The Journal of the 1942 Civil Rebellion*, Calcutta (forthcoming)

Chakrabarty, Dipesh. *Rethinking Working Class History: Bengal, 1890-1940*, Oxford University Press, Delhi, 1989.

Chatterjee, Bhola. *Aspects of Bengal Politics in the Early Nineteen-Thirties*, Calcutta, 1969.

Chatterjee, Partha. *Bengal, 1920-47: the Land Question*, Vol. 1, K. P. Bagchi, Calcutta, 1984.

——.*Nationalist thought and the Colonial World: a derivative discourse?*, Oxford University Press, Delhi, 1986.

——.*The Nation and its Fragments: colonial and postcolonial histories*, Oxford University Press, Delhi,. 1994.

Chaudhuri, Nirad C. *An Autobiography of an Unknown Indian*, New York, 1951

——.*Thy Hand Great Anarch*, Chatto and Windus, London, 1988.

Chopra, P. N. (ed.). *The Quit India movement: British secret reports*, Thompson Press, Faridabad, 1976.

——.*The Quit India Movement: the role of big business*, Imrpint, New Delhi, 1991.

Collected Works of Mahatma Gandhi, Ministry of Information and Broadcasting, Government of India, New Delhi (relevant years).

Coupland, R. *Indian politics, 1936-42: the report of the constitutional problem in India*, Oxford University Press, Madras, 1944.

Damodaran, Vinita. *Broken Promises: popular protest, Indian Nationalism and the Congress Party in Bihar, 1936-1946*, Oxford University Press, Delhi, 1992.

Das, N. N. *History of Midnapur*, Part II, Midnapur Samskriti Parishad, Calcutta, 1969.

Dasgupta, Ranajit. *Economy, Society and Politics in Bengal: Jalpaiguri, 1869-1947*, Oxford University Press, Delhi, 1992.

Deutsch, Karl. *Nationalism and Social Communication*, MIT Press, Cambridge, 1966.

Dhara, Sushil., *Prabaha* (Bengali), Midnapur, 1977.

Dobbin, Christine. *Urban Leadership in Western India: politics and communities in Bombay city, 1840-1885*, Oxford University Press, London, 1972.

Gellner, Ernest. *Nations and Nationalism*, Basil Blackwell, Oxford, 1983.

Gillion, K. L. *Ahmedabad: a study in Indian urban history*, California University Press, Berkeley, 1968.

Gopal, S. *The Viceroyalty of Lord Irwin, 1926-31*, Clarendon Press, Oxford, 1957.

Gordon, Leonard. *Bengal: the Nationalist Movement, 1876-1940*, Columbia University Press, New York, 1974.

Goswami, Gopinandan. *Midnipurer Shahid Parichay* (Bengali), Midnapur, 1977.

Gramsci, Antonio. *Selections from the Prison Notebooks*, Translated by Quintin Hoare and Geoffrey Nowell Smith, International Publishers, New York, 1971.

Greenough, Paul. *Prosperity and misery in modern Bengal: the famine, 1943-44*, Oxford University Press, New York, 1982.

Guha, Ranajit. *Subaltern Studies*, Vols. I-V, Oxford University Press, Delhi, 1983, 1984, 1985, 1986.

——.*Elementary Aspects of Peasant Insurgency in Colonial India*, Oxford University Press, Delhi, 1983.

——.*An Indian Historiography of India: a nineteenth century agenda and its implic ations*, K. P. Bagchi, Calcutta, 1988.

Haque, M. Azizul. *The Man Behind Plough*, Book Company, Calcutta, 1939.

Hardiman, David. *Peasant Nationalists of Gujrat, Kheda District, 1917-34*, Oxford University Press, Delhi, 1981.

Hasan, Mushirul (ed.). *India's Partition: process, strategy and mobilization*, Oxford University Press, Delhi, 1993.

Hees, Peter. *The Bomb in Bengal: the rise of revolutionary terrorism in India, 1900-1910*, Oxford University Press, Delhi, 1993.

Henningham, Stephen. *Peasant Movements in Colonial India: North Bihar, 1917-42*, Australian National University, Canberra, 1982.

Hobsbawm, E. *Revolutionaries*, Pantheon Books, New York, 1973.

Hopkins, A. G. and Dewey, C. (ed). *The Imperial Impact*, University of London, London, 1978.

Hutchins, F. G. *Spontaneous Revolution, the Quit India Movement*, Manohar, Delhi, 1971.

——.*India's revolution: Gandhi and the Quit India Movement*, Harvard University Press, Cambridge, 1973.

Inden, Ronald. *Imagining India*, Basil Blackwell, Oxford, 1990.

Islam, M. M. *Bengal Agriculture, 1920-47: A Quantitative Analysis*, Cambridge University Press, Cambridge, 1978.

Jalal, Ayesha. *The Sole Spokesman: Jinnah, the Muslim League and the Demand for Pakistan*, Cambridge University Press, Cambridge, 1985.

Joshi, P. C. *The Indian Communist Party: its policy and work in the war of liberation*, CPGB, London, 1942.

Juergensmeyer, Mark. *Religious Nationalism Confronts the Secular State*, Oxford University Press, Delhi, 1994.

Kanwar, Pamela. *Imperial Shimla: the political culture of the Raj*, Oxford University Press, Delhi, 1990.

Karlekar, Malavika. *Voices from Within: early personal narratives of Bengali women*, Oxford University Press, Delhi, 1991.

Kedurie, Elie (ed.). *Nationalism in Asia and Africa*, New American Library, New York, 1970.

Kohli, Atul. *The State and Poverty in India: the Politics of Reform*, Cambridge University Press, Cambridge, 1987.

Kumar, Nita. *The artisans of Banares: popular culture and identity, 1880-1986*, Princeton University Press, Princeton, 1988.

Laushy, David. *The Bengal Terrorists and Their Conversion to Marxism: Aspects of*

Regional Nationalism in India, 1905-42, Firma KLM, Calcutta, 1975.

Liddle, Joana and Roma Joshi. *Daughters of Independence: Gender, Caste and Class in India*, Kali for Women, New Delhi, 1986.

Low, D. A. (ed.). *Soundings in Modern South Asian History*, Weidenfeld, London, 1968.

——.*Congress and the Raj: Facets of the Indian Struggle, 1917-47*, Heinemann, London, 1977.

Majumdar, S. N. *In Search of a Revolutionary Ideology and Revolutionary Programme: a Study in the Transition from National Revolutionary Terrorism to Communism*, Peoples' Publishing House, New Delhi, 1979.

Mathur, Y. B. *The Quit India Movement*, Pragati, Delhi, 1979.

Meherally, Yusuf (ed.). *Towards Struggle*, Padma Publications, Bombay, 1946.

Minault, Gail. *The Khilafat Movement: Religious Symbolism and Political Mobilization in India*, Oxford University Press, New York, 1982.

Misra, B. B. *The Indian Middle Classes*, Oxford University Press, London, 1961.

Mitra, N. (ed.). *Indian Annual Register*, Delhi (relevant years).

Momen, Humaira. *Muslim Politics in Bengal: a Study of the Krishak Praja Party and the Elections of 1937*, Oxford University Press, Dhaka, 1972.

Moore, Barrington Jr. *The Social Origins of Dictatorship and Democracy: Lord and Peasant in the making of the Modern World*, Beacon Press, Boston, 1966.

Mukherjee, Jadugopal. *Biplabi Jibaner Smriti* (Bengali), Academic Publishers, Calcutta, 1982.

Mukherjee, Radhakamal. *Land Problems of India*, Longman, London, 1933.

Nandy, Ashis. *The Intimate Enemy: Loss and Recovery of Self under Colonialism*, Oxford University Press, Delhi, 1983.

——.*The Illegitimacy of Nationalism: Rabindranath Tagore and the politics of self*, Oxford University Press, Delhi, 1994.

Nehru, Jawaharlal. *An Autobiography*, Oxford University Press, Delhi, 1989.

——.*The Discovery of India*, Oxford University Press, Delhi, 1989.

O'Hanlon, Rosalind. *Caste, Conflict and Ideology: Mahatma Jotirao Phule and Low Caste Protest in Nineteenth Century Western India*, Cambridge University Press, Cambridge, 1985.

Oldenberg, Veena. *The making of colonial Lucknow, 1856-1877*, Princeton University Press, Princeton, 1984.

Page, David. *Prelude to Partition: the Indian Muslims and the Imperial System of Control, 1920-32*, Oxford University Press, Delhi, 1987.

Pandey, Gyanendra. *The Ascendancy of the Congress in Uttar Pradesh, 1926-34*, Oxford University Press, Delhi, 1973.

Pandey, Gyanendra (ed.). *The Indian Nation in 1942*, K. P. Bagchi, Calcutta, 1988.

——.*The Construction of Communalism in North India*, Oxford University Press, Delhi, 1993.

Parekh, Bhikhu. *Colonialism, Tradition and Reform: an Analysis of Gandhian Political Discourse*, Sage, Delhi, 1989.

Pati, Biswamoy. *Resisting Domination: Peasants, Tribals and the National Movement in Orissa, 1920-50*, Manohar, Delhi, 1993.

Potter, David. *India's Political Administrators, 1919-1983*, Clarendon Press, Oxford, 1986.

Ray, Rajat. *Social Conflict and Political Unrest in Bengal, 1875-1914*, Oxford University Press, Delhi, 1984.

Raychaudhuri, Tapan. *Europe Reconsidered: Perceptions of the West in Nineteenth Century Bengal*, Oxford University Press, Delhi, 1988.

Rumbold, Algernon. *Watershed in India, 1914-22*, The Athlone Press, London, 1979.

Samanta, Satish. *Sarvadhinayak* (Bengali), Midnapur, 1977.

Samanta, Satish. et al. *August Revolution and Two Years' National Government in Midnapur*, Part I (Tamluk), Orient Book Co, Calcutta, 1946.

Sarkar, Sumit. *The Swadeshi Movement in Bengal*, Peoples' Publishing House, Delhi, 1978.

——.*Modern India*, Macmillan and Company, Delhi, 1983.

——.*Popular Movements and Middle Class Leadership in Late Colonial India: Perspectives and Problems from a History from Below*, K. P. Bagchi, Calcutta, 1983.

——.*A Critique of Colonial Reason*, Papyrus, Calcutta, 1985.

Sarkar, Tanika. *Bengal: the Politics of Protest, 1928-1934*, Oxford University Press, Delhi, 1990.

Sathyamurthy, T. V. *State and Nation in the Context of Social Change*, Vol. 1, Oxford University Press, Delhi, 1994.

Scott, James. *Weapons of the Weak: Everyday Forms of Peasant Resistance*, Yale University Press, New Haven, 1985.

Seal, Anil. *The Emergence of Indian Nationalism, Competition and Collaboration in the late Nineteenth Century*, Cambridge University Press, Cambridge, 1968.

Sen, A. K. *Poverty and Famines: an Essay on Entitlement and Deprivation*, Clarendon Press, Oxford, 1981.

Sen, Amiya P. *Hindu Revivialism in Bengal, 1872-1905*, Oxford University Press, Delhi, 1993.

Sen, Asok. *et al. Three Studies on the Agrarian Structure in Pre-Partition Bengal*, Oxford University Press, Calcutta, 1982.

Sen, Shila. *Muslim Politics in Bengal*, Impex India, Delhi, 1976.

Sen, Sunil. *Working Class Movements in India, 1885-1975*, Oxford University Press, Delhi, 1994.

Shamsuddin, Abul Kalam. *Atit Diner Smriti* (Bengali), Nowroje Kitabistan, Dhaka, 1968.

Singh, Jasbir A. K. *Gandhi and Civil Disobedience*, India Office Library, London, 1980.

Sitaramaiah, B. Patabhi. *History of the Indian National Congress*, Vols. 1 and 2, Chand Publishers, Delhi, 1969.

Smith, Anthony D. *Theories of Nationalism*, Duckworth, London, 1971.
——.*Nationalism in the Twentieth Century*, Martin Robertson, Oxford, 1979.
Stokes, Eric. *The Peasant and the Raj: Studies in Agrarian Society and Peasant Rebellion in Colonial India*, Cambridge University Press, Cambridge, 1978.
Thomas, K. P. *Dr. B. C. Roy*, WBPCC, Calcutta, 1955.
Tripathy, Amalesh. *The Extremist Challenge*, Orient Longman, Calcutta, 1967.
——.*Swadhinata Sangrame Bharatio Jatio Congress* (Bengali), Ananda, Calcutta, 1990.
Umar, Badruddin. *Chirasthayi Bandobaste Bangladesher Krishak* (Bengali), Maola Brothers, Dhaka, 1974.
Washbrook, D. A. *The Emergence of Provincial Politics: the Madras Presidency*, 1870-1920, Oxford University Press, Delhi, 1970.
Wavell. *The Viceroy Journal* (edited by Penderel Moon). Oxford University Press, Delhi, 1977.
Zaidi, A. M. *The Way Out to Freedom*, Orientalia, New Delhi, 1973.
——.*The Encyclopaedia of the Indian National Congress*, Vols. I-IV, S. Chand & Co, New Delhi, 1982-88.
Zetland. *Essayez: Memoirs of Lawrence of Marquess of Zetland*, London, 1956.

Index